It's Just the Way It Was

Inside the War on the New England Mob and other stories

It's Just the Way It Was

Inside the War on the New England Mob and other stories

By Joe Broadmeadow
and
Brendan Doherty

JEBWizard Publishing

Cranston, RI 02920

JEBWizardPublishing@gmail.com

Ordering Information:

Quantity sales. Special discounts are available on quantity purchases by corporations, associations, and others. For details, contact the "Special Sales Department" at the email address above.

It's Just the Way It Was: Inside the War on the New England Mob and other stories —1st ed.

ISBN 978-1-7335264-0-1

Library of Congress Control Number:2019913101

Also by Joe Broadmeadow

Choices: You Make 'em You Own 'em (The Jerry Tillinghast Story)

UnMade: Honor Loyalty Redemption (with Bobby Walason)

A Change of Hate

Silenced Justice

Collision Course

Saving the Last Dragon

Dedication

No one writes a book alone. The pages you are reading are just the visible piece of a more considerable effort. Those behind the scene are the key to any success.

The writing of this book is no different.

Beginning with Brendan's first discussion with the late Channel 10 NBC reporter Jim Taricani, who encouraged Brendan to tell his story, to Attorney Tom Briody suggesting Brendan contact me to help write the book, this has been a team effort.

None of this would have happened without them and a host of others.

There isn't much more to say about Jim Taricani as a reporter and a man that hasn't already been said. He symbolized the commitment to a free and open press not just in his work as a reporter but by willingly sacrificing his freedom to protect a source.

Unlike the misplaced appellation co-opted by made men in organized crime, Taricani was a true man of honor. He didn't just voice his support of the First Amendment, he lived it. And he strove to tell the good story.

We dedicate this book to Jim and all the others who sought to uncover the truth and shine light into the shadows. And to the police officers, troopers, and agents who daily risk their lives in combatting crime and stopping those who would victimize society.

We owe them, and people like Jim Taricani, a debt of gratitude for their courage.

Joe Broadmeadow Brendan Doherty

Table of Contents

True North

On March 14, 1986, a dark, cold, and quiet night in Providence, Rhode Island, an ex-con with a penchant for violence, dropped into a local bar. He didn't realize he'd just entered jackal territory, and the jackals were hunting.

Dennis Wilmot, recently released from the Rhode Island Adult Correctional Institution (ACI) after serving several years in maximum-security for his involvement in a shooting, thought he was invincible in a world where the biggest lie was longevity.

Committing violent acts all over the United States, he'd established a reputation within organized crime. He was a guy you just didn't screw around with.

In his mind, this raised him to a higher status. He grew up in Providence, Rhode Island, a place with a national reputation as a hub of organized crime. His roots here, he believed, preordained his involvement with the mob.

Dennis thought of himself as a wiseguy because the wiseguys often used his skills. He protected their interest. In his mind, by relying on him, they'd tacitly accepted him into their world. He figured if he could work for them, he could hang out with them. He convinced himself he belonged.

His thinking, delusional and as misguided as his moral compass, would prove cataclysmic. To the wiseguys, Dennis was a junkyard dog; they let him off the chain when needed, then chained him up again until the next time. Sometimes they fed him, sometimes they kept him hungry to remind him of his place.

He was not, and never would be, one of them.

The wiseguys had rules. They had deep family connections. Did the guy pay his dues? Did he wait in line to deserve this status? Did he pay proper respect to the old-school mobsters? Would he take care of another guy's family when the guy was in the joint?

And most important, was he of Italian descent?

A guy can't just point to a fondness for violence on his street resume and expect to be one of them. Violent men were as ordinary as they were disposable. You needed to meet other criteria. Dennis was far from getting a button; the code word for becoming a 'made' man.

That had its own set of rules. Violence was Dennis's stock-in-trade. It made him merely useful, not eligible for inclusion.

Dennis built a reputation for extreme violence. He wasn't a moneymaker; he was a money collector. A bone breaker. He didn't negotiate, he knocked you out. They turned him loose when they needed more than intimidation.

They used his talents in matters of mutual concern. Dennis gave many beatings for them, extorted people on their behalf, collected unlawful debts, damaged property, committed larcenies, staged robberies, and did whatever else they asked of him.

During his investigation into this crew, Doherty and his colleagues found information about a beating for hire and the theft of hundreds of TV's taken from a local department store storage area. While the information was useful, there was nothing about Dennis Wilmot's threatening LaSorsa and Leonardo. That information came later.

As it played out, Dennis may have signed his own death warrant by threatening those guys.

When Dennis drove to the bar on Federal Hill that night, he had no idea how much trouble he'd caused himself.

After parking his car on the corner of Africa Street and DePasquale Avenue, he walked the short distance to the bar, taking a seat at a high-top. He noticed an associate of the Lasorsa-Leonardo crew staring at him, but the guy left shortly after that.

Dennis should have left as well. Instead, he ordered a drink. He had no fear, a warped sense of invulnerability, and his problem radar, never effective, was off-line.

The bartender looked at Dennis while making the drink. Dennis tugged on the cuff of his warm-up jacket. A not-so-subtle sign the drink was on credit, "on the cuff" as they say. The bartender knew that he'd never see the money, but he wasn't foolish enough to refuse, or ask Dennis to leave. It would have been better for Dennis if he had, but the bartender just made the drink. It was the cost of doing business with these guys.

Dennis had a couple of drinks, all on the never-pay-plan, then left about forty-five minutes later.

As he approached his car, LaSorsa and Leonardo ambushed Dennis. The terrifying staccato sound of shotgun and semi-automatic pistol fire echoed in the night. Bullets riddled the misguided bone breakers body. Dennis took rounds in the stomach, arms, legs, groin, head, and right wrist. The shotgun blasts were 12-gauge buckshot, one was a deer slug.

All were intended to kill him.

Over thirty rounds struck Dennis as he rolled on the ground, hoping the rain of bullets would soon stop. At the sound of approaching sirens, his assailants ran from the scene. Dennis could hear the ambulance getting closer as he lay bleeding and spitting blood. They took him to Rhode Island Hospital.

And he lived to tell the tale.

Doherty had never heard of anyone surviving such an onslaught of bullets. Dennis later described the pain from the shots like dozens of cigars burning his body. He felt his life force slipping out of him. He thought it was beautiful, as he looked up at the streetlights, knowing "this is how I died, on the streets."

Determined not to tell the police who was responsible if they arrived before he checked out, Dennis endured the pain. It was his code of honor.

It wasn't until the next day, when he awoke in the hospital, that he realized he was still alive and needed to retaliate. He also understood the severity of the damage he'd endured made vengeance unlikely. The damage to his right wrist was so bad it made him incapable of handling a gun. His injuries were so severe he realized he was just a sitting duck, prone, and waiting for them to finish the job. He needed to pay them back in a way that didn't depend on his violent temperament.

His retaliation was to contact Brendan Doherty; the code of silence abandoned for revenge.

Doherty spent the next few months with members of the State Police Intelligence Unit, Providence Police, and federal agencies debriefing Dennis about his life of crime. Because of his cooperation and other corroborating evidence, the State Police arrested several people. Some went to prison.

While interviewing Dennis, staying with him for several weeks and talking about his violent actions, the prison culture, and his "graveyard beef" with Vinny and Bruce, Doherty realized he was a long way from home. A long way from the black and white difference between right and wrong of his world. Doherty's ability to relate to Dennis and understand his rationalizing cooperation as a means of seeking retribution amazed him.

Doherty found this empathy for Wilmot troubling. He understood how Dennis turned bad and, with his reputation, why they tried to kill him. Doherty came to understand the reasons Dennis had to do what he did. It's a complicated, mixed-up world for these guys. Working it day in and day out gave Doherty an insight. He was learning to understand the way they thought.

The skill would prove invaluable.

Doherty came from a different place, just down the street from guys like Dennis Wilmot but a world apart. Through the fortunes of birth, Doherty grew up in different circumstances. He was lucky to have a solid foundation and a reliable barometer for right and wrong. While Doherty recognized the difference between men like Dennis Wilmot and himself, he understood their mind-set.

As Doherty became more exposed to this unique form of street justice, he learned the rules and the excuses employed by these guys. To work organized crime cases, you need a fundamental understanding of the way they thought.

It was like learning a new language. You had to train your mind to think in different patterns. As Brendan became more fluent in the culture of the mob, he tried to pass that on to those working with him.

Part 1: Changing Plans and New Opportunities

Chapter 1 Beginnings

Eighteen years old and on the brink of graduating from Bishop Feehan, a small Catholic high school in Attleboro, Massachusetts, life was good for Brendan Doherty. The future seemed bright, promising a world of possibilities there for the grasping. But he was about to learn a lesson in how life can change in an instant.

My dad, a dental surgeon, grew ill. Like most people his age, he had not planned for a sudden illness. It was a difficult time. Overheard discussions about problems paying bills altered my reality. The innocence of youth shattered against the realities of life.

I'd hear my parents talk about not having enough money to get the family through the next month. Because my dad was a sole practitioner, he never thought he would need insurance to cover a lack of wages.

My older brother, Ed, was in college at the University of South Florida, and my younger brother, Chris, was about to enter high school. Chris was too young to realize the weight of this. I planned to attend Bryant College, now Bryant University, in the fall.

It was the only school I applied to.

I was planning to live with three high school pals in an apartment off-campus. It probably wasn't the best choice for my academic success, but it sounded like a great adventure. Our first foray in adult independence.

It was not to be. The harsh realities of changing fortunes derailed those plans. In a way Brendan never could have expected.

One of his buddies, and future roommate, Arthur Boulet, died in a car accident in Rhode Island. The intimacy of his death, a stark reality check, coupled with the financial woes at home, thrust the real-world uncertainty of life front and center.

A few days before school started, Brendan withdrew from Bryant and applied at a less expensive state school. He decided on his own, unwilling to add to his parents' burden. It would be an early lesson in life's difficult choices.

Driving to Rhode Island College, Brendan filled out the requisite paperwork and waited in the lobby for a few hours for an emergency or hardship admission decision. The RIC basketball coach shepherded through his application, and Brendan was all set to attend the state college.

I was a little nervous. Who applies for a college two or three days before school starts? My dream was to play basketball at Bryant and major in business. Instead, I found myself in a different school with no idea how this would all play out.

Where this would lead, I had no idea.

Shortly after the RIC basketball season began, Brendan left the team. Balancing grades, basketball practice, and work schedule became burdensome. He needed to work to make ends meet.

Something had to give.

Dropping out of school was not an option. Education was essential to Brendan's parents—his father used to hitchhike from his job to college classes.

Brendan would stay in school.

I recall holding my school bill in hand, sitting in the living room with my mom and dad. The odor of smoke as my dad enjoyed his long cigars permeated the air. On the mantel were photos of Pope John Paul, President John F. Kennedy Jr., and my parents with Hubert Humphrey and Ed Muskie, both future Democratic Presidential hopefuls.

Brendan's parents were staunch Irish Catholic Democrats. JFK, the first Irish Catholic President, would come up in many conversations. His humor, his quotes, and his charm, everything JFK represented, was music to their ears.

Brendan's dad, Dr. Edward Doherty, son of Maybelle Hollihan, and his mom, Carol Flynn, daughter of Margaret Brady, were both from Taunton, Massachusetts.

Taunton was then an Irish enclave with ties to beautiful County Cavan, about an hour south of Belfast. Cavan is a poor county where the people are frugal.

There's a running joke about Cavanman. They are so poor that when they move, they take their wallpaper with them.

Coming to terms with the financial woes of his parents forced him to grow up, focus on school, and leave the childhood dreams of playing college basketball behind him.

Chapter 2 Security with a Twist

In 1978, nineteen-years-old, Brendan got a job working security at the Providence Civic Center, now the Dunkin Donuts Center. It was the experience of a lifetime.

During the late 1970s, concerts were very popular. You name it, they played the Civic Center. Elton John, Billy Joel, Aerosmith, Sinatra, Kiss, Dianna Ross, Bruce Springsteen, Jackson Brown, Neil Diamond, Donna Summer, and others all played there.

The sporting events were a huge attraction. Providence College moved their games from the on-campus Alumni Hall to the Civic Center. If I couldn't play for PC, at least I could see all their home games. I watched Marvin Barnes, Ernie DiGregorio, known by all as Ernie D., Kevin Stacom, and another hometown star, Joey Hassett, put Providence on the map.

In 1973, Ernie D., Marvin Barnes, and Stacom went to the Final Four in the NCAA tournament. It was exciting to watch these future NBA stars play, and I had the best seats in the house.

Boxing was big then. Middleweight Champ Marvin Hagler and Sugar Ray Leonard graced the squared circle, and the Boston Bruins and Celtics would play a game or two per season.

It was here in the Civic Center Brendan got his first look at the reach of organized crime and their influence in the state. Some wiseguys would come to the events, treated with reverence by some hang-around guys in the stage crew. It bordered on hero worship.

This odd affinity for the wiseguys was all new to Brendan. Unfamiliar with the fascination many in Rhode Island had for the mob, it was a phenomenon he would experience repeatedly.

Brendan kept his focus on doing his job and studying, unimpressed with the wiseguy love affair, but he found another interest to occupy his time, boxing.

I was balancing school, work, and my newest hobby, boxing. My foot speed was questionable, but my hand speed wasn't. My father loved the fight game. Growing up, there were always fights in my yard. My dad refereed some. If there was a neighborhood disagreement, we settled it in the back yard.

My dad was a huge Rocky Marciano fan and attended a few of his fights. Back in Taunton, my father's family ran the Parker House, a private social club. Boxing, gambling, and bootleg booze during Prohibition were their pastimes. My dad would work as a bartender at the Parker House until late at night and then hitch-hike to Stonehill College early the next morning. His Irish uncles insisted he got his education.

My dad and I had something else in common. We both bore an unexpected heavy burden before college. His dad and my grandfather, Thomas F. Doherty, was convicted for violating the National Prohibition Act, also known as the Volstead Act, and went to federal prison.

It wasn't something I spoke about when asked about my family history, but the fact is my grandfather was a bootlegger.

Sometimes things come full circle, and you learn to cope and adjust. My brother Ed later obtained a copy of my grandfather's *Application for Commutation of Sentence* which read;

> *"Federal Prohibition Agents, on October 17, 1931, made a purchase from him of one pint of moonshine alcohol, and on searching the premises found two quarts of alcohol and fifteen bottles of beer behind a ten-foot*

> *bar which was set up in one of the rear rooms.*
> *The family, consisting of the wife of the prisoner, her uncle, and three children, were living in a comfortably furnished, single house, assessed at $5000 against which there is a mortgage in the amount of $7000. The applicant's wife stated that her financial status was very poor and it would only be a matter of a short time before the family would be receiving assistance from local charitable organizations, as it had been necessary to borrow money to pay the taxes last year.*
> *She further stated that since her husband's incarceration her uncle had attempted to operate the store but was taken ill, and that* **since that time** *she,* ***in addition to*** *taking care of the home, was trying to conduct the store but* **was unable to** *do so as effectively as her husband, who was the sole manager."*

My grandfather was one of the kindest men I have ever met. I remember him fondly. I can still picture him wearing a fedora and a long overcoat. He always stressed being a gentleman and on your best behavior around women.

He died when I was around eleven. I was the last one to see him alive.

Family folklore said Tom was a shrewd operator of an organized group of Irish bootleggers, and the agents didn't get the stash-house. But, as George Santayana once said, "History is a bunch of lies about events that never happened told by people who weren't there."

Sixty-five years later, in another full circle event, Tom Doherty's grandson, my brother Chris, purchased the 19th Hole Tavern in Hyannis and sold the same product legally. The 19th Hole, the oldest bar on Cape Cod, was a known speak-easy during Prohibition. The secret basement room is still there today.

The "family" business ran deep in the Doherty bloodline.

Prohibition, in effect between 1920-1933, is considered the birth of Organized Crime in America. The irony for Brendan is that later in life he became an Adjunct Professor at Roger Williams University and taught a course on this very topic. It was a fascinating time, and the family connection made it more personal.

In an interesting dichotomy, Brendan's other grandfather, Jack Flynn, a big rugged man with forearms the size of a loaf of bread, was very popular in the city of Taunton. He became the first detective on the police force.

Detective Jack Flynn was one tough guy.

He would tell me story after story about safe crackers, bank robbers, and bootleggers. He refused to talk about Irish suppression, but my mother told me when he went looking for a job the "Irish Need Not Apply" signs troubled him.

Believe it or not, once, Americans considered the Irish undesirable and a risk to the country. It would seem everyone goes through the process.

In 1862, at the height of the Civil War, John Poole, an Irish immigrant, wrote what would become a popular song about the phenomenon.

No Irish Need Apply

"Ould Ireland on the battle-field a lasting fame has made;
We all have heard of Meagher's men, and Corcorans brigade.
Though fools may flout and bigots rave, and fanatics may cry,
Yet when they want good fighting-men, the Irish may apply,
And when for freedom and the right they raise the battle-cry,
Then the Rebel ranks begin to think: No Irish need apply."

My grandfather felt inferior to the "Swamp Yankees" or nativists, who ran government and businesses in those days. He had an honest reputation when corruption was rampant in policing. That time in policing was called the Corruption Era. Some acceptable practices back then would be frowned upon today.

Despite the obstacles, Jack Flynn maintained his integrity and built a reputation as a no-nonsense, honest cop.

Both my grandfathers were good to me, but Jack Flynn and Tom Doherty were not friends. Now that I realize the dynamics of this, I recall they would never mention one another. At family parties, they would sit in different rooms. I never remember a holiday without one of them and very few with both.

Irishmen might take offense and stand together when others try to exclude them or ignore them, that was one thing. But within the Irish community, stubborn adherence to grudges or disagreements is an art form.

I was raised in an Irish Catholic family where religion, education, politics, love of family, and fighting all mixed. It created a cognitive dissonance I still haven't reconciled.

One thing was for sure; my dad was of high moral fiber. He wouldn't take a dime that didn't belong to him and stressed those values. He also emphasized not to ever let anyone step on your toes. It was advice I took to heart.

Chapter 3 Grundy's Gym

In 1978, Brendan walked in the door of Grundy's Gym in Central Falls, Rhode Island. The experience here would have a lifelong impact on Brendan. Something he could never imagine when he first went in.

It was a real boxing gym, not a studio with mirrors where guys hit the bag and brag to girls that they're fighters. Like most hard-core boxing gyms, it didn't have the luxury of a quality cleaning service.

Pungent sweat, punctuated by the snap of leather on leather, engulfed you. Grunts, groans, and the shouts of trainers added to the mix. Marinated in the blood, sweat, and tears from years of boxers chasing glory, the building held the echoes of dreams, despair, and determination.

It was where the thrill of victory rarely interrupted the agony of defeat. Most guys were just happy to survive. It was all part of the less glamorous reality of the boxing world.

Old fight promotion posters and pictures of boxers covered the walls. Fighters who never made it to the main bout yet showed enough heart to earn a place on that wall. Making the wall was an accomplishment, perhaps their only one, but here it meant something.

Dried blood stains covered the floor of the ring, known as the canvas, serving as reminders of bouts that went beyond sparring. There was no Rocky-style soundtrack to underscore the punishing pain. The dingy walls, gray shades of age, echoed and amplified the sounds. It wasn't music, but it held a certain charm to those immersed in the sport. The only color, besides the boxing trunks, was the purplish-red splotches on bruised bodies.

This place was the real deal.

The owner, Bob Grundy, who later became like an uncle to Brendan, was a character out of central casting for a tough guy movie. He was a Marine Raider in World War II, fighting in the extended operation on Guadalcanal, considered the turning point of the war in the Pacific. He came up the hard way, born and raised in a one-room, cold-water flat in the Darlington section of Pawtucket, Rhode Island.

He worked hard, opened his own construction company, and did well. He was a generous man who gave back to his community. He started his gym after the Notre Dame Boxing Club closed. Bob understood the gym was the only thing between jail and the streets for some young men.

Bob charged no one for membership. The gym was free if you comported yourself like a gentleman. It was an exciting mix of characters, including ex-cons, pro fighters, cops, and con men.

If Grundy's gym was the real deal, the authenticity came from Bob Grundy. Bob's son, Peter, a football star at Bishop Feehan who later became one hell of a fighter, introduced Brendan to the place.

Peter and I used to fight on the lawn behind his house, graduating to the gym when his dad thought we were ready. We were ready when fights behind the house became too bloody and uncontrolled. We'd have to knock on the neighbor's door, covered in blood, to ask the neighbor to re-tie our gloves.

One of the pro fighters in the gym was John "Dino" Denis, the New England Heavyweight Champion. John was tough as nails and a good guy. By this time, 1978, John, previously undefeated, lost his first professional fight in a TKO (technical knockout) to George Foreman. Yeah, that George Foreman.

John was about ten years older than us and kind to the younger guys.

Another stablemate at the gym was Raphael Lopez, who had just turned professional. He was a friendly kid from the Dominican Republic looking for a better life here in the U.S. These guys, and others, added to the charm of the gym.

Yet places like this attracted another, less admirably charismatic, type of individual.

Occasionally, wiseguys would come in. They were former fighters or pretending to be. It wasn't uncommon to hear someone refer to "Raymond." I soon learned this one name title was the not-so-subtle reference to Raymond L.S. Patriarca, Sr., the boss of the New England La Cosa Nostra. My first experience with the reverence many attached to the Patriarca reputation. Something I would come to know well, but never quite understand.

I got to know these guys. Some were formidable fighters, meaning the real deal, and others were wannabe mobsters. Some were tough. Others couldn't break an egg, but they looked the part. Some of these wannabe guys watched a lot of movies and spent time looking in the mirror, practicing their tough-guy looks. Hollywood tough guys. Paper tigers.

I just minded my own business.

Even though he mixed in with this questionable crowd, Brendan always fell back on his parent's moral teachings and the faith instilled at Bishop Feehan High. But it was impossible not to see and hear things back then. Deals were going on all the time.

But not in front of Bob Grundy. They knew better.

There was a guy named Freddy who would come in and sell watches and gold chains out of a briefcase. There were conversations about guys who needed a beating and guys selling stolen suits out of their cars. You couldn't help hearing terms they used like paying juice, or rent, or the vig or vigorish, earner, stooge, loan shark, or the money guy behind a bookmaking operation as a banker.

They would brag about doing a bid or a guy being away at college. It all made sense to them. I was learning the differences between their world and mine.

Juice or rent refers to paying the bosses, like Patriarca, for the privilege of doing business in his territory. Be it as a bookmaker or running a crap (dice) game. Vigorish, or vig, is the interest on a loan from a loan shark.

Loan sharks would lend money to gamblers, and it became a never-ending cycle. Borrow one hundred dollars, pay twenty-five dollars a week "interest" and still owe the hundred dollars.

Few guys ever escaped the black hole of borrowing money from loan sharks to fund gambling.

Going to prison was doing a bid. Being away for some time was in the joint, away at college, on vacation, or spending time at a gated community.

None of this mattered. I was just there to learn how to fight and doing well at it. But at Grundy's, I got an advanced degree in the language and customs of the street and the mob. I didn't know it then, but it would give me an advantage.

One of the retired fighters, Dickie Gambino, was a tough-looking guy. His real name was Richard Quattrocchi. What is it about these guys and their names and nicknames? It did little by way of hiding their identity.

Gambino was a rough character. An associate of Gambino's, Dickie Callei, a "made" guy or full member of the mob, had been killed in a mob-related hit. It put a lot of stress on Gambino. Yet Gambino took a liking to Brendan, giving him advice before Brendan even knew about his mob affiliation.

I talked at the gym about a problem I had with an auto mechanic who overcharged me for some repairs. Gambino told me I should learn a lesson. He told me never to do business with anybody unless someone from the gym referred me. That way, he explained, someone had to okay it. It creates an opportunity for negotiation.

He said, "If Pete over there referred you to this guy that means he's ok and Pete is somewhat responsible for the price and the work."

I was confused but just went along with him.

Then he said, "Give me the name of the place, and I'll go see the guy and negotiate that right down."

I was thrilled to hear that because I couldn't pick up my car until I had full payment. Asking my dad was out of the question, and I was a few dollars short. Fifty dollars short, which was all I made per week at my part-time job.

I thought he'd solved my problem.

When Bob Grundy heard this, he stepped in and politely told Gambino it's all set. Already taking care of it. I didn't know what he was talking about because Bob didn't even know where my car was. Bob took me aside and told me he feared how Gambino would handle the situation. He explained that if the car guy became disrespectful, then Gambino would give him a beating and take the car. It wouldn't look good if the police got involved. Bob liked Gambino. He didn't want to put him on the spot, he just wanted to avoid any problems.

"Use your head," Bob said.

Frankly, the environment I came from doesn't make you think that way. I just assumed this guy was trying to help me. It never occurred to me, if it doesn't go the way Gambino wanted it to go, someone's getting a bad beating. Bob gave me a ride to the car place, and the owner was understanding. He took what I had and gave me my car. He was nice about it. I remember thinking this hard-working guy might have gotten a beating and it would have been my fault.

Somehow my father discovered I'd become friendly with Dick Gambino and told me to stay away from him. I later learned my dad did some dental work for him. Dickie wanted me to contact my dad, get his x-rays, and bring them to the gym. My dad told me to stay out of it and had them delivered.

Dickie moved shortly after that to Las Vegas. I never learned if anyone ever needed the x-rays, but I am sure Dickie didn't want them for his new dentist.

The gym was an exciting place with colorful people. Grundy made it a demilitarized zone; neutral ground for good guys and bad guys. Play by Bob's rules, you were welcome. Break the rules, and you were gone.

There was a guy who I would see around Grundy's Gym sometimes. His nickname was Whacko, and I used to play basketball with him at an old playground not far away.

I told him more than once to drop by to watch the fights. But he always had some excuse not to come in. Years later, I wondered if he owed somebody money or something. Whacko reminded me of the characters that Jimmy Breslin, the New York City columnist, wrote about.

Breslin had a masterful way of capturing the essence of a city in a few words. He wrote, "the best thieves in the world come from Providence, Rhode Island." It was a point I came to understand as time went on, and Whacko played a bit part in my education.

I saw Whacko on Broad Street in Central Falls one day. He was very cordial, but I never trusted him. He asked if I wanted to make a few bucks. A new venture helping a local charity. And what that might look like I asked. He told me he was selling raffle tickets. One dollar each or a book of six for five dollars.

The prizes were a big screen TV for the winner and something like $500 and $250 for the next two in the drawing. I was interested but didn't trust him. I could tell he was getting a little irritated with my questions. He wanted me to take a couple hundred booklets of tickets, and I'd get half the proceeds. Just "move" as many as you could he told me. Sell them to everyone I know, including my family.

I asked how long we had to "move" these tickets.

"As long as you need," he said, "as long as you need, but it's on the honor system."

He said I needed to meet him weekly to turn over proceeds. Just take them, he insisted, trying to hand me boxes of tickets. I resisted. He turned red in the face.

I wasn't worried about him because I knew him to be a scam artist and a quick buck guy. He knew if he went too far, I could face plant him in the street corner.

I asked, "When is the drawing?"

"The drawing?" he said, the frustration in his voice rising, "The drawing? There is no fucking drawing, there is no fucking TV. Do you get it now? We split the money. Are you in?"

"No, I'm not in. See you later."

Two weeks later, one of the new guys in the gym pulled me aside.

"Hey man, are you interested in winning a TV or cash prizes from a local raffle drawing?"

I shook my head. “No thanks, pal," and went about my business.

Brendan continued to pay his dues (putting in his time) in the gym, catching what Dino called, "the bug." He sparred with Dino because, regardless of Brendan’s lack of experience, he needed heavyweights in front of him and there weren't too many around.

Dino was a good sport. He would pepper me with jabs but hold back with the hammer, his big right hand. It was invaluable training for a young fighter. As I became more experienced, he would go harder and harder. Before the Foreman loss, Dino defeated Joe 'King' Roman and Scotty 'The Frenchman' LeDoux. Now, he was training for the main bout at Madison Square Garden against Gerry Cooney. I learned a great deal sparring with a boxer of his caliber.

Dino was in New York training in a local gym under the direction of his trainer Al Braverman. Several of us planned on driving to Manhattan in the morning for the Cooney/Denis fight, so I stopped by the gym kind of late for a quick workout. Rafael was the only one left training, and he asked me if I would work with him for a few rounds.

It was really a *faux pas* for a fighter to be sparring without his trainer present, but he needed the work. Even though I was much bigger, he needed the sparring for an upcoming fight, and I agreed.

Everyone was leaving, so I enlisted the help of a guy who was there to watch. He helped with our gloves and put Vaseline around our eyes. After the first round, he was the only one left in the gym. In the second round, Rafael hit me with an overhand right that caught me between my headgear and eyebrow.

It opened a massive gash over my eye.

Rafael thought I was mad and jumped out of the ring. Within a minute of the spectator trying to get my gloves off, we were both covered in blood. Facial cuts bleed a lot, and this was a good one. I remember feeling paranoid because I thought I would pass out from losing too much blood.

The guy offered to bring me to the emergency room at the old Notre Dame Hospital in Central Falls. When I walked in, wearing hand wraps, Everlast shorts, and Everlast shoes holding a blood-drenched towel, the receptionist said, "let me guess how this happened."

I thought that was cute.

I needed ten stitches in my eyebrow, but it didn't stop me from heading to Manhattan the next morning.

Cooney KO'd Dino in three rounds. Raphael was with us, and there were no hard feelings. It's boxing, and things happen.

He was a nice guy on his way to a promising career, chasing that boxing dream at the end of the rainbow with a big payday. He did become the New England Welterweight Champ but suffered a loss to Hector "Macho" Camacho. He was a clean-living guy but lived in a tough area. It was, perhaps, the last time I saw him. He was later stabbed to death in an argument with a guy in Pawtucket.

The lessons about the other side of life at Grundy's took hold. Brendan learned how to deal with guys who looked at the world as a glass half empty with someone trying to steal it from them. It would serve him well when he encountered these guys under very different, and no longer neutral, circumstances.

Chapter 4 Bob Grundy: The Law of the Jungle

Grundy's gym, like most gritty American boxing gyms, was a continuous lesson in life and Bob Grundy was the Dean of Students. One could learn more about the real world, and randomness of fortune, in a day at the gym than years anywhere else.

One day an up and coming pro, who Brendan sparred with once before, came in the gym with an attitude. He was about eight years older than Brendan and people called him CJ. When Brendan first sparred with him, it was during the day, which was unusual. Most of the sparring went on at night.

One of CJ's friends told Brendan CJ couldn't be seen during regular hours. Brendan didn't question it. It wasn't any of his business, and it worked better with his schedule. The guy needed a heavyweight to spar, and there weren't many around. When he was there was irrelevant.

The guy was a big heavyweight if out of shape, standing about 6'2" and 275 pounds. We sparred four rounds. Although I was in better condition, he was like a bull and more experienced. He threw a couple of punches that missed but caught me with an elbow on the jaw. I thought it was intentional, he didn't care.

The elbow shot didn't improve the situation between him and me.

Because I wouldn't give him the wiseguy respect he expected, we didn't hit it off. He boasted to everyone how many guys he's "straightened out for Gerry." I didn't stick around for the tough guy stories.

He was holding court, I wasn't interested. I came here to fight, not listen to war stories from the streets.

I heard this guy was an enforcer for some mob faction and a fugitive from justice. My disinterest in his stories may have sent a message, and not a helpful one. I had a choice to make. Either I go back to school for Dr. Sapinsly's Economics class at RIC or I sit with these tough guys, listening to how often he can bust a guy up and how much money he could net from that.

Either way, it's economics.

Before our sparring sessions, his friends conducted countersurveillance in the neighborhood looking for cops. At least that's what I thought they were doing. Later, when I'd run my own surveillances, it confirmed my suspicions.

They'd ask me a few questions, i.e., you didn't tell anyone where or who you were meeting did you? I didn't want to say to his buddies I had no one to tell and I didn't even know the guy's real name.

Brendan would learn CJ's real name. He was Carl Justice Nordstrom, also known as Carl Vescio. And Brendan would come to realize he was a very tough guy.

A couple of years went by where I didn't see CJ in the gym. The next time I ran into him, no longer among the missing and now fighting pro, I discovered he'd done a few years in 'college' on that fugitive bid. I learned other interesting things about CJ. He was a hardcore biker at odds for years with the Hells Angels and affiliated with traditional organized crime guys including brothers Gerard and Johnny Ouimette and Jerry Tillinghast.

One day, CJ was shadow boxing in the ring. I was in street clothes off to the side near a set of heavy bags. He made a snide comment, calling me a preppie. I was, but I didn't back down from guys like him, no matter how tough they might be.

I snapped right back at him.

"Hey, CJ, where did you get that new tattoo, K-mart?"

Covered with tattoos, CJ was very proud of them. Some were cool looking. He didn't take my answer well.

"How would you like me to wipe it off on your fucking face?" CJ said.

He wasn't smiling, and neither was I. A few guys heard it. The gym went deadly quiet.

My youth and enthusiasm overruled my common sense.

"I'd like to see that happen."

On reflection, it may not have been the best answer.

He climbed out of the ring, taped up but no gloves, and I realized this was not what I expected for a workout today. Bob Grundy came out of nowhere, grabbed me, and told me to go outside. He looked at CJ and said, "Keep working out and mind your business."

Outside the gym, under a beautiful moonlit night in Central Falls, Brendan got a quick, yet lasting lesson in life. One of many under the wise counsel of Bob Grundy.

"You don't let people mistreat you," Grundy said, "but he's in another league. Pick your fights – pick your disagreements—because no matter how that turned out, you lose."

Grundy could tell Brendan wasn't getting it.

"It's just the way he grew up," Grundy said, pausing a moment. "Let me say this; you might be willing to mix it up with him, but are you ready to die? Seriously, in his world, he can't let you disrespect him. I'll ask again, are you ready to die over something like that?"

He didn't wait for an answer.

"Of course not. Look, stick to college, and your good values. These guys are from another world. Now get in there, tell him you're sorry, and it's all set."

Apologizing was hard to do, so Brendan just nodded at CJ. CJ smiled back. They became cordial after that, but Brendan never trusted him.

Nor would he take a ride with him, although he tried to get Brendan to go with him several times. Take a ride with a guy like that, and you might end up dead or find yourself in some crazy beef with outlaw motorcycle gangs.

Many of CJ's friends took that ride, and it didn't end well. One of them was a reputed underworld figure named George Basmajian. Another tough guy shot and killed around that time.

I interviewed CJ in 2019. He is a version much older than the man Brendan encountered all those years ago, but no less intimidating. CJ had a different memory of the incident in the gym.

This is how CJ recalled it.

"I sparred with Brendan a few times, and he could punch. He was a smart fighter and a big bastard. Back then, I wasn't afraid of anybody. Still not. But Brendan presented a challenge.

"I busted his balls a bit, and he came right back at me. Usually, I can just intimidate guys. Now this preppy prick was willing to go toe to toe with me. I couldn't let that go."

"Bob Grundy saw it happening. He never missed anything in that place. Bob stepped in, told me to knock it off, and pulled Brendan outside. A couple of minutes later, Brendan came back in and nodded at me. I nodded back, and that was it.

"I didn't let Brendan know it, I wouldn't let anyone know it, but Brendan was skilled enough to give me a fight. I probably would have won, but I'd have taken some punches.

"I'm glad it never came to that. Brendan was smart as well. Knew enough to learn by sparring with me, watching me in the ring, but he also knew to keep his distance."

In 2009, at the former Topside Lounge in Bristol, CJ's long-running beef with the Hell's Angels boiled over into a confrontation. An Angel, flying his colors (wearing the famous full patch vest), came in. Words flew, threats made, and tempers flared.

CJ didn't back down. The Angel shoved him. CJ smiled and put the Angel's lights out with a single punch. In the world of biker gangs, such an act is an insult to the entire club. Not for the first time, CJ, never popular with the outlaw biker crowd, became a target.

He didn't care.

Despite approaches by various biker gangs to become a member, he thought it beneath his dignity. Stubbornly clinging to his independence, he refused all invitations.

But in that world, bullets generally win out over balls and brawn.

In 2017, a rival faction shot CJ in the face. He healed well. The round lodged behind the eyeball, yet the surgeons removed the bullet without causing damage to his sight.

Who gets that lucky?

Chapter 5 Looking for Something More

Brendan kept training at the gym, going to classes at RIC, and working at the Civic Center. He was busy but needed all three to stay on track.

One time, there was a lot of talk about a union dispute between management and the full-time crew at the Civic Center. It didn't affect the security guys because most were part-time workers, but Brendan got to know the union guys in the staging crew. Angry comments went back and forth. It was apparent a confrontation was inevitable, once the event was over.

Leaving the building around 1:00 a.m., I saw a guy I knew hurry across the parking lot. His right hand was inside a brown paper bag. He got into a crouched position, raised his right hand, and opened fire on a car.

I froze at the noise and muzzle flash of five or six shots. The windows exploded; shattered but still in place. I couldn't see inside the car because of the clouded and splintered effect from the bullets.

The guy ran off. I thought I'd just witnessed a homicide.

After a moment, I walked up to the car and looked in. No one was in the car. It was a message, severe but crude.

An Irish guy I knew came up to me.

"Hey, what're ya doing? You're with us. Don't get involved. Ya didn't see nothing here, did you?"

I told the guy that if there was a dead guy in that car, I did see something. He looked at me with disgust and walked away. As he walked away, I shouted,

"And by the way- I'm not with anyone."

I saw him again one day when I was sparring with Dino in an exhibition for charity. He and a couple of other guys, who thought they were Irish mobsters, invited me to go with them to a pub in the Smith Hill section of Providence.

I declined.

It was an amateurish recruiting attempt, and not the last one, by some guys looking for an identity. They would use the name 'Jerry' often. It was an attempt to underscore they were connected. Trying to impress Brendan and implying they had ties to Jerry Tillinghast, in prison for the murder of George Basmajian.

It wasn't cockiness, just self-confidence. The lure of the wannabe wiseguys didn't impress Brendan. He would see these guys occasionally at other boxing events but quickly distanced himself from them.

These guys thrived on people fearing or following them. In Brendan, they could make no headway.

The Civic Center was a strange place back then. It had a reputation as a place where wiseguys could get on the payroll and not have to go to work. In the early 80's several employees were arrested as no-show workers. All kinds of exciting things happened in that building, and it attracted top performers.

In 1979, Mayor Vincent A."Buddy" Cianci named Frank Sinatra an honorary fire chief with a helmet bearing the name "Ol' Blue Eyes."

That same year Cianci canceled a concert by The Who because of a stampede by fans at another show at the Cincinnati Coliseum.

The Who returned to Providence thirty-four years later in 2013 and honored tickets from anyone who had purchased them for the 1979 concert. Ironic how the band who Cianci feared would wreak havoc on the city ultimately showed more character than the mayor who sullied it.

You cannot make this stuff up.

On another night in 1979, Brendan was working the night shift at the boat show. The entire building was full of boats. All the spectators left the building by 9:00 p.m. and security locked the doors at 11:00 p.m. once the vendors had all gone.

After 11:00 p.m. there were four people in the building, the midnight facilities man and three members of the security team, including myself. All three of the security personnel were college students. It was customary on the graveyard shift for people inside the building to go off on their own to study, rest, or whatever else helps them pass the time.

No need to check doors or be on constant lookout. We were all secure and felt comfortable in this vast dark monstrous building. Policing the building was not cops-and-robbers.

It wouldn't be uncommon for the guys to hop on one of the yachts and relax. The other two security guys were college football players and needed their rest. I remembered studying for an exam for several hours and hearing nothing out of the ordinary.

Any sounds in the building were typical background noise. If you heard something, you'd assume it was a rat in the rubbish, not crime in progress. I studied, and I thought the other guys were sleeping somewhere on a boat.

At 6:00 a.m., the operations guys and the clean-up crew banged on the rear metal overhead doors. One guy let them in. We knew around 7:00 a.m. the boat show employees and vendors would show up to prepare for their day. We could leave at 8:00 a.m. The Civic Center started another day as our shift ended.

Just before 8:00 a.m. I heard a boat vendor yelling about one of his boats missing. I couldn't imagine how that could happen. If someone stole a yacht, it would make a lot of noise.

Nobody could mistake it for a rat in the rubbish.

I discovered later, after talking to a Providence Police officer, a new twelve or fourteen-foot Zodiac inflatable boat with an expensive outboard motor attached went missing.

It wasn't a yacht, but someone was out a few thousand.

They never solved the theft. I always thought it was one of the other security guys. The opportunity, timeline, and type of boat made it seem the most logical explanation. Someone intent on stealing a Zodiac could turn sideways and walk it out the crash doors.

We would have heard nothing.

Several years later the name changed from the Civic Center to the Dunkin Donuts Center. Brendan was at a Special Olympics meeting in 2012 and told one of the building administrators the zodiac story.

The administrator almost fell off his chair.

He told Brendan between 2005 – 2008, during an eighty-million-dollar renovation, they'd found a large zodiac boat—deflated, folded, and still with its motor—neatly tucked away in the ceiling.

It had lain hidden there for over 25 years.

Who stole it, and why was it left behind? One can only speculate. They were fired, locked up in prison, or both, no longer able to reap the benefits of the Great Disappearing Zodiac Caper.

Part II: The Rhode Island State Police

In the Service of the State

Chapter 6 A Select Few

In 1979, Brendan was hunting around for something to do. Mixed in with good guys and bad guys, he wanted to let everyone know where he stood.

The Civic Center was a job, not a career. Boxing was a hobby, not a serious calling. And school, while relevant, had opened no possibilities that caught his eye.

Once again, sage advice from Bob Grundy would steer Brendan toward a career he might never have otherwise considered. It is often these little happenstances of life which make the most significant impact on the future.

I did a little research. Bob Grundy introduced me to John Partington, at the time a Deputy U.S. Marshal, and John's brother, Bill Partington, a retired State Police Captain. I was fortunate to ask for advice from the Partington brothers.

John Partington, once a Cumberland Police Officer, had joined the Marshals Service looking to expand his career horizons. As the Feds improved their investigative tools against Organized Crime, cooperating witnesses became critical to their cases. Protecting them became a priority. John helped to set up the Federal Witness Protection Program, helping relocate witnesses in criminal cases.

Cooperating individuals, if left in their old neighborhood or routine, were at risk. On the street or in jail, many witnesses to crimes or criminal conspiracies who turn on their former partners need witness protection.

The United States Federal Marshals Service manages the program. John handled many high-profile witnesses. The program, in its early days, depended upon deputies to be innovative and creative. John would use his own house as a mail drop for mobsters and cooperators relocated across the country, using marshals to deliver the packages to the secret locations.

Both Partington brothers gave me good advice. I applied to the State Police, focusing on becoming a state trooper. The Partington brothers' stories gave me a goal of one day working in the Organized Crime Unit.

The night I fought the exhibition round with Dino Denis, I met a Rhode Island State Trooper. He'd come into the locker room to meet me after someone told him I had applied to be a trooper.

The trooper epitomized the concept of squared away; exuding honesty and integrity. Polite, well-groomed, well-dressed, carrying himself with confidence. I said to myself; *I want to do this.* The mob may have thought they had a mystique about them, but the Rhode Island State Police had the real thing.

I was now sure of my path. I was on a mission to become a state trooper.

As soon as I applied, the rumor hit the gym. Pete Grundy thought it was a good fit. So did Dino, but he needed to distance himself because he was friends with the wiseguys.

I felt the change in attitudes. The guys in the gym would say nothing, but it was like I was trying to elevate myself to something unattainable to them. Misery likes company.

Doug Mallette, who grew up in a tough part of Providence and later became a professional fighter, wouldn't even acknowledge me in the gym. That was fine, I wasn't there to make friends.

Dino's manager, Eddie Iamondi, tried to talk me out of it. Eddie was always the first in line for a good deal. He was known as a mover and shaker. A used car dealer, he always drove high-end cars. Eddie was a classic throwback, right out of the movies. He told me that with my boxing skills, I could make a lot of money.

“Don't forget,” Eddie told me, “Dino is on his way out. You could be the next boxing celebrity from this area. A white Irish kid with a left jab can make millions."

I did have an excellent left jab, but Eddie didn't realize that my Aunt Helen had a better right hand. There's no place in the heavyweight division for one-handed fighters.

It was enticing for a few moments.

Eddie wanted me to meet B.A. Dario, the former owner of the Lincoln Dog Track, who could help to secure fights. He would talk about Raymond in front of me with reverence. Eddie just couldn't understand why I would pass on this opportunity. He would respectfully try to encourage me to pursue a boxing career and to do it his way.

It didn't sway me.

If there wasn't such a mob overtone to it, I might have given it more thought. But I focused on becoming a member of the State Police. I believed in the system of justice and my quest to help people who can't help themselves. Through my classes on criminology and political science, I learned there are people, many lacking any resources, who need help. I thought the more good people in the system, the stronger the system would be. I wanted to be part of those who protect those in need.

I made it clear to Eddie and the others, ethics and being what they derisively called a "white knight" was important to me. Eddie was a decent guy. I think he admired that in his own way even if he couldn't understand my decision.

Eddie was impressed when I had a fight at Grundy's Gym with a street kid from Providence named Bobby Walason. Walason was a tough brawler with serious punching power. When he hit the heavy bag, it shook the support beams. He weighed in around 180 pounds, so I used my size and reach to overpower him. But there was no doubt he could punch.

Eddie heard about it and got excited. Walason had a well-deserved reputation as a tough guy. A lot of guys feared him.

A boxing exhibition was coming to the Civic Center. Eddie said he might get me on the card as one of the sparring partners for Muhammad Ali. Ali was the heavyweight champ at the time and the most prominent name for the event.

I thought it was a ridiculous idea. I was interested, but unsure of what that would entail. It's an honor to say you stepped in the ring with the greatest fighter of all time, but common sense would dictate he can knock you out any time he chose.

As the event drew closer, I realized Eddie was serious. There were rules for the opportunity. Don't try to upstage the champ. Don't take any cheap shots. It's an exhibition. Ali was not to look bad or else. The “or else” part was simple to understand. If you forced Ali to exert more energy than was necessary, you'd pay for your amateurish move.

And come to appreciate why he was the world champion.

A couple of days before the event, the Ali camp rejected the offer. I was too green and too much of a liability. The exhibition did take place on March 12, 1979. Ali boxed a few rounds with several professional heavyweights, including Dino Denis. I did get invited to his penthouse suite at the Providence Biltmore Hotel, where I listened as the champ told story after story.

Bob and Peter Grundy were with me that night at the Biltmore. We enjoyed Ali's magnanimous personality. At one point, Ali was joking with the other fighters. He looked over at me and said, "What are you looking at?" slapped me with a quick, playful light-handed touch, and then laughed.

I laughed with him; getting mad wouldn't have ended well for me.

Those were good times. I was involved with so many personalities with diverse ideas, goals, and perspectives. Peter Grundy won the New England Golden Gloves Championship. Eddie Iamondi trained other fighters. He eventually ended up in federal prison on a public corruption case. Doug Mallette served a life sentence in prison for murder, and Bobby Walason went on to a career as a racketeer and underworld figure.

Those stories will unfold in due time. For now, boxing remained a crucial element in my life.

In the Rhode Island boxing world, Brendan may have been a prospect in the eyes of some. But Brendan had other ideas, just wanting to do his own thing. He may not have understood everything about the dark underside of the boxing world and those who lurk there, but he knew enough to stay at arm's length from most. He would learn from them, spar with them, but not hang with them. That was a path contrary to a long, healthy, prison-free life.

Eddie Iamondi remembers Brendan from those days. He saw an opportunity in Brendan. A new face in the Rhode Island boxing world who could draw people to boxing matches.

Eddie also knew Brendan didn't fit the mold of many of these guys. Brendan had choices, opportunities, a future outside of boxing. For many guys in Grundy's gym, and gyms around the country, boxing was the only thing between them, the streets, or a prison cell.

I interviewed Eddie about his memories of Brendan. He said this.

"If Brendan really wanted it, I could have gotten him fights with some big names. He was smart, could punch, could take a punch, and he wasn't easily intimidated.

"He might not have been the most talented boxer at the time, but he had the heart. And that can make up for a lot of shortcomings.

"But, in hindsight, Brendan made the right choice. A boxer, even the best ones, don't last forever. Once that is over, there aren't a lot of career choices. Brendan could have done well by me. I took care of guys who worked for me. But he did okay with the State Police and who can say anything bad about that?"

I would travel to different gyms around the area to spar with other heavyweights who needed the work. One guy was going to Petronelli's Gym in Brockton, Massachusetts to spar with Marvin Hagler. His name was Fernando Fernandez, and he was the New England Welterweight Champ.

Fernando was a good man and was a friend of Marvin's. I would go to watch because it was a treat to see Marvin Hagler train.

One day, Goody Petronelli, Marvin's trainer, asked if I would spar with their up-and-coming heavyweight, Steve Zouski. I agreed and went three rounds with Zouski, who was very deceiving. He wasn't big, probably six-one, two hundred twenty pounds, but he could punch like a mule.

He hit me with several left hooks that caused me to hear my mother calling me for lunch. I went home with a concussion. Zouski later lost bouts to Mike Tyson and George Foreman.

While waiting for the State Police academy to start, I had another fight in Boston. I fought on the same card as Vinny Pazienza. Vinny was a great fighter with a big heart. I made twenty-five dollars for the fight. They couldn't pay us because that would constitute a professional status, but they could give us travel money. They named Pazienza the fighter of the night, and he got something like thirty dollars.

What a racket those promoters controlled.

There we so many good fighters from Rhode Island during that era who just didn't make it. To fight and win as a boxer was their reason for living, but such a life eludes most. Boxing was their only thing, and they had nothing to fall back on. Paul Simon said it best in the Simon & Garfunkel tune, "The Boxer":

"In the clearing stands a boxer, and a
fighter by his trade,
And he carries the reminders of ev'ry glove
that laid him down, or cut him
till he cried out, In his anger and his
shame,
I am leaving, I am leaving.

But the fighter still *remains...*[1] "

Brendan knew instinctively he did not want to be that guy; chasing a dream until it became a nightmare. He was a fighter, of that there was no doubt. He'd demonstrated it often.

He wasn't afraid to face a challenge in the ring, but he knew it was not his life. Not his reason for getting up in the morning. His calling would come from a different set of challenges.

He would face a more sinister group of opponents. In contests where the stakes were life and death, and they did not abide by Marquess of Queensbury rules.

And he would remain guided by the lessons of Grundy's gym and his own true north.

---

[1] Songwriters: PAUL SIMON

The Boxer lyrics © Universal Music Publishing Group

Chapter 7 RISP Recruit Academy

In July 1980 Brendan started as a recruit in the Rhode Island State Police Academy.

It is a proud organization with a tradition of excellence that all starts in the academy. This class started with twenty-three recruits during a ferocious heatwave. By the end of training in October, there were fourteen people left.

One instructor was a former Navy Seal. He trained us to be ready for any situation or event. His name was Gerry Brissette. He wanted no one to get through without earning his respect.

I was an excellent swimmer and enjoyed showing him my strength. I particularly enjoyed the exercise where he would tie a baby doll to a cinder block, throw it in the deep end of the Olympic size pool and time us in the retrieval.

The academy was a twenty-four-hour, six-days-a-week torture show. It was every man for himself. I remember a recruit who was a good runner ask me to go easy on him in boxing.

Come on," he said, "You know, just go through the motions and make it look good."

"Are you going to wait for me in the long runs?" I answered. We would sometimes go out in ninety-degree temperatures for a ten-mile run.

"You know I can't do that."

I gave him his answer. I fought that guy and knocked him out cold. It's not that I was any tougher than anyone else, I just had the experience.

Graduating from the academy in October 1980 was a proud day. My dad was still alive but very sick. He knew I left college to go to the academy. He made it clear he was pleased, but I had to go back to earn my degree. I promised I would.

It took some time, but I graduated from Roger Williams University and earned a master's degree in Criminal Justice from Anna Maria College in Paxton, Massachusetts.

A promise is a promise.

The military drill, Esprit de corps, and paramilitary bearing during the academy's graduation ceremony amused my parents. But it made me what we would call "squared away."

One of the academy staff would always say, "You need to be squared away. At all times. At any cost."

That stayed with me for life.

Chapter 8 Dark Nights Working the Street

Brendan was now a trooper with the elite Rhode Island State Police. But the most dangerous thing in the world is a new anything. The academy is the foundation of a good trooper. It tests your mettle, your determination, your ability to endure for the greater good.

But a foundation is not a complete structure. There's a lot of building and finishing work yet to do. The academy teaches you how to wear the uniform, how to look the part, what the department expects from you.

It does not make you a good cop.

It doesn't make you a cop at all—that can only happen on the street. Like a newly minted doctor, you have the title, but no one wants you to operate on them.

My first assignment was the Hope Valley Barracks. It was like the Wild West in Hope Valley. About forty minutes south of Providence on Rt. 95, you may as well be in another country.

At least back then.

Now, new housing developments provide a short commute to nearby Connecticut or downtown Providence. The cost and quality of housing increased over the years. But then it wasn't unusual to respond to a one-room, cold-water house with dirt floors and an out-house or a trailer with no plumbing.

It was unlike anything I had ever experienced.

One night, the barracks received a call for shots fired. I was still a probationary trooper riding with a senior trooper named Pat McQueeney. Pat was the son of Chief Walter McQueeney from Providence. He was also the brother of Sgt. Bob McQueeney from the State Police and brother of Det. Gerry McQueeney of Providence PD.

Nepotism and legacies were not unheard of in Rhode Island law enforcement circles. Nothing wrong with that. But it was tough to compete for advancement when your dad was a dentist and others had titles in their families that sounded like they had their own army.

We responded to the shots fired call. Pat was a cool, calm, and collected guy. Younger troopers looked up to him because he had a lot of institutional knowledge and was happy to teach the younger guys. When we pulled onto the road, it was about 2:00 a.m. with no streetlights. Pat told me this street was usually well lit. There were no outside lights on, and all the houses were dark.

As if a call for shots fired wasn't enough, now darkness enveloped us.

The only light was a full moon lighting a path through the pine trees. It was winter with a little snow cover, quiet and still.

Suddenly, we heard five or six quick shots. We were close. Pat pulled the marked cruiser over and shut off the lights. He told me to be mindful of the interior light in the car. He wanted to make sure I got out quickly and stepped away from the vehicle. Our interior light had not been disconnected yet as it was a relatively new cruiser.

I recall him saying, "Are you ready, kid?"

"Ready for what, sir?"

His response was precious. "Whatever it is we need to be ready for!"

"Yes, I am, sir." Although I wasn't convinced of it.

I remember thinking I had no idea what he was thinking, but this may not end well.

He suggested we walk toward where we thought we heard the shots. The barracks radioed us, telling us people reported a power outage. Trying to make our way toward the gunfire in the dark, this just added to the joy.

The homes were spread out, three to four-hundred yards apart. People may not even know their next-door neighbor. We tiptoed, just outside the moonlit walk, up a hill toward the transformers supplying the power. Just then, only two minutes into this exploratory walk, a guy popped out from behind shrubs, dressed in camouflage and wearing full military garb, yelling at us to stop.

He pointed his rifle at me.

Pat yelled back; the guy yelled over him.

"Hands up!" the guy yelled.

Pat yelled back, "Drop the gun."

I recall thinking there was something wrong with this – his gun is pointed at me, and Pat is yelling at him. *Should I drop and roll or just comply? And is this how I will die?*

Pat told him that everything would be ok. That it was time to sit down and talk, trying to calm the guy. The soldier dropped to one knee and put his gun against a nearby tree. Pat McQueeney was a compassionate guy, and it didn't take a psychiatrist to recognize this guy needed help. He was suffering from post-traumatic stress disorder or, as it was known back then, "shell shock."

Pat notified the officer in charge (OIC), a Viet Nam veteran, who agreed the guy needed help. He didn't point the gun at anyone else (except me and I guess I didn't count.) We seized his weapon, drove him to Providence for mental health evaluation, and reported the outage to the electric company.

No arrest, no sensationalized grab, no perp walks, just doing what is right. All in a day's work out of the Hope Valley Barracks of the Rhode Island State Police.

We followed through with his family, safe-guarded the weapon, and made a note about his condition if we ever heard from him again. I learned he had a stellar military career. The guy cried in our back seat. How many of our veterans have come home like that and are ignored by society?

I learned a lot that day.

I enjoyed my days as a uniform trooper but always had an interest in the Intelligence Unit. I understood the underworld, the wiseguys, mobsters, button men, whatever you want to call them. They're the same characters whether you are in The Bronx, Providence, Boston, Chicago, Hoboken, or Philly.

A wise guy is a wise guy.

Whether it's Irish mobsters, renegades, or La Cosa Nostra, they are all the same. There's one good reason for that – they all watch mob movies and TV shows: *Good Fellas, Godfather, State of Grace, The Sopranos*, etc. You name it, they watch it, and they learn.

Some guys I have known with a proclivity for mob life could have succeeded in some other business, but they needed respect, or in old school Mafioso, "rispetto." A man of honor. They live by "Omerta," the Mafia Code of Conduct.

Be respectful but don't talk to law enforcement and never be a "rat."

I understood their world, their allegiances, and their fears because they weren't all tough guys. Most were not tough. I knew it and wanted to play in that arena. To show them I could be fair, play by the rules, and put cases together that others might not because I knew them.

I got my break on St. Patrick's Day in 1986. I received a call notifying me of my promotion to the State Police Intelligence Unit, essentially the Organized Crime Unit. Raymond Loretto Salvatore Patriarca, Sr., the same 'Raymond' whose name I'd heard so often from wiseguys and wannabes, had just died.

The New England mob, better known as the Patriarca family, was in a state of flux. Raymond left quite a legacy. He was a man who did time and had close, often secret ties to legitimate businesses, the police, the clergy, politicians, judiciary, and the average guy on the street. He was a gentleman unless you crossed him.

In 1981, while in uniform, I was assigned to watch him for a few days at Miriam Hospital. Charged in an indictment, he became ill and couldn't stay in prison. While I sat in the room with him, Raymond asked me if I wanted a Whitman Sampler chocolate. I declined. I had just come out of the academy still brainwashed that if you accept ANY form of graft, you are "bought and paid for," corrupt, and subject to termination at the very least.

Raymond could tell I would have loved a piece of chocolate, but he smiled and told me to help myself.

That's how legitimate members of society saw Raymond. He held immense power over career criminals. They would not dare to cross him. There is no better teacher than the past. Raymond's methods worked.

It's just the way it was.

Chapter 9 Patrol to Chasing Mobsters

Assignment to the State Police Intelligence Unit is an honor. The unit carries a secretive reputation. Covert and surreptitious was the order of the day. Most surveillances concerned mobsters or career criminals, but occasionally the boss would give Brendan other confidential assignments.

They operated on a need-to-know basis.

In the mob, wiseguys refer to the person who sanctioned them as their godfather. To enter that secret society, you need a sponsor. The sponsor is responsible for your actions. In the Intelligence Unit, they joked about the same nicknames or nomenclature. It was the same thing.

My mentor, who some would call my godfather, was the legendary Col. Walter E. Stone. He took a liking to me, and I was fortunate to have caught his attention. Many members of the State Police saw the man less than a dozen times in their career.

He was getting up in age by the time I met him.

I was with the Colonel one day, and he quizzed me on criminals and politicians with criminal ties. I passed the test. I provided intelligence not only on each one, but I believe I knew more about them than he did.

One person he was interested in was Chief Justice of the Rhode Island Supreme Court, Joseph Bevilacqua. After passing the test, I would often receive a particular assignment that would range from delivering a personal message, providing a sealed envelope to the Providence Journal, or just attending an event with him.

Col. Stone was the last of the old school. He survived the transition to the modern era of policing even though there was nothing modern about him, aside from his immaculate style of dressing. He was a former Providence policeman, beginning his law enforcement career in 1931, and worked his way up to become the Chief of Rhode Island's capital city.

In 1959, he was appointed the Superintendent of the RI State Police and held that position until 1961. He was reappointed in 1963, by then-Governor John Chafee, who later became a U.S. Senator.

The reappointment of Col. Stone would become a significant issue in Chafee's campaign for governor. Chafee painted the picture that the mob didn't want Col. Stone back in office and capitalized on the idea the RI mob had ties to political insiders.

In 1963, Col. Stone testified in Washington before a subcommittee on organized crime identifying Raymond L.S. Patriarca Sr. as the head of the mob in New England. He described him as a man who "runs a strong-arm operation" and cleverly conceals his role.

This was after Senator Kefauver's Committee described Patriarca as the "king of the rackets" in New England.

The Colonel and Raymond were each other's nemesis. Col. Stone had old school members of the Intelligence Unit, Tony Mancuso, Vin Vespia, Pete Benjamin, Mike Urso, Lou Reali, Johnston police officer Marty Cappelli, and others keep close tabs on Raymond's activities.

Throughout this time, other State Police detectives focused on cases involving the mob. Ed Pare, Joe Broadmeadow, Ed Correia, and Don Boddington worked with Providence Police and the FBI on mob killings and criminal activities.

To the Rhode Island State Police, the Patriarca organization was always a high priority.

Patriarca's criminal record is an intriguing document. Reading between the lines of the numerous indictments, dismissals for failure to stand trial for health reasons, federal and state incarcerations dating back to 1926, one realizes Patriarca served little time in prison.

Through the influence of the mob, reaching into higher political offices, Patriarca once served only six months of a fifteen-year sentence for armed robbery after receiving a pardon from the Governor of Massachusetts. The resulting scandal, once the word got out, caused the resignation of a members of the Governor's staff.

Yet Patriarca kept his pardon and headed back to Providence.

The Colonel remained in office until 1990. While his longevity as an agency leader was unmatched, the changing face of law enforcement; women, minorities, outside scrutiny of operations, took their toll. The times were changing. It was time for the Colonel to step aside.

The Colonel outlived Raymond by six years, dying in 1992. One man knew just by his position, the other known only by his first name created an enduring part of Rhode Island history.

No matter the criticisms leveled at the Colonel, his concern for preserving an unblemished reputation and continuing success of the Rhode Island State Police was one of the most significant factors in the organization's evolution.

He gave me his entire uniform on the day of his retirement. He was a hard man to work for, but compassionate. He was exceptionally sympathetic to victims of crime. If the victim was a woman, it would draw even more attention, and he expected justice. Justice came in different shapes and sizes. He walked tall, carried a big stick, but was seldom seen in public.

From my first day in the Intelligence Unit, I always respected the role and learned from past members. We were up against some of the most dangerous career criminals in the northeast. We played by the rules but needed to be resilient. We showed the mob element we were not afraid under any circumstances.

It's just not in our DNA.

Most of the bad guys understood the unwritten rule against threatening or retaliating against cops. But not everyone got along all the time—there may have been some personality differences—but if anyone threatened or harmed one us or a member of our families, we would come together and set an example.

It wasn't a significant concern, the only bad guys who would step outside of those boundaries would be amateurs, albeit some dangerous and violent. Raymond always impressed upon his followers the need to be respectful. He was savvy enough to know that if wiseguys under his direction were disrespectful to the FBI, State Police, or any police officers, it would just bring more heat on him and the organization.

I was in the Intelligence Unit for about a week. Everyone had a desk except me. I was using different spaces to call informants or study old intelligence reports. I asked if I could get a desk. The head of the Intelligence Unit, Lieutenant (later Captain) Mike Urso, said, "You'll get one when you earn one."

About a week later, I arrested a guy for bookmaking with ties to "The Office," the main bookmaking operation. I got a desk and a car along with a new assignment. I was to run surveillances on two criminal associates of Judge Joseph Bevilacqua, the Chief Justice of the Rhode Island Supreme Court.

As my investigation was just starting, a photo of a woman exiting a hotel in Smithfield, R.I. with Judge Bevilacqua appeared on the front-page Sunday edition of the Providence Journal. It created a controversy. But the Colonel stood behind us, the investigation, and the surveillance operation.

Bevilacqua, known as "the Chief," was a political powerhouse in the 70s and 80s. A former Speaker of the House of Representatives in Rhode Island, he was, by most accounts, an excellent jurist.

One of his failings, in the eyes of some, was his ties to organized crime. Not one to turn his back on guys from the old neighborhood or the old social clubs, "the Chief" maintained relationships with many people both in and close to the mob.

Back then, if you grew up in an ethnic neighborhood in inner-city America, whether it be Irish, Italian or otherwise, you knew everyone. The family and neighborhood relationships—the good guys and the bad guys—all coexisted, mixed in the same socio-economic chess game, it was a custom hard to break.

It's just the way it was.

This was Rhode Island, where there is only one degree of separation. The Robber Barons all played in the same sandbox; anointing political leaders and earning riches from their machinations.

"The Chief" was a known associate of Eddie Lato, who was on his way to earn his "button," and Rocco Argenti, a strong-arm guy who already had his button.

Both Lato and Argenti had reputations as hitmen.

The photo of "the Chief" coming out of a room at the Alpine hotel was significant. There was no checking in or out. "The Chief" had a key in advance.

The owner of the hotel, Eugene Carlino, had a criminal record. News stories and subsequent testimony before the Rhode Island Judiciary Committee revealed reputed mob associate Robert Barbato arranged for Bevilacqua to have undocumented access to rooms at the hotel. The photo, taken by then Lieutenant Mike Urso, somehow ended up in the hands of the Providence Journal.

A move was on to unseat the Chief Justice. He would be no easy target.

One obstacle was his son John, a well-known attorney, who held the leadership of the Rhode Island Senate. Well-liked, John would do whatever he could to defend his father. Another obstacle was John's brother, Joseph Jr., who was a prominent criminal defense attorney in Rhode Island.

John later became the President of the Senate. Joe went off to prison, not his finest moment.

In 1986, politics and the mob met at an intersection of common interest. Hearings began before the House Judiciary Committee with former United States Attorney General Benjamin Civiletti serving as special counsel to the House. Civiletti served as the Attorney General in the Carter administration.

The frenzy of building a case was intense.

Surveillances and subpoenas were full speed ahead. Some subpoenas services turned into investigation reports. Often, when we located the person and served the summons, they were with people they wouldn't usually be with. These links added to our understanding of the organization, the way they sought to protect themselves, and just how significant "the Chief" was to them.

These guys preferred anonymity. They operated through go-betweens to avoid direct ties. Yet the seriousness drove them to risk our discovering these previously unknown associations. The RICO (Racketeer Influenced and Corrupt Organizations) statute was a powerful tool in investigating and prosecuting organized crime. They knew we might later use this information to tie them to criminal activity in subsequent indictments.

RICO (Racketeer Influenced and Corrupt Organizations) statute 18 U.S.C. §§ 1961–1968 is one of the most effective investigative tools in combatting organized crime, both traditional and other groups.

Under the statute, the head of an organization faces prosecution for the acts of those acting on his orders or under his direction.

> *Predicate offenses such as narcotics trafficking, murder, robbery, extortion, etc., committed as part of a continuing criminal enterprise encompassed a wide range of prosecutable crimes.*
>
> *Where bosses once insulated themselves from the acts of subordinates, they now faced prosecution as if they had pulled the trigger.*
>
> *Applying the RICO statutes in organized crime cases was the most significant factor in the demise of traditional organized crime and other organized criminal groups such as outlaw biker groups, drug cartels, and street gangs.*

In the intelligence world, associates are the key to any organization. It wasn't a lot of fun, but the overall objective was to impeach the Chief Justice because of this shadow of corruption over the courts.

People were running scared, and tempers were flaring in both circles.

Subpoenas were issued for many of the upper echelon mob. We brought in Nicky Bianco, aka "Providence Nick," who had ties to the New York mob. Raymond Jr. was another. We believed Junior took over as "Boss" after his dad died. Bianco later became the titular head of the family when Junior went to prison after the FBI intercept of the induction ceremony in October 1989.

Nicky faced an indictment shortly after that because of a RICO charge in Connecticut, and I testified at the trial in Hartford. I have to say, Nicky always carried himself with class. We passed one another as I arrived in the Federal Courthouse in Hartford.

He was an old school La Cosa Nostra. Always cordial, he said hello, but wouldn't give you the time of day beyond that. He died in federal prison.

The FBI introduced incredible evidence at the trial confirming the structure and organization of the mob. Its impact on the case was immeasurable.

The FBI recording of the Mafia induction ceremony was one incredible investigative effort. The recording corroborated testimony about the Mafia, or La Cosa Nostra, in the United States Senate known the Valachi Hearings.

Joseph Valachi, a New York mob affiliate, was the first to violate the Omerta code. Omerta was the code of silence—no discussing family business outside the family, no cooperation with authorities—and until Valachi testified, it had never been broken before.

Valachi detailed the structure, organization, and described the ceremony used to induct new members. Such a ceremony—long rumored to be real—was rarely discussed until Valachi testified, and no one had ever said it with such clarity.

Valachi provided riveting testimony before the hearing committee. Yet, there was nothing more than Valachi's word. Those suspected of being members, suspected of going through the ceremony, denied the existence of La Cosa Nostra.

In 1971, another Mafia soldier, Vincent "Fat Vinny" Teresa, a member of the Patriarca organization, talked. As is often the case, the motivation wasn't fear of prison (he was already serving time) but lack of respect — offering too little or no money — that Teresa believed was owed to him and his family.

More information leaked out about the Mafia, confirming much of what Valachi said. Yet no independent evidence corroborated the sensational revelations, leaving the ceremony to speculation and imagination.

The ceremony— the words, the burning of Saint's card in the hands, the pledge of leaving only by death—with a history reaching back to the origins of the Sicilian roots of the Mafia, became the thing of legend.

Now, for the first time, the FBI captured it on tape.

There was friction between Boston, Hartford, and Providence factions of the New England mob. Frank "Cadillac" Salemme of Boston and Sharon, Massachusetts, newly released after spending considerable time in prison, reasserted control over contested territory. Summonsed to a meeting in Saugus Massachusetts, gunmen ambushed Salemme, shooting him several times. But Cadillac survived.

On or around the same date, William "Wild Guy" Grasso, of Connecticut, believed to be the "Underboss," was shot and killed.

Within a week of the Grasso/Salemme shootings Brendan accompanied Col. Stone and Maj. Lionel Benjamin, the State Police Executive Officer, to a briefing with Col. Jack "O D" O'Donovan of Massachusetts State Police, the FBI, and the Boston PD.

Word filtered through various sources that the New England mob was looking to restore peace. Trying to broker peace among the factions, they called for an induction ceremony. The FBI, through an outstanding intelligence operation, developed adequate probable cause, obtained necessary electronic surveillance warrants, and prepared to wire the location.

Operating with limited advance notice, the FBI pulled off the intelligence operation of the century in the long battle against Organized Crime.

Raymond Patriarca Jr. presided over the ceremony.

"We're all here to bring in some new members into our family, and more than that, to start maybe a new beginning. Put all that's got started behind us. Cause they come into our Family to start a new thing with us...."

The consigliere of the family, Joe Russo of Boston, introduced the prospects to the other members. One of the men receiving his button was Robert "Bobby" Deluca of Lincoln, R.I. The newest members took the required oath.

"I want to enter into this organization to protect my family and protect all of my friends. I swear not to divulge this secret and to obey with love and Omerta...."[2]

This investigation by the FBI was one of the most significant single events in dismantling the New England mob.

One guy whose stock went up after the induction ceremony was Robert "Bobby" Deluca, known as "Cigars" because of the large cigars he favored. The cigars were so large they often obstructed surveillance photos.

[2] Organized Crime Sixth Edition by Howard Abadinsky Wadsworth COPYRIGHT 2000

After Raymond Sr died, there was a shuffling of the deck. Deluca's elevation to made status raised eyebrows. A lot of old school wiseguys watched in amazement. Bobby was not a tough guy. Many of the old breed could not understand why he was elevated.

What did he do to deserve a button?

The bottom line was Raymond Sr., and Raymond Jr. trusted him. After the induction ceremony, "Junior" went away to federal prison and Bobby quickly aligned with Frankie Salemme.

He became Frankie's trusted confidant and given the tough assignments. Bobby handled meetings with the Whitey Bulger crew, Chucky Flynn, a career criminal and participant in the famed Bonded Vault robbery, and others, clarifying who was the new boss.

Frankie, having survived an assassination attempt in Saugus where gunmen shot him several times in the stomach, a shooting we'll discuss more later, needed to limit his exposure, and Bobby was the perfect man for the job. He would be Frankie's eyes and ears on the street and his messenger.

FBI agent, Chuck Robbins, and I became Bobby's shadow. Bobby was good at his job. That job was avoiding a hit by the bad guys and avoiding detection or electronic intercepts by the good guys.

Bobby rented cars weekly and switched cell phones almost as often. His main hangouts were a couple of Rhode Island restaurants and the Lincoln Greyhound Park. Bobby would often spot us at those venues. He was street savy guy.

A wiseguy reported to Deluca we tried to flip him; now Bobby knew he was a target. He wouldn't talk to people unless they had years of experience together.

But Bobby needed to keep doing what he did best because the rent had to be collected. Frankie was the boss, and he had a lot of financial making up to do. Frankie spent a lot of time in prison for this organization and a lot of time thinking about recovering what others owed him.

Frankie needed to keep his accounts receivable current, and Bobby was the voice delivering those messages.

Everybody who ran an illicit business within reach of his guys had to pay rent. Bookie's, bars involved in the drug or gambling business, and strip joints either paid up or went out of business, involuntarily.

Bobby was good at making surveillance teams. He'd think nothing of walking over to confront someone. Bobby saw us even when we weren't there. He'd tell guys at his table at the track that the guy in the blue coat with the white hat is undercover for Doherty or Robbins. It would get back to us, and we weren't even on him that day. He saw ghosts, so we knew we were getting to him.

He'd spend his day with guys like Poochie, Eddie Lato, Harpo, or Rocky, and then slip away to meet Frankie. Bobby's rise continued with his elevation to Capo (Captain) in Salemme's crew. This enabled him to make decisions.

Col. Stone kept hearing the name and wanted a photo of Frank Salemme delivered to his desk.

We didn't have a recent photo of Frank Salemme, but if the Colonel wanted one, it was priority number one. I had a source who would contact me with updates on Frankie; Frankie was on "The Hill." Frankie was on a side street with Louie in conversation. Frankie just walked into a restaurant through the back door and was meeting Bobby.

After several trips to different locations and striking out, I finally found him. The source told me Frank was standing in the entrance of Casa Christina on Atwells Avenue in Providence with his son, "Frankie Boy."

By the time I got there, they were about to leave. When I walked in, two guys I didn't know left in a hurry through the kitchen, apparently not wanting me to see them with Frank. I said hello to Frank Sr, identified myself, and asked that he walk outside.

He did.

I introduced myself, and he said he'd been wondering what I looked like. He was very cordial and smiling. I had a camera in my hand. Frankie Boy got up on the side of me, and I felt a little uncomfortable.

I wanted them to know that I was only there for a photo, we could do that standing right there on Atwells Avenue, then everyone would be free to go. I told Frank it wasn't my preference to confront him with his son present, but since we're here, we might as well get this over with.

I didn't like to bother people with family members around.

Frank Sr. joked around, and I asked him how he was recuperating from his shooting. He told me he was doing well and those twenty-plus years of doing sit-ups all day gave him a washboard stomach that helped absorb the bullets. By the shape he was in, it was almost believable.

Frankie Boy never said a word.

I said we needed a photo of each and the cordial nature of our conversation dissolved. Frank Sr. said there would be no photos taken.

"My lawyer has requested no photos."

"We can take the photo here right now, or we're all going back to State Police Headquarters," I replied.

Frank Sr. asked if I had a warrant. I said no.

He asked what powers I had to bring them in? I told him he'd be placed under arrest per order of Col. Walter Stone.

Frankie Boy got fidgety, and it looked like he might try to impress his dad. I stepped back so he couldn't sucker punch me.

Frank Sr. said, "Take the photo." He looked at Frankie Boy. "Just stand for the photo and let's get this over with."

I took the photos, said thank you, and we all went our way.

Salemme's growing influence after the death of Raymond, Sr., became a concern. Much of this intersected with the hearings for Chief Justice Bevilacqua's impeachment proceedings.

Former US Attorney Benjamin Civiletti, in charge of the impeachment process, directed many upper echelon members of the New England mob subpoenaed to testify. No surprise here, most invoked their fifth amendment privilege.

Public sentiment was somewhat mixed. Some thought it was a cheap shot. Some thought it was based upon mere speculation and appearances of impropriety. Some political neophytes saw it as retribution.

One thing was sure, Col. Stone had the intestinal fortitude to pursue the matter.

The Senate conducted a hearing into how the Providence Journal obtained a copy of the State Police surveillance photo of the Judge leaving the hotel.

There were implied threats to the detectives serving subpoenas, including me. All part of the job.

But other regular citizens thought it was the right thing to do. It was amazing to see people, some politically connected, offering up information. Trying to discern what was real and what was just political revenge was tricky. Loyalty in politics is like flowing water—direction can change in an instant or, in a drought, dry it up.

Chief Justice Joseph A. Bevilacqua resigned on May 31, 1986. When asked by the New York Times about taking the case further, Benjamin Civiletti said, "It seems to me that enough is enough."

A battle won, and the war raged on.

Chapter 10 Providence and the Mob

Rhode Island has a reputation as a target-rich environment of political corruption. The media often repeats the words of the muckraking journalist, Lincoln Steffens, who, when writing about cities and states in America, said, "Rhode Island is a state for sale, and cheap."

Corruption is no more prevalent in Rhode Island than anywhere else inhabited by humans. It's the size of the state that makes it more visible. Rhode Island is a small state with an active media. They did an excellent job of exposing corruption.

Yet it is not isolated to Rhode Island. Just look at our surrounding states, many public officials have gone to prison or resigned because of law enforcement or media exposure. Massachusetts and Connecticut are replete with Governors, Speakers, Mayors, and other public officials who have walked the plank.

What makes Rhode Island different is it's likely you're related to, went to school with, hung around with, or sought favor from the corrupt politician who may have once been an honest citizen. Everybody knows everybody here in Little Rhody. It makes it difficult for checks and balances to work correctly.

Early organized crime and corruption took root in the northeast. In the later part of the 19th century, organized crime and political corruption were the Robber Barons. They saw an opportunity and seized it. Industrialists and businessmen acquired tremendous wealth through questionable tactics and political hubris. American capitalists grew wealthy wielding government influence. They controlled the politicians who passed laws and reduced oversight to benefit their wealthy benefactors.

It was a self-sustaining cycle. Control the government, dictate to the legislature, and reap the benefits, allowing you to exert more control.

Many summered in Newport, Rhode Island. Their opulent, sea-side mansions an obscene testament to the enormous wealth. They amassed fortunes through political maneuvering before organized crime was a concept. Organized crime often hides under the patina of successful businessmen. Capitalism for a select few in a rigged game.

It wasn't until others rigged their own rackets it became criminal.

Until Irish and Italian immigrants seized the opportunities created by Prohibition, organized crime was an unknown concept. The Volstead Act, commonly known as Prohibition, enacted in 1920 and repealed in 1933, gave birth to systematic and widespread violations of the law.

Some historians believe Prohibition sparked traditional organized crime in America. There were conflicts and cognitive dissonance in inner-city neighborhoods. Studies show, in specific communities, ethnic succession and differential association, i.e., learned behaviors, attracted young men to the wiseguy or racketeer lifestyle.

Being a wiseguy was a dream career in the eyes of many young men in Providence. It was a badge of honor for some of these guys. It's a total elevation of status in the neighborhood. It does not happen overnight. Like any other job, it can take years to get recognized. But once known for doing something outstanding or achieving success, you might just get a bump. Even the mob recognizes "success."

It was "making your bones" before anyone knew what that meant.

In corporate America, one might get a promotion or a favorable performance evaluation that bodes well for the future. In a police department, you might get a promotion or a transfer to a more favorable shift or assignment. In the mob, you get a smile or a nod as acceptance from one of the guys in the upper echelon. It might not even be the boss. If you're an associate, you wouldn't be able to just walk up to a boss and talk about criminal conspiracies. A smart boss is too cautious and insulated for that to happen.

But if you're a tough young guy, and you've just impressed a made guy, then you've raised your stock. You get a little more respect. The made guys may ask you to take a ride or let you remain in the room when they force a stooge or a lackey to leave.

In that world, respect is what it is all about. Eventually, if you do something big enough, you might even get your "button." If you get a button, you have lifelong respect, and so does your family.

I knew a guy who was an associate, not a made guy, and his son got involved in the life. The son got his button. The father looked up to his son. It would be like a hard-working guy, with no formal education, whose son gets an MBA from a top tier school. The father, proud of his son, living vicariously through the son's achievement.

That's what it was like with this guy. Because the son got his button, the father was proud. The son killed a guy, and he earned respect in that world. If that's not something for a father to be proud of, what is?

Edwin Southerland, considered one of the most influential criminologists of the 20th century, called this Differential Association Theory. Learned values, behaviors, and attitudes are all part of that mindset. It's just the way it was. Everyone needs a goal; organized crime became a goal for many tough young guys influenced by their environment.

Even wannabe mobsters have dreams and aspirations. Why not me, they say, why not me?

Chapter 11 Who Chooses the Mob?

Despite the public fascination with organized crime, most people cannot fathom such a life. While the mob has more than its fair share of sociopaths, lunatics, and evil individuals, many members and associates are intelligent, articulate, even charming.

What lures such men to the mobster's life?

I was having lunch one day with Chazz Palminteri and Joseph "Joey Pants" Pantoliano at the Providence Westin a few years back, and we got into this conversation about why a guy would resort to that lifestyle.

Respect and status seemed to be a common theme.

Those guys know a little about what I was talking about, Joey grew up in Hoboken and had his head cut off by Tony Soprano, albeit through the wonders of special effects.

Chazz grew up in the Bronx, NY, and wrote and starred in the movie, "A Bronx Tale." They're two of the best wise-guy actors of our time. Chazz also played Raymond Patriarca, Sr. in the 2019 movie, "Vault."

My thing was monitoring and building cases against real mob guys. They knew me, and I knew them. Even guys like Gerard 'Gerry' Ouimette, who was in federal prison for much of the time I worked OC, knew about me.

I would talk to guys on the street and ask questions about Gerard; who he's in touch with, what he controls, and so on. Some would report back to Gerry and repeat the questions I'd asked.

We'd float a fabricated story to a confidential informant in touch with Gerard when we suspected the informer was a double agent. It happens often. Some guys play a dangerous game by feeding you with information then twisting the story around to the target of the investigation, playing both sides.

Misinformation and psychological warfare, like tracers, work in both directions.

I had a guy talking once, we'll call him "Slats." I interviewed Slats at a local police department that knew I had an interest in him. I was clear with Slats as to what recommendations I would offer on his criminal charges. My help was contingent on him delivering credible information on a couple of renegade Irish guys from the Ouimette crew.

We had a cordial conversation. Slats provided information, putting a few missing pieces of a puzzle together for us. We released him, and he agreed to meet again.

Shortly after that, we learned he'd put everything "on record" with the targets of our case. He crafted the story to make it appear he wasn't cooperating. He wanted the targets to know, "Doherty was asking me about things." He said I slapped him in the face several times, but he refused to talk.

Playing the tough guy, he wanted them to believe he was not a rat. I never touched the guy, didn't have to. Most of these guys fold like a cheap suit, but he'd play the stand-up guy when he was with them.

Then, he'd give us more information.

You cannot make this stuff up.

In the 70s, 80s, 90s, until the day he died in federal prison in April 2015, Gerard Ouimette was a significant player in the New England mob. His closest confidants were his brothers, Johnny, who spent considerable time in MCI Walpole in Massachusetts, and Freddy, who spent his time at the ACI in Cranston, R.I., known affectionately as the Cranston Hilton.

Others in his crew included Chuckie Flynn, Richie Gomes, Jerry Tillinghast, Ronnie Sweet, and many others. All in the same mold. Feared on the street and in prison, they were a formidable group.

Then there were non-violent guys, moneymakers like Charlie Kennedy, Anthony Fiore, and Johnny Geremia. Many of his crew members or associates died a violent death.

Gerard spent forty-six years of his life behind bars. He was a handsome, charismatic guy with a lot of juice on the street, an ally of John Gotti, the boss of the Gambino family in New York, and close to Raymond Patriarca Jr. and Sr.

He could never become a made guy because he was not of Italian descent, but Patriarca trusted him. It gave him the gravitas of a Capo, or street Captain. The guys on the street called him, "The Frenchman," and others called him, "The Irishman," because his mother was of Irish descent.

Gerard could get a job done from far and wide. He was careful not to step on toes in the Boston area. Those jurisdictions were carved out long before his ascension to power, but he did have strong ties with both the Angiulo faction and the Bulger faction.

If birth by an Italian mother was a requisite for becoming a made man, usefulness as an enforcer, hitman, earner, or loan shark granted one access to the mob regardless of one's pedigree.

Sometimes the man, by fortunes of birth, chooses the mob and sometimes, by necessity, the mob chooses the man.

The mob chose Gerard Ouimette because of his usefulness, and Gerard chose those useful to him. He had an uncanny ability to engender loyalty to himself and his crew.

Johnny Geremia is the best example of the loyalty Gerard Ouimette engendered. A lot of these guys wouldn't stand up to a slight breeze, Johnny Geremia would stand in a hurricane if Ouimette asked him.

Gerard would be careful as to how he utilized Johnny. He understood the division of labor and managing resources. Some guys were expendable; send them to do whatever, casualties are part of war. But Johnny Geremia was someone to protect. Gerard wanted him on the street, not dead or locked up. Gerard had plenty of violent guys he could call upon, but he needed earners to survive. And Geremia was trustworthy. He was a guy who could deliver a message without ever sharing it with anyone.

Geremia was so loyal, he'd never flip. He'd do time for Gerard or his brothers if need be. Johnny knew how to keep his mouth shut.

The best illustration of his loyalty to Gerard involved an incident with another notorious mobster, Frank 'Bobo' Marrapese. Geremia walked into the middle of a disagreement between Bobo and some other guys.

Shots rang out, and Johnny took a round in his backside. He wasn't Bobo's intended target, but the bullet didn't know that. It didn't matter to the police either. If they could jam up 'Bobo' on a gun charge, it was okay with them.

Geremia would have no part of it.

While recuperating, he sent a message to Bobo; he'd never talk to the police. Johnny didn't want Gerard to find out either. Gerard was away doing one of his many stints in the joint. If he found out about the shooting—accidental or otherwise—he might call for a meeting or, what the wiseguys call, a sit-down.

Those rarely ended well.

It's hard to believe 'Bobo' shot one of Gerard's confidants, and there was no retaliation. But Johnny wanted to keep the peace.

That's loyalty.

Sometimes, when there's a sit-down, the boss might impose fines or bar the offender from a particular club or area of town. Johnny was a moneymaker though, so the show must go on. There was no time to dwell on mobsters with a lousy aim.

One Saturday afternoon in 1990, Johnny Geremia was driving a van on Rt-6 on the Johnston–Providence line. An unmarked State Police detective vehicle passed him. John could smell those cars and spotted the driver, Rhode Island State Police Detective Gregory Long.

Greg was working weekends, recently assigned to the Organized Crime Intelligence Unit.

Johnny and Greg made eye contact, both familiar with one another. Johnny looked suspicious, a natural state with these guys. It was apparent to Greg the van was full of boxes, obstructing Geremia's side and rearview.

Greg pulled the van over just before the Hartford Avenue exit near the Providence line. It was full of Reebok sneakers. According to Greg, there were hundreds of boxes of sneakers. It was so full Johnny couldn't fit one more box in the back. Reebok boxes filled the front passenger seat and floor well to the roof of the van.

Detaining Johnny for investigation after he failed to come to some logical reason for possessing so many boxes, Greg knew he could only hold Mr. Geremia for so long.

Greg called in a request for help, other detectives contacted Reebok to verify the lot numbers. In a short time, Reebok confirmed the sneakers were stolen from a trailer in Massachusetts. Greg called me to assist in the investigation. While there was the assumption Gerard was involved, it remained an assumption.

And Johnny wasn't cooperating with any information.

Intelligence sources pointed to Anthony "The Saint" St Laurent being involved in the score, earmarked to go to New York City. We knew Geremia frequented Ozone Park from his time working in the city. He also took trips to New York with Gerard to see John Gotti at the Bergin Hunt and Fish Club.

We were convinced the load was going to Ozone Park. We also believed there were more sneakers than just the ones seized in the van. Detectives, armed with a search warrant, went to Geremia's home in the Thornton section of Cranston, Rhode Island to search for and seize Reebok sneakers.

At the house, Greg Long found hundreds of more Reeboks in the basement and another load in the back seat and trunk of a parked Cadillac in the driveway. When interviewed, Johnny Geremia insisted the hundreds of pairs of brand-new Reebok sneakers were "legit."

Once we broached the subject of his cooperating with us in exchange for a deal, he refused to say anything else.

There would be no talk of Gerard. No talk of The Saint. No talking period. He was Gerard's guy and proud of it. Today when people talk about Gerard, Johnny always lets them know he was the last crew member to see Gerard alive in federal prison.

Loyal even in death.

Chapter 12 Cases: Big and Bigger

The Hill

The once primarily Italo-American neighborhood, at the center of the universe for organized crime, is known as Federal Hill. Once almost exclusively Italian in character, time and changing demographics have altered the place in recent years.

While the made men of the mob are all Italian, it is but a tiny percentage of the Italian culture.

Italian culture is more vibrant with examples like Leonardo da Vinci, Michelangelo, Verdi, Christopher Columbus, and rooted in the Roman Empire with all the classics of Latin writings and history. The mob is no more representative of the Italian culture than Adolph Hitler is representative of Germany. They may be a better-known aspect of the culture, but these exceptions do not reflect the true nature of the Italian culture.

Federal Hill is still a place where people can go to eat the best Italian food in the country, see the old-school Italian culture, and relax with friends and family. It may not be as exclusively Italian as it once was, but the influence of Italian culture endures.

Back in the 30s and 40s, there were peddlers with food and produce, storefronts, restaurants, and people milling along the sidewalk, hurrying about their business.

And, in the 60s and 70s, one might glimpse Raymond L.S. Patriarca, Sr., sitting outside Coin-O-Matic, his vending machine business, a cigarette dangling from his mouth, lording over his kingdom.

"The Hill," as it was known, produced some of the most respected citizens of Rhode Island, including the Calenda family and E. James Monti, lawyers; Judge Frank Caprio and family, priests; Bishop Robert Evans, politicians; longtime councilman John Lombardi and Lt. Governor Thomas DiLuglio; doctors; entrepreneurs; athletes; and one of Providence's most beloved residents, Senator John O. Pastore.

John Pastore became the 61st Governor of the State of RI and then a United States Senator from 1950 to 1976. He was a true statesman. Known for many pieces of legislation and his chairmanship of Senate committees, the testimony of Fred Rogers (of Mr. Rogers' Neighborhood fame) before Pastore, seeking funding for public television, is one of his most endearing.

If John Pastore and others like him were the bright spots of "the Hill," different, less admirable denizens lurk about a darker side.

Away from the patina of the good life, the restaurants, and the bars. Apart from the Saturday night crowds. Lacking the trappings of congenial society. Hidden by the happy façade and slinking about in the shadows. The hopeless, desperate, and depressed, whose survival is moment-to-moment, also lived there. On the side of the Hill most feared to tread.

I know kids who grew up on the Hill and experienced a different version of the neighborhood. Dragged into the dark side because of limited opportunity, they wanted out. Conversations with them would remind me of the lyrics in Springsteen's Born to Run.

> *"...this town rips the bones from you back,*
> *it's a death trap, it's a suicide rap, we gotta*
> *get out while we're young...."* [3]

---

[3] Songwriter Bruce Springsteen Born To Run lyrics © Downtown Music Publishing

Getting out wasn't possible for twenty-two-year-old Raymond "Pumpkin" Marzullo. I knew Raymond well. Someone fired a round through the front window and killed the young man as he sat in his living room. It was a shame that the wiseguys couldn't give him a pass.

This was not just an Italian American phenomenon. Like any other ethnic enclave, we see the good and the bad.

South Boston, once the center of Irish immigration, has a similar history. There were success stories and criminal enterprise. The Irish mob in Boston's "Southie" had similar anecdotal stories. The corrupt FBI agents, a cop whose brother was a bookie, the Senate President whose brother ran the Irish mob, and so on and so forth.

But I love those neighborhoods. My familiarity with them illuminates the good, forcing the evil deeper into the shadows.

I recall one day around 1994, I was on the Hill to meet a friend for lunch at one of my favorite restaurants, Angelo's. Before we met, I thought I'd take a swing by the Acorn Athletic Club where Dickie Callie, a made guy, was murdered in 1977. The owner, Frank "Bobo" Marrapese, was serving time for the mob hit.

I figured I'd see if any of the guys were around. Guys known by colorful nicknames from their younger years—Beans, The Kook, Rocky, Poochie, Chi-Chi, Gigo, Slick, Bozo, Blackie, Red Ball, Tilly, Buckles, The Blind Pig, The Animal, The Barber, Patsie, Tootsie, Johnny Shags. Some guys assumed nicknames kept them anonymous to all except those in the know. Nothing could be further from the truth.

I was looking for LaLa, Chippy, Blackjack, The Saint, or even young Raymond "Scarface" Jenkins. I would note who was hanging with who. It was good intelligence. It might be useful later when we' be looking for certain guys. We'd know where to look and who they might be with.

Much to my surprise, I saw two guys acting suspiciously on a corner of a side street away from the wiseguys. They were counting money and holding a jewelry box. It was Anthony Meo and Louis Marchetti, two up-and-coming guys from a group known as the Golden Nugget Crew.

I didn't know them well, but intelligence sources indicated they were committing house invasions, robberies, and B&Es all over the state. A lot of innovation went into pulling off these scores. They thrived on inside information, surveillance, Ninja bikes, boats, snowmobiles, etc. We had been trying to get close to them and catch them in the act, so far with little success.

It was early 1994, and Detective Joe DelPrete was on their case building reliable intelligence through a cooperating individual. Joe was very good at flipping career criminals.

He didn't lie to them or try to trick them. He just let them know that sooner or later they will need a little help. May as well put one in the bank to establish a relationship as a confidential informant. Some people called them rats or snitches. We'd downplayed those terms and called them confidential informants or cooperating individuals depending on the level of exposure.

There were very few who didn't offer cooperation. The hard cases took the hit and went to prison rather than cooperating. But they were the exception, not the rule.

Protecting the identities of those who cooperated was critical to our success. Investigators in ongoing matters like organized crime or narcotics are only as good as their source of information. No informants, no cases. There would be a shock wave through the crime community if they learned the identities of the people who cooperated with us.

Look no further than what happened when the full story of Whitey Bulger broke.

Back to the bad guys. I stopped my unmarked State Police vehicle, and they both looked over at me. They knew me better than I knew them. It was part of their success, to keep aware of who might be interested in them. As soon as I got out, they ran in separate directions. I stayed with Meo for a short period. Remember, I have no foot speed, and he was wearing felony flyers.

They got away.

We learned later they did a "score" the night before and the "office" called it back in. They robbed the wrong guy. Detective DelPrete discovered that while they were splitting the loot, or "whacking it up," they got a call from a made guy. He gave them orders to bring the loot back. I just pulled up on their 24-hour return policy in progress.

With the guidance of the best prosecutors in the business, Joe DelPrete put together an incredible case on the Golden Nugget Crew. Bill Ferland—in charge of the Organized Crime Unit at the Attorney General's office—and Paul Daly—a workout fanatic who looked like he jumped out of GQ magazine—worked hard at crafting a bulletproof prosecution.

We indicted several members of the crew. Their innovation and creativity set these guys apart from common thieves. They would use bold ideas to gain the advantage in their choice of vehicles or planning their getaway route. By focusing on intelligence-gathering tactics to obtain information about their intended targets, they minimized risk and targeted high-value locations. They ran surveillances and made pretext calls to back up their knowledge.

They had big pump, too. In October 1994 Trooper Jim Manni (now the 14th and newest Superintendent of the RISP) was driving through Western Cranston. Manni spotted a suspicious vehicle parked on the side of an ornate house with a large gate. It was around 8:00 p.m. and, responding purely on instinct, Trooper Manni swung around to investigate.

Something just didn't look right.

The vehicle, stolen as part of their regular method of doing scores, took off at a high rate of speed. The chase was on. Manni believed, and we later confirmed, he was chasing Anthony Meo and Louis Marchetti. The chase proceeded down Pippen Orchard Road at speeds close to three times the speed limit of thirty-five.

With Jim Manni close behind, the vehicle slowed. The driver, Meo, jumped out as the car plowed through a front yard. Marchetti followed his partners lead and tried to jump from the driver's side. Marchetti's foot caught in the steering wheel. He hung sideways for a short period before momentum tossed him from the vehicle.

An acrobatic performance that would have injured, if not killed, most people.

But as often is the luck of bad guys, both men escaped unscathed and were now on foot running toward a dark wooded area. Jim Manni got out of his marked cruiser while other State and Cranston police cruisers responded.

Manni ran after the two. But as he approached the wooded area, he knew it would be inadvisable to proceed. The two men, not yet positively identified, escaped.

We later learned it was a good move for Jim Manni to maintain the perimeter instead of chasing them into the woods. Our investigation determined both men were armed, and they had no intention of being caught.

These guys were cunning, determined, and disinclined to follow the unwritten mob rule against fighting with or shooting at cops. With these guys, if it kept them out of jail, they were willing and capable of anything.

Returning to their old habits, the incident was just a minor interruption in the gang's activities. Resuming the usual methods of operation, often using diversions to draw the police away from their targets, the gang located and hit more targets.

On at least one score, they reported a serious accident on the opposite side of town knowing in a small police department all cars would respond. The crew needed just four or five minutes inside a target home or business to complete their job.

By the time the local police determined it was a false call, the gang would be long gone.

They usually knew the location of a hidden safe or a stash based upon their intelligence sources. How would they know of private family things like safes or hidden items of value?

Because people are too trusting. Who could provide such valuable inside information? Relatives, carpet installers, housekeepers, contractors, alarm company employees, and others.

Often the victims themselves would unwittingly reveal information. The husband or wife at a cocktail reception boasting about how secure their house is and how they leave all their valuables in the bathroom linen closet or the drop ceiling in their basement.

These guys would never hit a place without having an edge.

Once inside, organized, methodical, and quick, the gang moved with deliberate precision. They'd communicate with outside lookouts via walkie-talkie. If they suspected the occupants were home, they'd wear tightly fitted masks.

Though none were of Latino descent, they'd sometimes speak Spanish. With the job done, they'd dump the getaway vehicles far from their own neighborhoods to discourage police hunches or suspicions.

Once, they were casing a jewelry store under the guise of looking for a specific piece of jewelry. Two of the crew members, well-dressed and working together, played the part of legitimate customers.

While they were doing their thing, they made mental notes as to camera locations, how many store employees, busy times, buzzer locations, and other useful information.

A man walked in and introduced himself to the store manager. He was a traveling jewelry salesman with a briefcase loaded with high-end chains, rings, and pendants. During the conversation, the two crew members heard the salesman talking about easy access inventory he keeps at his own home in Warwick, RI.

Bingo. Alarms sounded in their heads, red flags raised, flashing lights, and voices. All these guys needed to do was look at each other. There was no need to discuss further. They walked outside and took a position in their vehicles.

They waited for the salesman to come out, followed him to a few more stops, and then to his home. They jotted down his registration, confirming it was his house through registration data.

By monitoring a local police department radios, they got the code word for the Registry of Motor Vehicles for releasing confidential, protected information to law enforcement. A code word never intended for broadcast, but mistakes happen.

Pretext calls to the Registry of Motor Vehicles provided the confidential phone number to a back office. One of the crew leaders practiced his conversations with the registration section to make himself sound like a police officer calling in a legitimate request.

The crew planned the score and ran sporadic surveillance of the neighborhood. They needed to make sure the target's neighbors didn't randomly drop by, determine if a cop lived in the area, or and if the owner had a cleaning service. They looked for patterns of behavior to narrow down the best window of opportunity.

It was an affluent neighborhood in Warwick and a busy street. They preferred to hit the place with no one home. Their experience and organization gave them an edge. By following a successful pattern, they could minimize their exposure.

The crew was aware we were building intelligence information on them, but they were close to impossible to follow. Always alert to police surveillance, they thought we were behind them even when we weren't. Just because you're paranoid, doesn't mean we aren't after you.

Here, their paranoia was an extra level of protection.

The troopers knew of scores they pulled off through police reports. Through street sources, they'd uncovered other, unreported ones, they were supposed to have pulled off. The problem with an active crew like this is that, in such a small state, every score or robbery with an innovative angle is attributed to them.

It made targeting them difficult; not knowing where they were operating. Cooperation among agencies was often an issue, although Brendan contacted other agencies.

I would trade information with Bob Lauro from Providence PD. He had a good handle on these guys. They would try to avoid Providence because cops knew them better there.

We had names of players, some were in and out of jail. As soon as we conducted interviews with local police officers, the word got out that we're actively pursuing these guys.

The bad guys are as interested in what we're doing as we are in them, Some will play the game and give a little information. Some will take their chances in court. Those who offer information also feed their friends in the crew a different story of how standup they were. They convey the questions we asked. Those questions tell a story and indicate how close we are even if they deny giving information to us.

Joe DelPrete had done his thing. He flipped one of them for good. Joe got some useful information on their next score.

It was late January 1995, and the forecast for that night predicted the worst snowstorm in years. The owner of the house, after we explained the situation, turned the house over to State Police detectives.

By midnight on game day, a Friday night, we were in. In a rare occurrence, the forecast was on the money. It was snowing like hell. We drove the van right into the attached garage, unwilling to take the risk of parking cars in the neighborhood for fear they would spot the out of place cars from prior surveillance.

To complicate matters, there was a parking ban. Wouldn't do to have undercover State Police cars towed for violating the ban.

Through Delprete's intelligence information, we believed they knew no one would be home that weekend. The owner confirmed it was a planned weekend away. The only vehicle we had was the one parked in the garage.

We notified Warwick Police in case we needed immediate assistance. They were part of a statewide task force formed to take these guys out. The interest in these guys was mounting, and their potential for violence escalating.

In one home invasion, they threatened to cut a woman's finger off because she couldn't get her diamond off quickly enough.

In charge of the overnight surveillance, Brendan faced no easy task. He had to anticipate various points of entry, likely the front door but had to plan for all possibilities. These guys sometimes took doors right off the hinges like a police raid. But what if they go to the back? Unlikely since they had at least a foot of snow on the ground and it was lit up like daylight.

But nothing was a guarantee with these guys.

These situations are nothing like TV shows, whatever was the worst possible occurrence was the most likely, and hardest to plan for.

The troopers sat in darkness; furniture overturned as shields toward the possible entry points. If the bad guys had guns, Brendan had to situate everyone so none of the detectives might hit by friendly fire. He needed to anticipate a myriad of possibilities with little to go on but instinct and experience.

Time slows. The slightest sound amplified. Darkness envelopes everything. Waiting is the worst part.

And the uncertainty.

At 2:00 a.m., the phone rang. It was a weird feeling knowing who was most likely on the other end. The caller left no message.

Shortly after that, a vehicle pulled in the driveway. The tracks of our surveillance vehicle, secreted in the garage, were evident in the snow. An earlier counter-surveillance hadn't allowed enough time for the tire tracks to fill in.

You can't make this up. Why did they have to pick a snowstorm?

The vehicle backed out of the driveway and left the area. Joe DelPrete tried to get info, but his source was unable to get an update. We knew if the source pushed too hard, he might expose himself.

Joe had information on another one of their targets. Several members of the team went out with me to assist Joe and Rich Ryan. They'd spotted Meo and Marchetti on snowmobiles in West Warwick casing another house.

We caught them by surprise. Usually, in a snowstorm, the snowmobile wins. But Meo and Marchetti weren't aware of who was pulling up and jumping out on them.

Meo tried to fight his way out. He lost in a unanimous decision.

They were both brought in but refused to talk about the events of that night. Through further investigation, and a grand jury proceeding led by Bill Ferland and Paul Daly, we broke the case.

Strategizing as to who was most likely to cooperate, we identified the weakest link. We gathered sufficient information to proceed and executed search warrants seizing additional evidence.

In July 1995, a statewide grand jury indicted forty-four people on 721 counts of home invasion, burglary, grand theft, larcenies, and receiving stolen goods. The case, mainly based on the State Police investigation, decimated the Golden Nugget gang. But the case succeeded because of cooperation between many police departments. Investigators from Johnston, East Providence, Warwick, and Cumberland all contributed to the case

It didn't end with just indictments or prison for every gang member. One guy met his demise before we could dismantle the crew.

His name was Barry Kourmpates, a vital member of the crew. A terrible thing happened to this young man. Evidently, the gang hit the wrong house or crossed the wrong person. Barry paid the price for the gang's mistake, or because of intra-gang paranoia.

On Mother's Day, May 8, 1994, a passerby found Barry's body. Shot multiple times in the head and set ablaze in Beavertail State Park in Jamestown, R.I. Barry never lived to face criminal charges.

Sometimes paranoia isn't adequate protection and works in both directions. There is little honor among thieves.

The case remains unsolved. But the full story may yet emerge from the decades-old slaying.

Dead men tell no tales, but the people who helped make them dead often do.

Chapter 13 Going Inside

In 1992, Brendan enlisted two State Police detectives to go undercover targeting wiseguys. The two troopers, Joe DelPrete and Steve O'Donnell, looked and talked the part. Working in tandem to infiltrate the organization, they played the role of two up-and-coming local wiseguys. The operation required a convincing story.

Brendan wrote the script and arranged for an introduction to Bobby Almonte, an aging old-school mob associate. They believed, with the right approach, Almonte would bring them into contact with the more active guys. Almonte was the way in, not the primary target.

The two undercover detectives hung around with Bobby. Almonte was a loner in mob circles. Most of his friends were either dead, most by murder, or in jail where they would die. Brendan discovered late in the case Almonte had memory problems. Age had taken its toll.

As the case progressed and they got closer to Almonte, once a force within the mob, it became apparent he was a shadow of his former self.

Had I known earlier about Almonte's mental state, I would have passed on the case. There is an unwritten code of ethics with the wiseguys and how far we'll go to make the case.

Bobby was a close associate of Richard "Red Bird," Gomes, a member of the Ouimette crew, and a former driver for John Gotti in New York City.

Richard was a feared guy.

A team of detectives once arrested him as he crossed over the Rhode Island border, on his way back from New Bedford, Massachusetts, transporting a large quantity of cocaine. He was with another mob associate, Albino "Albi" Folcarelli. It was a long surveillance. Fortunately, my partner, Steven Pare, had hawk eyes. We'd lost them for a few minutes but Pare picked them out of a parking lot as they firmed up their plans.

When we got them, because of their status, Folcarelli took the hit. He said the cocaine was all his so Gomes would walk. But Gomes was a violator on another case. Albi received a substantial prison sentence.

I testified against Gomes at a Providence Superior Court violation hearing before Judge Thomas Calderone. Attorney Jack Cicilline Sr. represented Gomes. Richie sat in the defendant's chair, smiling at me during cross-examination. Cicilline was tough, and he was on his game this day, although there wasn't too much to attack.

At one point, Jack reached over and grabbed a small piece of paper in my hand. I should have known it was discoverable but hadn't included it. I held my end, and Jack asked the judge to instruct the witness, me, to let go of the paper.

It had only a few notes, such as exit numbers and times I would have had trouble remembering, but Gomes thought I was in trouble with the judge. He rocked back and forth in his chair, one hand over his mouth and one hand pointing at me, laughing.

This was a full-grown man in his 60s, on trial in Superior Court, acting like a child in kindergarten.

More *Sesame Street* than *Goodfellas*.

Albino Folcarelli took the fall for the drugs, allowing Gomes to walk on the violation. But his time on the outside was fleeting. Subsequent cases put him back behind bars. Released after serving several years on other charges, his return to the street underscored by his propensity to violence.

Sometimes justice takes time to come full circle. After a lengthy investigation, Providence Police charged Gomes with attempted murder for shooting two men during a confrontation back in 1985.

The shooting, in Gomes old haunt in the Olneyville section of Providence, happened because Gomes took offense at a look the two men gave him. Respect compelled at the point of a gun. This put him in prison for his last time.

Gomes served sixteen years until his release in 2005, a shadow of his former self. He died in 2006 still clinging to the old ways even though time had passed him by. But Gomes left an impressive, if evil, legacy.

According to several sources, Gomes was one of eight men in John Gotti's crew who made John Favara disappear, forever. Favara's crime? He struck and killed John Gotti's twelve-year-old son with his car in what investigators ruled an accident.

Favara's disappearance was no accident.

The only ruling that mattered to men like Gomes was the mob's rule.

Another close associate of Almonte was Kevin Hanrahan, a tough kid with a troubled past. The son of an attorney, Kevin was one of several boys brought up by their mom after their father died at a young age.

She was a good woman in difficult circumstances.

Kevin hung around with a questionable crowd. His toughness attracted the attention of the Ouimette faction. Gerard took Kevin under his wing, and the rest is history. Schooled by the Ouimette crew, enamored with being a mob tough guy, Kevin found a niche. He was tough, smart, and good looking.

He played the part of mob wiseguy, he just didn't dress the part. Rather than the classic black leather coat with black slacks—the mob uniform of the day—Kevin often wore button-down dress shirts or polo shirts and tan pants. This made him less likely to stand out in a crowd, and more dangerous to those looking for the standard wiseguy.

People like Kevin operated in a straightforward world. Whoever was in charge would point out someone needing an attitude adjustment. Names, locations, and instructions provided simple guidelines.

Such beatings took place in the manner of a typical mob messenger delivery service. Two men arrive at a reluctant individual's home or office. When he answers the door, they'd punch him in the face and offer a cryptic, but unmistakable, rebuke to his resistance to their demands.

If this guy didn't "get" the message, the next one would be easier to understand. It would be his final, fatal message. Ouimette didn't take no for an answer. Kevin was often the messenger to remind guys of this fact of life.

I grabbed Kevin for possessing a truckload of stolen furniture. It was a masterful scheme he put together using the identity of a guy named Clancy. Kevin didn't take the arrest well, refusing to talk to me for a while.

Kevin married a nice girl from Federal Hill and raised a family. He looked like a debonair gentleman you might see sipping a Guinness on a bar stool in Dublin. La Cosa Nostra members lionized him because he was known for violence. They played to his ego and used him as needed.

Kevin controlled a small bookmaking operation, dabbled in other crimes, but denounced the use of drugs. He once ridiculed another mobster accused of rape.

It's strange the moral compass of these guys. Certain things are acceptable, and other things are not. At least as a man who insisted on being a man of honor, he was a defender of women.

He later became a close associate of and reputed enforcer for Raymond “Junior” Patriarca. Kevin would lead an interesting if all too brief life.

One day, while on surveillance on Branch Avenue in Providence unrelated to organized crime, I backed into a space near a Dunkin Donuts. I sat watching a car that caught my attention.

I noticed a young man staring at me. I was driving an off- white Cadillac at the time and thought he was looking at the car, but it became apparent he was looking at me.

I knew I should recognize him, but his boyish look seemed out of context. I thought he might be the son of a friend or other acquaintance. I smiled. He nodded, got out of his car, and walked toward me.

Putting my window down, uncertain as to how I knew him, I said, "Hey, what's up?",

‘Are you…?’ pausing in mid-sentence. I could hear the uncertainty in his voice.

I thought he just had me confused with someone else..

"I'm Brendan," I said, hoping to get a response.

He looked like he'd seen a ghost, hurried back to his car, and sat there staring straight ahead. What a mistake I'd made. I wonder what message I would have received if I said, ‘Yeah pal, get in the car.’

Seconds later, a white Cadillac pulled into the parking lot. Kevin Hanrahan got out, motioning to the young man to follow him into the Dunkin Donuts. They obviously had never met, but Kevin knew what car to look for.

When they shook hands, the younger man must have told him of our encounter. Kevin turned and looked right at me, even as I nestled behind a couple of cars. This whole thing was weird. I drove around the block, grabbing this guy's plate.

When I checked the registration data, I almost fell out of my car. The car belonged to Christopher Patriarca, the son of Junior Patriarca.

Raymond Jr. was in federal prison and could have very few visitors. Chris was one of them. Now that I knew I missed a perfect opportunity. I swung back in the lot and walked in to get a coffee. Chris and Kevin watched me come in. They were the only people in the shop.

I walked over and sat in the booth right next to them. Kevin looked over at me.

"Is this necessary, Brendan?"

I forget what my response was, but in a cat-and-mouse game, I was not bending the rules. They got up and walked out.

I spent a lot of time on Kevin over the years as did the Providence Police and FBI. At the risk of understating knowledge of his activities by other agencies, I made it my business to know everything about him.

I knew who he served federal prison time with; one was Henry Hill of Goodfellas. I knew his relatives, where he ate, where he banked. I knew when and where he worked out. When he went to the local fights where he would set up meetings with other mobsters. Where he would be late at night—usually the Arch on Federal Hill. His brothers' names and license plates if he was using their cars. His barber, gambling customers, people who feared him. People who didn't. Anything and everything that might help me in investigating his activities.

We had a non-confrontational relationship; cautiously cordial to one another. It was Kevin's choice. I would rather have it that way, but I could play the other role if necessary. He knew he didn't intimidate me. I came close to pinching him on a couple of felony assaults, but the witnesses turned out to be less than credible.

The courtroom dynamics are a culture unknown to most people. The system works for guys like Kevin. Who the hell wants to appear at several court dates, stand in the hallways with other witnesses or relatives of the accused, and take time out of work just to point the finger at a guy who might try to retaliate?

That's where Kevin knew I drew a line in the sand.

If someone came forward, showing the temerity to testify against these guys, then the witness is with my mob and me. We had more resources than them. Play by the rules, or you may force me to bend them.

Kevin knew the rules in that respect, but he got lucky with a few cases.

One day, he flagged me down on Federal Hill. He looked excited. He told me his wife just gave birth to a baby boy, and he named him Brendan. I congratulated him. He said he always respected me because I would never fabricate evidence to pin a case on him, and he hopes his son learns the same honesty.

He didn't say he was naming him after me, but it was a paradoxical position to be in. I wished him well and, as he was walking away, I gave him a hard time for having green shoelaces. He came right back with "they were Irish shoelaces."

"So, I guess as a new father, this means you'll walk the straight and narrow now?"

He just smiled and walked away.

Late at night on September 18, 1992, as he was leaving the Arch Restaurant on Federal Hill, a gunman ambushed Kevin, shooting and killing him. The murder, as is often the case in mob hits, remained unsolved for years until someone cooperated.

On January 17, 2017, Robert "Bobby" DeLuca admitted in Federal Court to conspiring to murder Hanrahan. This was part of plea negotiations and mea culpa for his participation in other crimes, of which there were many.

One was DeLuca's involvement in the 1993 murder of Providence native, and Boston nightclub owner, Steven DiSarro. In March 2016, based on Deluca's information, police recovered DiSarro's body from a makeshift grave near Branch Avenue in Providence.

In June 2018, in Federal Court in Boston, a jury found Francis "Cadillac" Salemme Sr., age 85, and Paul Weadick, 62, guilty of DiSarro's murder. Deluca's testimony was an essential part.

Deluca testified that Francis "Frankie Boy" Salemme, Frank "Cadillac" Salemme's son, who died long before Deluca's cooperation, strangled DiSarro in the senior Salemme's garage because they feared he may be cooperating with authorities.

DeLuca testified against his old boss in the trial and denounced his membership in the Mafia. Only the best of prosecutors can put a twenty-five-year-old case together and get a conviction. Veteran Assistant U.S. Attorneys Fred Wyshak and Bill Ferland prosecuted the case.

Families get closure and killers face accounting for their crimes, even if they are old and feeble. Sometimes justice takes time, but it never gives up.

While Bobby Almonte wasn't in his prime, his familiarity with all these wiseguys and players was the perfect way in.

Brendan and his team were about to prove it.

Chapter 14 A Cast of Characters

Robert "Bobby" Almonte and Infiltrating the Ouimette crew

Brendan and his undercover troopers knew Bobby Almonte, a longtime associate of Raymond Patriarca Sr., was their best chance to get inside. Involved in the rackets his whole life, he'd never pass up an opportunity to get a piece of easy action from guys trying to break in with the mob. A shadow of his former self, but still open to possibilities. Old habits die hard.

It was in his blood, and they knew it.

Joe DelPrete befriended him first, then introduced Steve O'Donnell as his partner in crime. Weaving their story and dangling the bait, they built credibility and let nature take its course.

The wiseguy moniker may not be an accurate portrayal of the intellectual capacity of many of these guys, but for sensing bullshit, they were savants. One needed patience, poise, and perseverance. And balls.

We concocted stories and scenarios we hoped would prompt Bobby to introduce them to other career criminals. At one point, I had them discuss a truck hijacking from a liquor distributor in Boston. I knew the story would get them some respect from Bobby, and who knows where it would go from there.

Two Rhode Island guys pulling a score in Boston showed Bobby these guys had balls. It could earn a meeting with the Winter Hill guys to give them their end.

Instead of Boston, we ended up with the Ouimette crew at their social club, St. Rocco's, in Cranston.

Back in those days, the Ouimette crew wouldn't check with Jimmy Bulger and the Winter Hill guys to do a score because they were just as ruthless. If nothing else, our story might spark a sit down between the two factions.

Johnny Ouimette knew the Bulger crew from his time in Walpole State Prison in Massachusetts, now known as Cedar Junction. I wasn't concerned about the venue we chose. Either way, was a win.

Gerard Ouimette still sat in prison, but his brother Freddy, out after serving time on a murder bid, hung around their social club. John Ouimette also frequented the club.

John Ouimette was the mastermind behind one of the nation's most massive heists, The Bonded Vault robbery. The vault was a secret, invitation-only, safe deposit box facility used by wiseguys to hide their loot. Several mob luminaries, allegedly on the orders of Raymond L.S. Patriarca Sr., took the place down in 1976.

Once again, a perceived lack of respect by failing to offer proper tribute and financial support while Raymond Sr. served time, demanded satisfaction. Patriarca hit them where it would hurt most, their money, and cause him no risk. How can someone who stole something report it taken from them?

The perfect crime, almost.

The investigation and subsequent arrests sparked one of the most sensational criminal trials in Rhode Island history. The results of which had enormous implications in the coming years.

Although Raymond Sr. never faced charges, his presence permeated the courtroom. After a lengthy trial, a jury convicted John Ouimette and two others, Ralph "Skippy" Byrnes and Charles "Chucky" Flynn, based on the testimony of two fellow robbers, Robert "Deuce" Dussault and Joe "The Dancer" Danese.

The same jury found three other defendants, Jerry Tillinghast, Walter Ouimette, and Jacob "Jake" Tarzian, not guilty.

Despite a sentence of life in prison for the Bonded Vault conviction, John was once again out and about. It all depends on what you define as life. In Rhode Island, it was flexible.

The Ouimette's social club was a hang-out for mobsters who were not made-men in the traditional sense but mirrored the organized crime hierarchy. They bore a similarity to the Winter Hill Gang in Boston.

> *Under the umbrella of the New England mob, but never able to enjoy made status because of their non-Italian heritage, Ouimette's crew was one of the most feared and productive.*
>
> *Gerard Ouimette enjoyed a special bond with Patriarca, Sr. and Jr., and had a close relationship with John Gotti. These were real guys and well-connected. They were mutts, junkyard dogs, or mongrels in the eyes of some, but their productivity made them integral to Patriarca's organization.*
>
> *Gerard was known as a no-nonsense guy. Throughout the years many of his friends and associates died prematurely, never of natural causes. Some just disappeared.*

One afternoon, Bobby took the boys to Ouimette's social club. He introduced them as renegade wiseguys and friends of his. Bobby wasn't made, so his saying "friends of his" violated no mob protocols. If he was made, it would mean they were made.

It's a part of mob protocol and works this way—a made guy introduces someone to another made guy as "a friend of ours." It means he's with us and he's made too. There are rules and customs within the organization, even one driven by criminal activity.

But none of that mattered here because they weren't at that level.

The conversation turned to their score in Boston, Johnny took the hook. He asked what they could get and ordered up.

"It's hidden out in a warehouse," Joe said, "but we can get it here within a day."

Now, all we had to do was come up with the stuff.

We needed to deliver fifteen cases of Absolut Vodka and fifteen cases of Budweiser beer. I had to purchase the booze from a liquor store on the Connecticut line using an impress account credit card set up for this case.

Before they made the trip, I warned them these guys are the real deal. In this business, it's a mistake to judge a book by its cover.

Johnny Ouimette was slender in build and stood about five-foot-six. His stock-in-trade was not physical intimidation. But size was not important when the real possibility of a gun being pulled existed. If they profited from theft, they would take it at gunpoint if it suited them.

There is no honor among thieves, only opportunity.

I was in the Intelligence Unit for years before these young troopers and wanted them to benefit from that experience. It took courage and acting ability to go undercover. I didn't want courage to overcome caution. I gave them a historical overview of these guys and the crews they belonged to. Most of these guys earned their well-deserved reputations for violence before these undercover troopers were in high school.

I told them not to let the cordial and cavalier demeanor lull them into relaxing their guard. These guys will laugh and joke and buy you a drink, but they play for real. In their world, there's a fine line between friendly banter and opportunistic brutality.

Even though we were putting together a nickel and dime case, it was a way in the door. A way to gain their trust. The last thing we wanted was some stone killer who hung out there to think Joe and Steve were easy marks, or worse, informants.

If they thought they were cops, they'd walk away from the deal. If they suspected they were informants or smelled a rat, it'd be a different story.

Our undercover called ahead. Ouimette's sister answered the phone, and he talked to her about the deal. It just happened. We weren't trying to drag his sister into the score, but she answered the phone.

That conversation infuriated Johnny.

When the guys showed up to unload the shipment, Johnny called the two over to the side of the bar. He pulled a barstool close to Steve and Joe. He motioned them in for a close-talk huddle while his murderous colleagues looked on.

John put his hand on Joe's forearm and locked him in a stare.

"Look, we can do business. We can work together. But leave my sister out of any conversation." He let the words sink in. "Never make that mistake again. Are we clear?"

He looked at both undercover guys, making sure they got the message. Steve and Joe nodded. They'd made a mistake. It wouldn't happen again. Message received. For the rest of this counterfeit relationship, they played the subservient role.

Joe later said that when John looked in his eyes, all he could see was a cold, hollow stare. I think it reinforced the point I'd made earlier.

As the case progressed, Bobby's medical issues—failing health and memory loss—worsened. We could continue, keep getting him to introduce us to people, but we had to coach him, to remind him of the people we were targeting and how he knew them.

We realized he was sick and failing fast. From an investigative perspective, we wanted to keep it going. From an ethical and humanitarian perspective, we needed to end it.

I decided to pull the plug. We took down several defendants on a variety of charges including stolen goods and attempted stolen goods charges. i.e., the "stolen" liquor. The Ouimette's attorney, John Cicilline Jr., called it entrapment and a setup. He argued the defendants were not predisposed to the crime.

It troubled me that some believed we exploited Bobby's failing health. I always vowed to get bad guys by following the rules; not manufacturing probable cause or evidence. I built my reputation on it.

But this was a different spin. This questioned my humanity, even if the wiseguys had none.

After learning of Bobby's mounting health issues, I wasn't comfortable continuing. Not from a legal perspective; he made the introductions, but the others committed the criminal acts. I looked at it from my true north. I prided myself on following my guiding principles. We would never intentionally take advantage of his failing health and memory loss. It just took a while for us to understand how severe Almonte's health issues were.

Sources of mine told me Gerard was outraged when he heard his sister Carol's name came up. He wasn't happy about us jamming up Johnny and Freddy either. Family was important to him, no matter what crimes they may have committed.

Soon, he'd try to express his displeasure through subtle but deliberate intimidation.

Try but fail.

Chapter 15 Gerard and the Staring Contest

Within a year of the St. Rocco's case, Gerard walked out of prison and opened a business on Park Avenue in the city of Cranston. Surveillance revealed interesting characters visiting him, including New York registered vehicles.

Several agencies, from local to the Feds, had Gerard in their sights. The storefront offered surveillance and intelligence gathering opportunities, but Gerard was no fool. He was as aware of the police as they were of him and conducted his business to minimize his risk, but he also had an attitude.

Gerard knew me, and I knew Gerard, but we had never met.

I avoided him as best I could because I knew about an FBI and Providence Police investigation into Gerard extorting a local restaurant owner.

However, right across the street from Gerard's storefront was my barbershop, the Razors Edge. This is Rhode Island, after all, and I liked my barber.

Sal Pazienza, the uncle of five-time world boxing champion Vinny Pazienza, owned the barbershop. Everybody liked Sal. Sal was comfortable talking to anyone, from cops to wiseguys, but didn't want to get in the middle of their disputes. Sal was Switzerland, neutral territory, stuck between the cops and crooks.

One day I walked in and a member of Gerard's crew, John Geremia, was standing in front of the Ouimette Office. He said hello. I waved to him, then went into see Sal. The last time I'd seen Geremia was when we arrested him for the stolen Nike sneakers.

Since he saw me, I wondered how this would play out.

I got right in the chair. The seat gave me a view of the mirror, which gave me an excellent vantage point for activity across the street. Keeping an eye on things, I talked sports with Sal.

What happened next was unexpected.

Gerard showed up, walking right over to Geremia. Geremia was animated. Jawing away. Pointing to the barbershop.

I couldn't read lips, but I assumed they bandied about my name in a less than complimentary fashion. Gerard looked over toward the shop, a puzzled look on his face. Walking with purpose across the busy adjacent intersection, he came toward the shop.

I asked Sal to spin the chair around. Visions of all the mob assassinations in barbershops flashed through my head. I felt like a sitting duck, wondering if he would try something crazy. While mobsters rarely crossed the line with cops, rational behavior is not a strong point with these guys, Gerard more than most.

As I watched him make his way toward the shop, I thought, Gerard has some gall. Out of jail for a few months and he's coming over to create a problem.

With a trooper of all people.

We'd soon see what level he would take it. I could tell Sal wanted to be any other place on the planet besides the middle of a confrontation between Gerard Ouimette and me. It wasn't my idea of a fun time either, but sometimes it goes with the territory.

I decided, for Sal's sake, I would play this as cool as I can.

The door opened, and Gerard walked in. No urgency, no slamming of the door, just a casual entry into the shop. Nonchalant, almost oblivious, he looked at pictures on the wall. Ignoring me, at first.

"Hello, Gerry," Sal said like he was greeting the next customer, not a potential nightmare.

"I really like this barbershop," Gerard said. "I'd like to get my hair cut here someday."

"Any time, Gerry," Sal said, trying to stay calm.

Gerard looked at me and stared. It was weird because I'm sitting in a typical barber's chair, a barber's apron over me, my hand under the apron on a 9-millimeter semi-automatic, and this criminal legend is trying to intimidate me.

I do have to give him credit for the stare. It would have scared most people. About five seconds into our staring match, I broke the silence.

"Something you want to get off your chest, Gerard?"

"No. I just wanted to drop in to say hello."

"And to get a good look at me, right?"

Gerard smiled, turned, and walked out.

I thought Sal would have a heart attack. He grew up in the same neighborhood as Gerard and knew he struck fear in the hearts of many.

The next day, even though he was a target in an active case, I walked in his office. Just to see if he changed his mind about what he wanted to say in the barbershop. He wasn't there, but no doubt he got the message.

I went in alone to show his barbershop visit hadn't intimidated me.

Several days later, the Feds arrested Gerard Ouimette for extortion of a Warren, RI restaurant and a Providence strip club. He became the first criminal in New England to face a new federal statute known as *Three Strikes You're Out.*

The statute, The Violent Crime Control and Law Enforcement Act of 1994, provided a life sentence for anyone with three convictions for crimes of violence.

A federal jury convicted Gerard, and the judge sentenced him to the mandatory life in prison. When leaving Federal Court under the escort of the US marshals, a reporter asked how he felt about the sentence. Ouimette said, "It's just another day."

He died in prison on April 19, 2015.

Just another day.

Chapter 16 Stock Value

The mob has this odd sense of propriety and decorum. Certain things are acceptable, others repulsive. There is a standard of acceptable behavior challenging for most people to understand. They put great stock in respect, albeit a skewed concept of what most people would consider proper conduct.

Respect within the mob is just fear masquerading as reverence. Once greed or ambition outweighs the fear, respect dies at the point of a gun and under the blade of a shovel.

In the twisted minds of mobsters, they even hold cops to specific standards. As ludicrous as that might sound.

After the Almonte case, I ran into Louis "Baby Shacks" Manocchio, boss of New England mob. He told me my "stock" went down on the street because of those arrests. He joked there were no wiseguys left because the big liquor caper put them out of business.

I hadn't seen Louie in a long time. I kidded him about running crap games upstairs from his Nuevo lounge in The Café Verdi. He reminded me of our last conversation during the banking crisis.

That conversation went back to 1990. The owner of Heritage Loan, Joe Mollicone, who would become the face of the Rhode Island banking crisis, owned several buildings. Both buildings, located several miles apart, sustained significant vandalism in the same night in November 1989.

Now is that a coincidence or what?

Mollicone was close to Louie, and most of the wiseguys knew that. I'd heard about another mobster who didn't like Louie, but I didn't want to jump to conclusions. The FBI had no information, so I contacted my informants and street sources.

Louie was an interesting guy; a debonair and dapper dresser. An old-school Mafioso who, like other successful businessmen, drew animosity and jealousy from others.

Especially from others who couldn't, at least ostensibly, earn money by legitimate means.

In the rules of the mob, as nebulous as those may be, you can't make a move on a "made" guy without approval from the boss. It's against accepted mob etiquette. It's not that you can't kill a "made" guy, you must make a good argument to the boss *why* you need to kill him.

One of the best arguments is there would be more money for everyone after the hit. They would talk about insults or violations of honor as justification for their request to move on a "made" guy. But it was all a smokescreen to greed and jealousy over lucrative illegal operations or territories controlled by rivals.

Most followed the rules.

You can, however, send a message without asking the boss's permission; target a "made" guy's friends or damage their property. Made guys are off-limits; their friends and associates are fair game in this unfair game with ever-changing rules.

Somebody was sending Mollicone a message and the State Police were interested in knowing who, and why.

Another detective and I walked in unannounced to Mollicone's Atwells Avenue office on January 11, 1990.

Joc was an intelligent and well-spoken man. A graduate of Boston College, with many legitimate business friends, he just couldn't leave the old neighborhood or distance himself from the other side. His was a broad spectrum of friends and associates. One might see him having coffee with Louie in the morning, lunch with the mayor, and sipping cocktails at a fundraiser for the governor at night.

A bridge between polite society and society's less savory underbelly made him unique. He was a well-connected guy and an integral part of the who's who in the Rhode Island social scene.

But in the mob's world, unique means opportunity not immunity.

It was my first time in his office, and he invited us in for a coffee and a muffin. I wasted no time getting to the reason for our visit. He confirmed the reports of the damage, expressing outrage while professing ignorance as to who was responsible, as carpenters hammered background noise to the conversation.

I mentioned the name of the mobster that didn't like Baby Shacks. Joe became defensive. I told him, based on my information, this mobster may be responsible. Joe claimed he did not know of any problems with the guy.

Joe filed a complaint with the Providence Police, but the investigation would be perfunctory. The inherent lack of cooperation by the victim and a shortage of suspects would ensure the case remained unresolved, even if everyone knew who did it.

Some police reports are just formalities. Victims in these mob-related vendettas report the crime, offering little more than bare details because not reporting it might draw more unwanted attention. The main reason for the report was to file an insurance claim, the course of justice was of little consideration.

I gave Joe my business card and offered help if it got too hot. I shared the intelligence information with Bobby Lauro of the Providence Police and Bill Shea from the FBI. Each little piece of information builds on our collective knowledge of the inner workings, daily machinations, and trends within the mob.

Manocchio's walk down memory lane about Joe Mollicone's problems conveniently ignored the more significant issue.

Soon after Brendan's conversation with Mollicone about the vandalism problem, a problem bigger than building damage reared its ugly head. Joe's inability to stick to the legitimate side of life would make him one of the most wanted men in the world.

And the most hated man in Rhode Island.

Chapter 17 The Perfect Storm

In December 1990, Attorney General Jim O'Neill and one of his top prosecutors, Bob Craven, summoned the State Police to the Attorney General's office. Colonel Edmund Culhane, the Superintendent, selected two troopers to send to the meeting: Brendan, then a Detective Corporal, and Detective Lieutenant Jack Scuncio.

Gathered around the table, members of the Rhode Island Share, Deposit, and Indemnity Corporation (RISDIC) Board of Directors presented a sullen and somber visage.

This confidential meeting later became a thing of lore in Rhode Island history. Another of the many chapters of political corruption and inside baseball by those in power.

The RISDIC officials offered some staggering information. It would send shockwaves throughout the Rhode Island banking community, force the newly elected Governor, Bruce Sundlun, into a cataclysmic decision, and place thousands of Rhode Islanders in financial straits.

Rhode Island credit unions, under the auspices of RISDIC, faced insolvency because RISDIC reserves—the insurance fund protecting depositors—were gone. A run on the banks and the whole system would collapse.

It was one of the most unusual moments of my career. An audit of Heritage Loan, Joe Mollicone's bank, ordered by then Governor DiPrete in early November, discovered significant financial irregularities. They temporarily closed the bank to complete the audit. When the bank reopened on December 4th, customers withdrew their deposits from the eight million five hundred thousand dollars remaining, forcing RISDIC to infuse the remainder of their reserve.

Joe Mollicone, the bank President, was missing. But that wasn't all they revealed. RISDIC was teetering on collapse.

There was a stunned silence. The ramifications of the revelation took a moment to sink in. Jim O'Neill, to his credit, recognized the ominous portent. He stopped the meeting and asked Craven, Lt. Scuncio, and I to step out to the hallway.

We all agreed not to ask more questions of the RISDIC representatives. There was a chance they could be implicated in criminality. The real possibility existed we were looking at future criminal defendants sitting in the meeting with us.

Questions could come later as to what point the participants of the meeting might become suspects in the overall conspiracy. If they were, it entitled them to legal representation.

We needed to protect the integrity of the process. Returning to the room, O'Neill announced the meeting was over.

As soon as I returned to State Police Headquarters, I called the Mollicone residence. I spoke to Joyce, Joe's wife. Introducing myself, I asked for Joe. She became agitated and abrupt.

"Joe's not here. Don't call back." She hung up. Things continued to go downhill.

Joyce Mollicone's reluctance to cooperate added to the growing complications. Finding Joe became a high priority. State Police made several other attempts, contacting street sources and Joe's friends. No one knew or would say where he was.

Joe Mollicone had fled the jurisdiction and gone into hiding. Of that, the State Police were confident. I prepared a report for incoming Governor Bruce Sundlun, who would face making serious decisions within hours of assuming the office.

Mollicone and the money were in the wind. Subsequent investigations determined Mollicone's son dropped him off at Logan Airport on November 8th. The FBI could not locate a ticket for Joe Mollicone on any airline.

This was not a spur-of-the-moment trip.

On New Year's Day 1991, his second day in office, Governor Sundlun announced he was closing the credit unions in Rhode Island. I could not imagine the actions of one man, Joe Mollicone, could devastate the state's economy. The full story would reveal a lack of oversight, inaction by others, and the old- boy political network provided ample opportunity for Mollicone's actions.

Mollicone wasn't the main problem; the inside and insidious old boy network in Rhode Island was the problem. And the mob, through Joe and others, had a big part in the whole scam. But for the moment, Mollicone was the face of the disaster. Finding him, and getting to the bottom of the entire story, became critical.

Ordinary Rhode Islanders' life's savings were in those credit unions. But the Governor had no choice. Word leaked out. Rumors spread. The Governor feared a run on the banks. Sundlun ordered all accounts frozen and State Troopers posted at every credit union location throughout the state.

More than one billion dollars, belonging to over one hundred fifty thousand depositors, was now inaccessible.

Happy New Year.

State auditors sifted through records with the Attorney General's Office and State Police detectives. The criminal case was underway, and the target was Joseph Mollicone. It didn't take investigators long to determine what happened. Figuring out why, how, and who else was involved took a little longer.

Joe Mollicone was now a fugitive from justice. Eventually, he made the Top Ten on the FBI Most Wanted list. It put him in the same company as Osama bin Laden and Whitey Bulger. Even Raymond L.S. Patriarca never made that infamous list.

We focused on locating Mollicone.

Detective John LaCross, the trooper assigned to the fugitive case, and I met regularly with an investigator from the AG's office. They were perfunctory meetings, not a lot of exchange of intelligence. The sad reality of law enforcement is the childish jealousy over cases, big or small. Why this happens is anyone's guess, but it serves no purpose except to delay investigations.

Sometimes police departments act as if they're playing poker in a game against other agencies. Playing their hands close to the vest in fear of losing front-page headline stories to others.

In Rhode Island, with so many local, state, and federal agencies competing to justify their existence, it can have a paralyzing effect on the course of justice.

We were conducting interviews, offering rewards, doing surveillance, making rubbish pickups at known associates homes and businesses, but kept coming up empty. I knew from my informants that Joe was close to Baby Shacks, so I decided that it can't hurt to start the conversation.

Around that time, we were up on a wiretap of one of Baby Shacks bookmaking operations in Johnston. I showed up, unannounced, at the Café Verdi on Atwells Avenue in the Federal Hill section of Providence. Another detective kept watch, not out of any concern for safety, just to make sure we documented the meeting. I wouldn't want someone to misconstrue why I was there.

When I walked in the building, several guys—hang-around-guys we called them—were sitting at a table, no doubt wondering why the hell I was there. I saw Louie sitting alone in the back of the room. I'm sure he knew from his alert lookout when I walked across the street.

We made eye contact.

"Brendan, what brings you here? Are you slumming today?"

An attempt to lighten the conversation, I guess. I said hello, and Louie invited me to sit for an espresso. He's as sharp a tack, he knew what was on my mind, but he kept asking questions to stall.

At one point, he asked, “How are you doing in the gomatta category?” (*Gomatta* is Italian slang for a girlfriend.)

Before I could answer, he smiled.

“I'm just kidding with you. I know you're married.”

It was all a delaying tactic, a subtle way of breaking the ice and sending a message; *we know things about you.* Not that it mattered, we knew more about them. Salutations and manuevering aside, I told him it would be a feather in my cap if Joe Mollicone would return to Rhode Island and surrender to me.

“It would, wouldn't it?” Louie said.

“Yes, it would,” I replied.

He sat back and pondered for a while. It was only about ten seconds, but it seemed to last for minutes. I'm looking him in the eye, trying to read him.

"What's in it for me?"

"You'd have one in the bank."

I realized he'd never take me as serious, but I hoped it would keep the conversation going. Louie smirked, he was playing me.

"Ok," he said, "if I arrange to have Joe come back and turn himself in, I get to run crap games upstairs?"

Now I knew he was just playing with me, so I said, "If Joe surrenders to me, you can run crap games on the sidewalk."

He looked me in the eye and smiled. "You're an honest guy, keep doing what you're doing, but I can't help you."

We shook hands, and I left.

As I was walking out, a car stopped in the road. Eddie Lato leaned out of the car and yelled to Louie.

"There's a cop watching the building."

The cop he was talking about was my extra eyes and ears.

Louie laughed, because he knew I heard it. He shouted back, "Nice job," and smirked again.

Nothing about Mollicone came out of the meeting, but you never know how things might change. Louie was a loyal, old-school guy and he would protect Mollicone until it was no longer in his best interest to do so.

Mollicone was in the wind, we kept digging at it, but the world didn't stop turning for us to find Joe. We had other cases to work.

Chapter 18 Baby Shacks in Charge

One of Louie's most productive guys was Ronnie Coppola. Ronnie was a high-end earner for the mob. The State Police were looking at his high stakes card games.

He got a significant cut from the game. You paid him to sit at the table or by the hand, so he made money no matter if you won or lost. He ran them in a Cranston social club until 2:00 -3:00 a.m., twice a week.

A great deal of security and control protected the game and the location. This low-profile, well-hidden business generated significant profits for Coppola and Manocchio.

My source said close to $100,000 might be in the room at one time. No one would dare to rob the game. It was a mob sanctioned game and thus protected. Robbing the game would be signing your own death warrant. Security's primary function was to squash any internal arguments—people sometimes get emotional losing big stakes hands—and keep an eye out for us.

Ronnie was an up and comer, on his was to earn his "button." Moneymakers were the rock stars of the mob, and the mob protects their own.

Some people argue bookmaking and high-stakes gaming are victimless crimes. There is some validity to the argument. No one forces these guys to play. Back then, who would ever think thirty years hence we'd have on-line sports betting, fantasy games, and computerized football pools to satisfy the human predilection to bet, gamble, wager, on sports and games of chance?

But there's nothing sadder than hearing the stories of inveterate gamblers. They would beg, borrow, and steal from anyone—family, friends, employers—chasing that next sure thing. The next full house or straight flush. Each win would drive the need to play higher and higher. Each loss is seen as a momentary setback.

They saw the slim possibility of their next win as a matter of time, not continuous losses. The nefarious individuals behind the gambling operations knew this and fed the addiction. For that is what it was, an addiction as powerful as heroin or cocaine.

Once you rode the dragon, you'd sacrifice everything and everyone dear chasing the moment. An elusive fantasy, always one more bet away.

Those running the games almost always maintained a loansharking operation. If you were down to a point where you are behind three to four thousand dollars and playing catch up, you could find yourself down ten grand in short order.

Loansharking was a way to get blood from a stone. No money? No problem. We will loan it to you. We know you're good for it. Place your bets, we love your business. Win, and you're all set.

The ultimate sucker's bet.

I've seen young, otherwise intelligent men end up on the hook of a loan shark. It would force these guys to use every imaginable way to keep betting, trying to recoup their losses.

I've seen guys borrow from their parents, sell their car, steal from elderly relatives, and, in one case, a young man took his father's credit card, maxed it out at a jewelry store, then sold the jewelry back to the corrupt store owner at half price. Enough to satisfy the debt to the loan shark, leaving the father on the hook for the maxed-out card.

Our investigation into Louie's operation in Johnston, one of the largest and most successful bookmaking offices, required caution. We had to be careful about who knew of the wiretap. Back then, there were individuals throughout the court system interested in what we were doing, and willing to share the information.

If something compromised a case, it often tracked back to someone being sloppy and the information getting into the wrong hands.

Col. Stone warned us if anyone compromised an investigation, through carelessness or otherwise, he'd put them before a grand jury. It affected our dealings with other departments and the court system making us hyper cautious in sharing information.

We were fortunate to have a good relationship with the justices in Superior Court. We had immense respect, going back over thirty years, for Presiding Justices such as Anthony Giannini, Joseph Rodgers, and Alice Gibney.

Judge Rodgers was not only an honorable guy, sensitive to the need for confidentiality, but he was street smart. I recall him telling me to hold off for a few hours before bringing paperwork to his chambers. He knew certain people were present in the courthouse that day. People who would take an interest in seeing my entering the Judge's chambers.

The Presiding Justice is the only Judge who can sign wiretap applications and orders. Seeing me going into his office with a file wouldn't take much for them to draw a conclusion. Judge Rodgers knew connected guys were in the courthouse and didn't want them to put it together. Instead of going to his chambers, sometimes we'd meet in a parking lot far away from prying eyes.

While Mollicone was still on the lam, we received information related to the Manocchio wire I thought might help us track him down. Two bookies, in earshot of one informant, cryptically talked about Louie. Louie's name was in the Providence Journal that day. One bookie asked the other, "Did you read the story about our guy?" and then talked about the "other guy," who was away.

The conversation then segued toward having to pay their guy his "rent" money. They weren't talking about renting a room, but their rent, or tax, for doing business. The two bookies discussed how to get "that guy" his Christmas present and how they had to give "five dimes" or five thousand to an intermediary to get it to the man.

That was a nice piece of information, useful to know they were keeping tabs on Mollicone, but short of my objective of catching a location where we might find him. Bookies rarely possess such inside information. But one guy was good at moving money around that might tie into Joe. I had a hunch he'd be more helpful over his phone if we could get the probable cause to get up on it.

We were a long way from that.

One of the most frustrating things of the job was knowing something was going on but not having enough evidence to get a court order. The standard for obtaining a wiretap is a high hurdle, rightfully so, but it didn't make it any less difficult to accept.

We went back to the drawing board. Trying to build a case against Coppola and the operation.

Another one of Louie's earners was Raymond Lyons. Ray was also a sharp dresser in the mold of the old-school mobsters. He wasn't prone to violence but lived in that world and knew how to survive. He grew up in a mob environment, recognized the necessity for occasional violence, and understood the money side well.

Ray managed one of the largest "offices" in New England. Had dozens of bookies working for him and, at the close of business, all bets came into his office. He would move the office and phone number around every couple of weeks. It was probably the most innovative operation I've ever seen.

He used trusted, old-school guys like Howard and Milton Ride, Mike Mastrati, and Gabriele "Chubby" Presioso. Milton and Howard were loyal to him. The Lyons operation bridged the 80s and 90s. It wouldn't be unusual for an operation like that to manage a Monday Night Football game with $100,000 in overall wages.

Each office tried to "balance" its books. They would hand off bets to other offices, trying to get close to an even spread on each team.

That means there are fifty thousand dollars in winners and fifty thousand dollars in losers. The losers pay the "vig," or vigorish, the price of doing business, and that is ten percent. His operation would make five thousand dollars for the night.

That's just one office and one football game.

We focused our attention on the Lyons organization. Steve Foley, our undercover trooper's street name, infiltrated the operation. He was into Chubby pretty good. Steve met with Chubby and engaged in small talk on square up day. Chubby liked him until he started a losing streak.

Ironically, getting the losing streak started took longer than we anticipated. At the start of every week, I would sit down with Steve, look at the games, and bet to lose so we could test how they'd handle larger bets coming in. The problem was, for about three weeks, we kept winning.

Eventually, we fell behind by a few thousand. Chubby demanded payment. Steve intentionally made himself scarce, adding fuel to the fire. Chubby turned the account over to his boss. They summonsed our guy to meet the head of this operation. We didn't know who they would send and were surprised when Ray Lyons showed up.

He usually remained more insulated, but the surveillance team identified him right away.

They met on Water Street in the town of Warren, Rhode Island. Lyons motioned for the undercover trooper to follow him into an alleyway. Dressed up in his role as a house painter, with dry paint all over his clothes and boots, our guy followed Lyons down the alley. He pleaded for time, telling Ray he'd come upon tough times and couldn't come up with the three or four thousand he owed.

Ray told him, in what was an attempt at collecting an unlawful debt, he had a couple of guys with the "IQ of a kitten" and, when you least expect it, they will find you. He explained how years ago he invested in a small Rhode Island bank that eventually went under.

He'd lost money in the stock he explained, but understood it was the risk he took. Lyons told the undercover trooper he should look at it that way. You made a lousy investment, now you had to pay for your loss. It was the start of the extortion case against Ray Lyons.

We indicted Ray, Chubby, and several others. Ray was looking at a violation from a previous charge in Providence Superior Court. I testified about the surveillance and recorded conversations we used as evidence. It wouldn't be unusual for me to be in the hallway outside the courtroom with prosecutors, defense attorneys, defendants, cops, court officers, and courthouse hangers-on.

All mixed in pursuing justice but seeking different results.

The dynamics of the courthouse, out in the hallways and inside the courtrooms, are fascinating for those who experience it for the first time. I spent a lot of time in court, so I understood the environment.

At one point, Howard Ride approached me. I knew Howard because Peter Grundy and I used to go to his Pawtucket restaurant, Ride's Bar and Grille, when we were younger. Pete didn't drink, but he loved the food.

Grundy's gym was not far from the restaurant. Back then, I didn't know these guys were bookies. But to be honest, they were two of the nicest guys you could ever meet.

Howard was a friend and business colleague of Ray. He pulled me aside, away from others. Howard was about seventy-five years old but sharp as a tack. I didn't think he remembered me. He was very cordial and said that it would be "a shame" if Ray had to serve time for this. He told me I had an influence on whether we proceeded or not. It would be nice if the state would drop the felony and allow Ray to plead to a lesser charge.

That was the approach; they followed it with a sweetener. Using what they knew about me as best they could.

Howard asked me if I still liked to go to the fights. He reminded me they had junkets to Atlantic City. It would cost me nothing. Do this for them, they do something for me.

I could have pursued it for a bribery charge. But at Howard's age, he was a product of the era he grew up in, it was an ingrained habit. I thought it was best to let it go.

I was kind but left little room for doubt. "Ray's going away, and I'll buy my own fight tickets."

Nothing these guys did would, or could, be sweet enough to buy my integrity. People can take your property, your freedom, even your life without your consent, but they cannot take your integrity. Only you can give that away.

Chapter 19 Pizza Delivery

Ronnie Coppola was still making serious money running poker games, and rumor had it he was next in line to get his "button." He was with the in-crowd, the right "faction." You had to be to survive. In the mob, like in life, it's the politics of power.

I ran surveillance on his club on the corner of Park Ave and Gansett Ave in the city of Cranston. One night, at about 1:00 a.m., I was with another detective. We spotted a lookout. A paid knucklehead Ronnie posted to look for law enforcement or stick up guys. Considering it was a "protected" game, robbery was unlikely.

It's mob money. Only a crazy person, or someone with a death wish, would rob a sanctioned game.

The State Police were the bigger risk, and this guy wasn't very good at his job of spotting us.

We fought through briars in the back of the building and looked through a little vent. It added to the information we would put in the affidavit for a search warrant. We also noted the metal door that opened out when they let players in. A sturdy door and a problem if we needed to knock it down.

Why knock it down when you can be innovative?

During the surveillance, I could see thousands on the table. Ronnie was cutting the deck. From the back vent, we could see the lookout was doing a great job; he never left his post.

And he never saw us.

We obtained a search warrant based on our surveillance information.

The next day, around 1:00 a.m., John LaCross dressed up as a pizza delivery guy. We borrowed a local pizza chain uniform and roof sign for our car. John walked up to the door carrying two large pizzas. Several detectives waited at the corner of the building about fifteen feet away. When John knocked on the door, the lookout was watching him through the peephole.

“No one ordered a pizza here,” came the one-eyed voice from behind the door.

"What's this, a joke?" John said. "I'm trying to make a living."

"No one ordered it."

John said, "Well, this is the address. But if you say no one ordered it, then take it for free."

The door opened. John handed him the two large pizza boxes with one hand and spun him to the side with his other hand, securing the door for three or four detectives who quickly ran in.

We grabbed the evidence and money. Ronnie looked up at me and said, “Clever, very clever.”

We seized close to $40,000 from that game.

Later, in plea negotiation, Ronnie's defense attorney, David Cicilline, agreed to forfeit about half the money. I thought there were potential problems with the case if we went to a full hearing. The defense raised the issue of us looking through the vent without a warrant. If the court agreed and suppressed the evidence, we could lose it all. The AG's office concurred, and we accepted the deal.

A few weeks later, Ronnie saw me out to dinner with my wife Michele at the Capital Grille in Providence. We made eye contact and nodded. The waiter came to our table and said: "Mr. Coppola would like to send over a bottle of wine."

I said, “Tell Mr. Coppola, thank you, but I'm not drinking tonight.”

Ronnie never got his button. On April 1, 1994, in another Cranston social club, Coppola and his confidante, Peter Scarpellino, through their careless ignorance of mob protocols, met their ends at the hands of an aging, old-school—but still dangerous—mobster.

The price of disrespect in the mob is often deadly.

Chapter 20 Respect is the Only Thing

On April 1, 1994, Ronnie Coppola and Peter Scarpellino sat in a Cranston social club. Sitting nearby was Antonino "Nino" Cucinotta, the former driver for Raymond L. S. Patriarca Sr.

Tradition was about to confront the new generation.

An angry exchange of words, some insults traded, a status challenged, and that's all it took. The sensibilities of the old school mob code of honor demanded satisfaction.

Nino took offense at a perceived lack of respect by Ronnie. In Nino's world, that was unforgivable. Leaving the club, Nino went home, got a gun, and returned.

Walking into the club, he never said a
word. None needed. A lack of respect
demanded a response, often in fatal fury.
Shooting Coppola and Scarpellino dead,
Nino walked out. His honor now restored.

I still remember walking in the club with Cranston Police Chief Augie Comella and seeing the back of Ronnie's head stuck to the wall. At the time he was growing his hair long in the back, and the impact of the bullet lifted it up to about six-foot-four, much taller than Ronnie stood, and nailed it to the wall. Blood trickled through the hair, a dried trail of bloody tears.

He was larger in death than in life.

When Peter Scarpellino heard the first shot, he ran to the bathroom to seek cover. But, as he slammed the door shut, Nino opened fire through the door. He hit Peter several times, killing him.

Insult avenged.

Nino eventually turned himself into the East Providence Police. Bill Ferland, the Assistant AG in charge of organized crime cases, and I, along with Cranston Police, executed a search warrant at Nino's modest Johnston, Rhode Island apartment.

Meanwhile, Cranston Police divers searched the waters of Meshanticut Lake in Cranston for the murder weapon. They not only found the murder weapon, but another gun. What havoc the second gun raised we never found out.

While at Nino's house, Ferland—a great prosecutor and a great strategist who later convicted mob boss Louis "Baby Shacks" Manocchio—and I were stunned by an odd contradiction.

We both thought we'd seen it all. Yet Nino had a surprise waiting for us in his house we could never have anticipated.

Neatly arranged on the kitchen table were church envelopes and a budget indicating how much Nino was to give to the church that month.

The paradox startled both Bill and me.

Here was a guy who held a profound obligation of faith to support the church yet considered an act of disrespect enough grounds to kill two men.

Thou shalt not kill had exceptions in Nino's mind.

I have no doubt those envelopes would have made their way to the church had Nino not exacted revenge that night.

Cranston Police charged Nino with two counts of murder. The court ordered him held without bail at the RI Adult Correctional Institute. After about a week in prison, he asked a correctional officer to call me. Knowing he had Jack Cicilline as his attorney, I notified state prosecutors. I didn't want to interfere with any court proceedings or create complications with his right to counsel.

The fact he was a made guy caused me to consider the implications. It's rare for them to talk to the police, let alone ask for a meeting. These elements weighed on my mind.

I called a colleague from the FBI, Special Agent Bill Shay. We worked together on this faction of the New England mob. The State Police operated independently of the FBI in intelligence gathering, but Bill shared a lot of information with us. I felt the obligation to include him

I was a little reticent about seeing Nino without properly memorializing the conversation, so I wore a wire. In the parking lot, outside the prison, I told Agent Shay. He said it was against FBI policy, and he preferred that I did not record the conversation.

I understood, but I didn't tell him I wouldn't wear it. He was here at my invitation. I felt no need to comply with his agency's protocols if they conflicted with my best judgment.

During the two days we met with Nino, he talked about his induction to La Cosa Nostra ("baptized" in 1978 in Boston along with two other Rhode Island mobsters), and he provided details of significant Mafia activity. He filled in gaps in our intelligence information about who was with whom, why someone got their button, and so on. The full details of these meetings remain sealed in court proceedings or in State Police Intelligence Unit files.

Nino was the first made guy in Rhode Island to cooperate. This was a big deal. But it came with complications and questions.

What information is relevant? What can we corroborate? And more important, what can you do for a fifty-five-year-old career criminal who just shot and killed two unarmed men because of some broken Mafia code of respect owed for one's position in a criminal enterprise?

We could help in some respects, but we made no promises.

My decision to wear the wire, while lawful under state law, created issues for me with the Federal Court. Rhode Island state law permits one-party consent in recording conversations, and I was the one party. But the Federal Court took a dim view.

During the sentencing of Raymond Patriarca, Jr., I was on standby to testify against Raymond. The prosecutor, Assistant US Attorney Jeffery Auerhahn, after hearing the judge's concerns of my surreptitiously taping an inmate, opted to knock me off the witness list.

Since the defense and the court knew of the tape's existence, it became discoverable.

In Boston, US District Court Judge Mark Wolfe wanted prosecutors to look at whether it was unlawful for me to record a defendant in prison without a warrant.

That was comforting. While the inquiry amounted to nothing, it did not make me feel warm and fuzzy.

Judge Wolfe was the same judge who exposed the unholy alliance between certain FBI agents and James "Whitey" Bulger. Wolfe is a no-nonsense guy. It was a lousy situation for law enforcement, but I have the highest respect for Judge Wolfe's integrity. I agree with the adage, "better a hundred guilty men go free than one innocent man goes to jail."

The Bulger situation underscores the risk of crossing the line. Bulger bears much of the guilty for it all.

FBI agent John Connolly exercised bad judgment in his handling of confidential informants, allowing them to compromise himself and his agency.

After his conviction in 2000 for racketeering and obstruction, John Connolly went to federal prison. And, in 2008 while serving his sentence, a Florida jury convicted him on a charge of second-degree murder.

The circumstances surrounding the Bulger era, and how Connolly hurt the Bureau, are well known, and I see no need to revisit them except to set the record straight on my experience with the Bureau.

I've worked with great agents, and I am confident the problem was isolated. An aberration in one of the most respected law enforcement agencies in the world. When the information rose to the surface, they acted appropriately.

The agency rebounded.

If they had supervisors like Warren Bamford and Rich DesLauriers back then, the Bulger situation would never have happened. They are two of the most honorable people I have ever worked with. Both ran the Boston office after the aftermath of Bulger.

John Connolly's last effort to get out of federal prison was in October 2007 on an appeal No. 05-2772[4] before the First Circuit, and the court denied the motion.

Sitting on the First Circuit for the case, among others, was Senior Circuit Judge Bruce Selya, one of the nation's most respected judges. He is tough but fair. The decision by Justice Selya read like an eloquent mob movie script.

Enough said about the Bulger-Connolly debacle.

---

[4] https://law.justia.com/cases/federal/appellate-courts/ca1/05-2773/05-2772-01a-2011-02-25.html

Nino went away for a double life sentence and disappeared into the Federal Witness Protection Program. Guys like Nino were old school wise guys, they'd lived by inviolable rules.

In their world, there was no contradiction in filling in church donation envelopes and killing two men. Both actions comported with the rules. Nino saw the obligation to support his faith and the need to uphold his honor at the point of a gun as the same.

But the game was changing.

Just like politics, when your guy is out, you're out. Nino's guy, Raymond, Sr., was dead. The son, Raymond, Jr., was in prison and could no longer protect him.

Nino fell from grace, but he did not take the fall gracefully.

Judge Wolfe later lodged a complaint against AUSA Jeffrey Auerhahn in a different Organized Crime case against Mafia lieutenant Vincent Ferrara, known to the cops as "Vinnie the Animal."

The complaint alleged Auerhahn withheld exculpatory evidence of a witness lying under oath in Ferrara's trial for ordering a murder. The Justice Department privately sanctioned Auerhahn.

The First Circuit Court of Appeals upheld Judge Wolfe's allegation and referred the case to a disciplinary hearing. A panel of three Federal Judges ruled the claims of professional misconduct were not proven by "clear and convincing evidence."

Carl Justice "CJ" Nordstrum, renegade biker, sparred with Brendan at Grundy's

Grundy's Gym

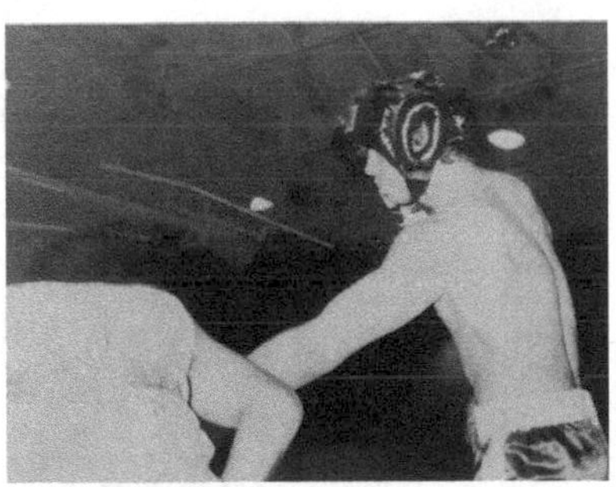

Brendan sparring with NE Champ Dino Denis

Colonel Walter Stone, a legend in Rhode Island law enforcement and Brendan's mentor, took a liking to the young trooper and promoted him to the Intelligence Unit

Corporal Brendan Doherty in the distinctive uniform of the Rhode Island State Police

Raymond L. S. Patriarca, Sr. led the New England Mob for decades

Raymond "Junior" Patriarca inherited the mantle of leadership when his father died

Nicholas "Providence Nick" Bianco

Gerard "The Frenchman" Ouimette Despite his lack of Italian heritage he was a powerful figure in the Patriarca Organization

Vincent "Fat Vinny" Teresa was the first New England mobster to break the Omerta code

Richie Gomes and Gerard Ouimette in prison. At the time, the inmates ran the prison.

Gerard, George Basmajian, and Joe Timpani deliver a message. Basmajian would be murdered a short time later and Timpani would go to Federal Prison.

Detectives Joe DelPrete and Brendan undercover

Richard Tiberi and Felix "LaLa" Dibenedetto Decatur Social Club Peephole in background.

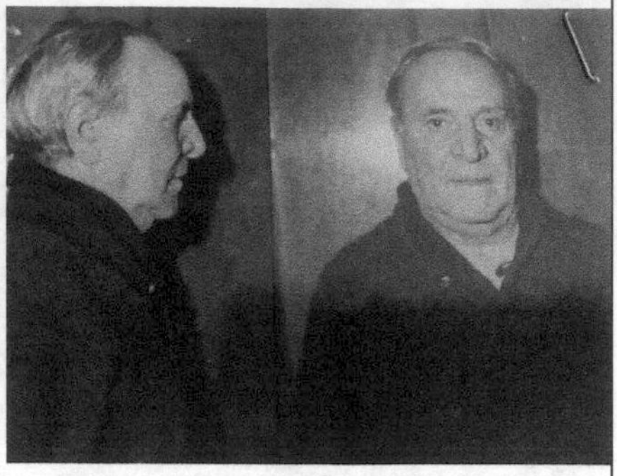

Bobby Almonte arrest photo RISP. Almonte introduced the undercover troopers to the Ouimette brothers.

Brendan encounters John Gotti outside the court at the trial in Hartford.

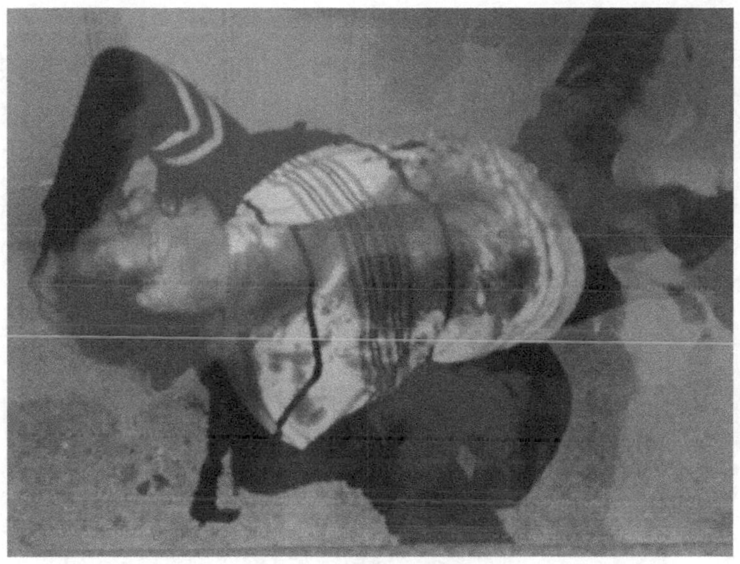

Dennis Wilmot shortly after the attempted hit

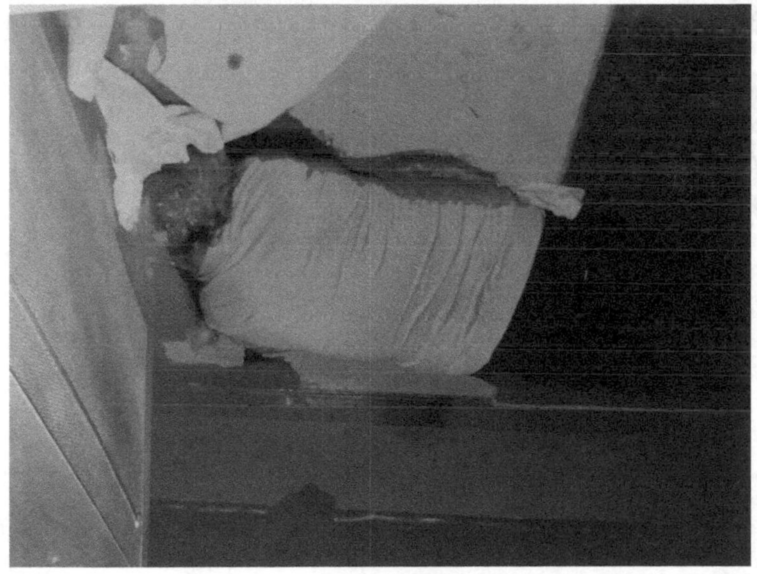

Ronnie Coppola lies dead in a Cranston social club...the price of respect

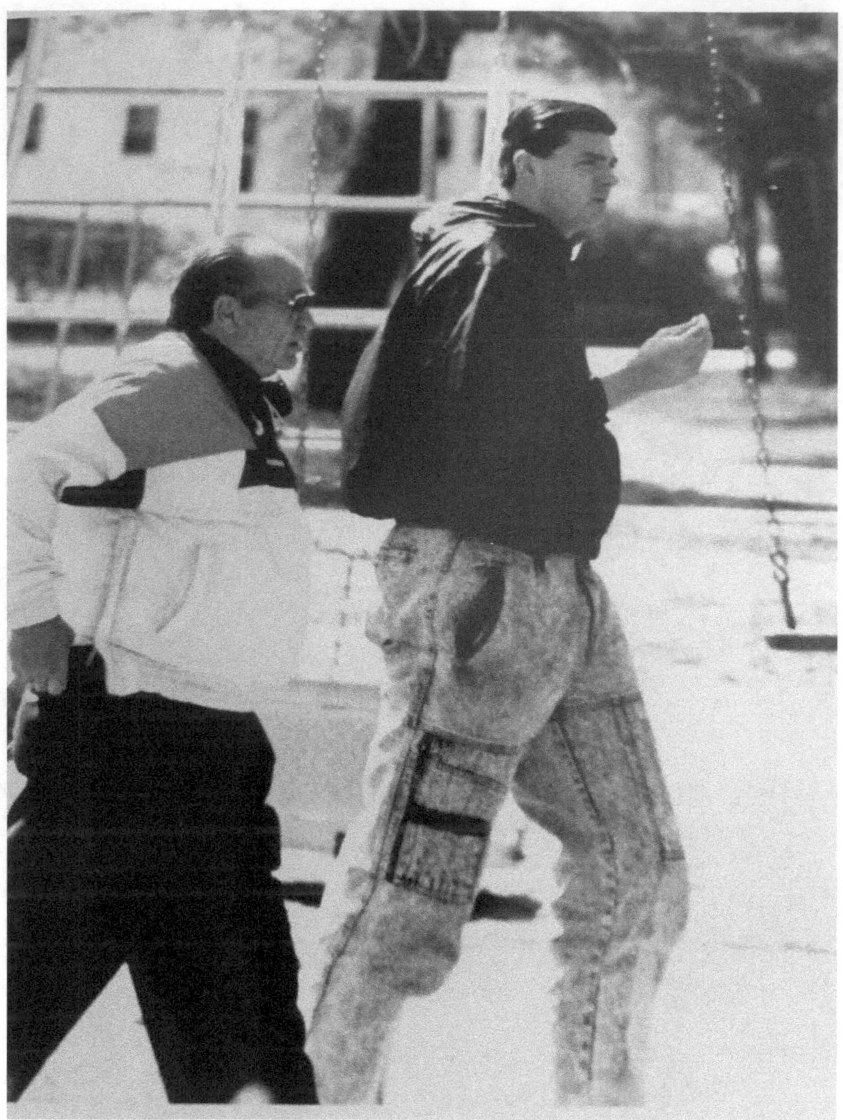

Brendan walks with Rudolph Sciarra, one of the most feared enforcers for the mob

Gerard Ouimette and Johnny Geremia shortly before Ouimette's death in federal prison. Geremia remained loyal to Ouimette.

Chapter 21 A Narrow Escape

One mob-connected guy who always got along with everyone was Blaise Marfeo. Blaise was a money-maker. A masterful bookmaker, booster, and loan shark, always with a deal in the works.

He sold knockoff designer clothing and bags before they were even a commodity in New York City. He had guys working the phones for sports bets, people in stores who would set up scores, and an eye for a new scam.

He was a jack of all trades in criminal matters.

Blaise bought a truckload of stolen high-end clothes; Hart Schaffner Marx, DKNY, Zegna, Gucci, Prada. You name it, he had it. I'd love to know what it cost him because I knocked his door down and we seized it all.

There were hundreds of suits.

Blaise called me over to the corner of the room during the inventory and told me that if I took a few for the case, but left the rest, everyone looked good.

"I'll hold a forty-eight extra-large Zegna here for you to pick up later," he added as an extra incentive.

I just smiled and walked away.

"Brendan," Blaise said, "you don't know how to play the game."

I knew exactly how they wanted me to play the game, and what the result would be. I wasn't interested. The bad guys would never steer me away from my true north.

Blaise had Joe Bevilacqua, Jr. for an attorney, so we knew the case would be contentious. There were so many suits with the labels and serial numbers razor-sliced out it was difficult to identify the victim stores. Those cases are more arduous than one would think. You needed to locate the store, have a store representative identify the suit as one missing from their inventory, and mark the evidence tag with his or her signature. Then they had to testify.

It was a tedious, time-consuming process. While we tried to identify the owners of the suits, Joe Jr. pulled a slick move. He tried to get a court order to return suits to their rightful owner, Blaise Marfeo. Absent proof to the contrary, he might have had a valid claim.

Seriously, you can't make this up. Luckily for the prosecution, we had Gerry Coyne. Gerry was a seasoned career Assistant AG, and won the argument, convincing the court to deny Bevilacqua's motion to return the suits.

Blaise negotiated a plea agreement. Part of the negotiation required Blaise to sign off on all clothing we couldn't identify and turn them over to a local private school for their charity drive.

Blaise served time for a variety of crimes. He wrote it off as the cost of doing business. The "business" ran in the family. His two uncles, involved in the same ventures as Blaise, having angered Raymond L.S. Patriarca Sr. were both shot to death.

A fatal mistake Blaise would not repeat.

Blaise was not a made guy. We believed he had the opportunity but refused it. His reputation as wealthy, generous, and charismatic grew over time. As a cover for his other business, he owned a popular restaurant on the affluent east side of Providence. The restaurant, Adesso, at 61 Cushing Street, was a popular venue for business meetings and office parties. Frequented by many of the misguided East-siders who wanted to say they were friends with a mobster.

I've never understood the mentality. Why do legitimate people want to say a friend is "in the mob?" Perhaps they saw it as a harmless flirtation with the dark side without getting their hands dirty. Or, they looked at it as an insurance policy against becoming a target.

It was a severe misjudgment of character.

One day in 1990, Blaise nearly met his demise in the parking lot of the restaurant if not for the sharp eye of an observant Providence Police Officer named Frank Moody.

Detective Moody spotted three men in a van. They aroused his suspicion. Inside the vehicle, police found the tools and ingredients for kidnap and torture. Two of the men were career criminals, one with ties to Boston's Irish mob.

Later, police charged Kevin Hanrahan as a co-conspirator in the abduction attempt. Providence and State Police learned from a cooperating witness the men planned to torture Blaise until he took them to an area where he kept large quantities of cash.

It's a good thing Blaise didn't take that ride.

The score confused investigators. How were those guys going to pull this off? You can't whack a guy like Blaise, an earner for other factions, without an okay from the boss.

Blaise was close to William "Billy Black" DelSanto, also known as Blackjack. Taking out an earner for Blackjack was not good policy if you valued your longevity.

Blackjack was a short, stout man, but charming to women. He was also a family man. One of the few mobsters I knew who was married and took care of his kids.

Blackjack was also a made guy.

He was close to Junior, and he ran the rackets on the Hill for twenty years. There were a lot of high-ranking guys on the Hill, but they didn't conduct business up there. Billy did. He had the juice behind him and the standing to make it happen.

We'd see him leaning against his car in his black leather coat. Someone would walk by, nod, shake hands with cash in palm, a subtle exchange, and keep walking.

It wouldn't be out of character to see him standing on the corner, a car with Massachusetts plates pull up, and Blackjack jump in. They'd ride around the block and Blackjack would get out at the exact spot where he'd been picked up.

Advice, intelligence, orders, or payments delivered. Business continuity mob-style. Blackjack owned a beach house in Narragansett; his business was good.

He was easy to watch but hard to pin a case on. One day I spotted Blaise and Blackjack, near a carload of men's suits, women's jackets, suit coats, and other accessories, parked on the Hill near Tony's Colonial Market.

From where I was sitting, I could see garments still had the store alarm system, called The Security Tag, attached to the clothing. When I saw those, my reaction was they must be stolen.

I assumed an inside guy let the clothes go out the back door instead of the front. There were so many plastic security tags, there would be several alarms going off if someone did a smash and grab.

Plenty of probable cause for me.

Pulling up to them, I jumped out.

"Hi, fellas."

Blaise turned and ignored me. Blackjack, who was holding several garments, said, "Hi, Brendan, let me explain."

There was no need to explain. Our intelligence information identified him as a made guy. We also know he's the sidewalk inspector for the City of Providence, which raised eyebrows knowing the way Providence City Hall worked. He was a man who lived a life of crime but had no criminal record. Now he's standing here with Blaise Marfeo, one of the most prolific boosters in the state, handling clothing still bearing security tags. I can see Blackjack's trunk is loaded with other high-end women's clothes.

It didn't take a leap of faith to know they were up to no good. Unless we'd missed something in his lifestyle, I was sure they weren't for him to wear. Taken together, there was only one conclusion.

I know what my job demands me to do.

Blackjack wanted to talk. I knew he would never give me information—he wasn't looking at a jail sentence since he had no criminal record—but it was apparent he had something to say.

And it was evident he needed to say it soon.

He sat handcuffed in my back seat. I was a gentleman to him. I was courteous. I didn't make one of the TV moves and slam him against my trunk or something worthy of cop show drama, but he was motioning me over.

By the time I spotted them, Blaise didn't have possession of any clothes, and there were none in his car. I thought it was fair enough letting Blackjack take the hit. After listening to Blaise tell me I was making a big mistake, the clothes were given to them, or they found them, or some other excuse that didn't make sense, I got back in my car.

That day, I was driving a black Ford LTD. The standard unmarked detectives car and I think he was angry he hadn't spotted me sooner. Blackjack said that before I embarrass myself, I should rethink this.

"I pay my dues," he said. "I buy my political tickets, and I know people at the statehouse." He paused a moment to let it sink in. "If you go ahead with this case, I'll make sure you never get promoted."

Subtlety was not his strong suit, stolen ones were.

I remember not knowing what to say other than telling him if I was ever reconsidering this arrest, it was never happening now.

I drove Blackjack to State Police Headquarters and locked him up.

We identified the items as stolen from various women's clothing stores throughout the northeast. I had to drive to upstate New York and then over to Cape Cod to identify where he'd stolen the clothes. After a lot of leg work, we convicted Mr. DelSanto for Felony Receiving Stolen Goods.

The criminal case was not without its moments as it progressed through the court system. Blackjack's attorney tried but failed to plead the case down to a misdemeanor while the lead prosecutor was on vacation.

Bill Ferland, the Assistant AG handling the case, was off for a summer vacation. Blackjack's lawyer, Jack Cicilline, tried to dispose of the matter with another prosecutor less familiar with the case.

But Bill Ferland and I had left a note not to dispose of the case without one of us present. The prosecutor, who didn't know Blackjack, was ready to allow a plea to a lesser charge when she discovered she had to give one of us a call.

Whack...good try. Blackjack had to live with his only criminal conviction.

Blackjack was once the sidewalk inspector for the City of Providence. A position he used for more than just the good of the city.

I had information Matty Guglielmetti—another made guy—was in cahoots with a guy named Mike Mendozzi to break up sidewalks during the night. Mike owned a concrete repair company in Johnston, Rhode Island.

Why would a made man waste time breaking up a sidewalk? Not exactly the stuff of mob movies. But they don't call them wiseguys for nothing. Scamming the public out of tax dollars is lucrative and low profile. A broken sidewalk doesn't lead the nightly news.

The sidewalks were Blackjack's responsibility, he was the inspector. A broken sidewalk qualifies as an emergency, triggering a no-bid contract to repair the "dangerous" condition.

Selecting the company to make the repair? Blackjack. Sidewalk inspector sounds like an innocuous job but mix in the mob penchant greed, it is the goose that laid the golden egg.

Whether this happened this way or not is open for conjecture. Would they damage a sidewalk and fix it or just put in the paperwork as if they did?

One day, when Brendan arrested Mendozzi with Anthony "The Saint" St. Laurent for extortion, he asked him that exact question.

"Look," Mendozzi said, "I work hard, and I don't know what you're talking about." End of story as far as he was concerned.

I knew Mike because we fought a three-round training session at Grundy's Gym several years before. Dino worked my corner. He had me throw an overhand right into Big Mike's face as he lunged in. Bingo, I caught the big fella right on the nose. He bled like a fire hose. I did have a little edge when I asked him something about his tough-guy reputation later.

He never confirmed the sidewalk gig. He did own an asphalt repair company in Johnston. He was friends with and came under the umbrella of Matty Guglielmetti.

We connected the dots. We know Blackjack is the sidewalk inspector and my information had them working together. A reasonable and prudent person would agree there was some validity to this conjecture.

But the cases were historical.

Blackjack sued the city after losing his job as a no-show worker. Mike died, and Matty served considerable time in federal prison. After Matty got out, it elevated his status within the organization. Things were changing, and new faces were rising to positions of command in the mob.

Chapter 22 A Delta Force Escape

Sgt. Marshall Brown

In June 1989, terror gripped Rhode Island because of a mysterious serial rapist. The suspect raped two women, at knifepoint, after breaking into their apartments. The most frightening aspect? The suspect climbed the outside of the buildings to enter the second-floor units.

Police arrested Marshall Brown, a US Army Sergeant and alleged member of Delta Force, who was in Rhode Island for training in Newport.

His arrest calmed the public, but it was a short reprieve. During a trip to Superior Court for a hearing, Brown escaped and disappeared into the streets of Providence East side near Brown University.

The terror returned as the public feared what might happen once again.

On July 30, 1989, Brown had a court date in Providence Superior Court. When the sheriff's van pulled up, the inmates on board, cuffed with waist chains and leg chains, started for the rear door. Sgt. Brown somehow removed the restraints, spun away from the others, and ran down South Main Street toward Brown University.

Within seconds he was gone.

It is unknown how he unlocked the chains, or if he had someone waiting, but he quickly became public enemy #1. In Rhode Island for his first time, at a nine-week training session in Newport, he didn't know the state. We later discovered that he used his charming personality to ingratiate himself with contacts in prison.

Sgt. Brown had the tools to survive. He was a member of the elite Delta Force and a former Golden Knight free-fall parachutist. He participated in the failed raid in Iran in 1979. His escape became front-page news in and about the Rhode Island area. Colonel Stone made it clear that he wanted his State Police to hunt him down.

After a week of soft clues (B&Es, stolen cars, etc.) indicating that he might still be in town, a uniform trooper received a call from a guy who did not want to give his name. He told the trooper that Brown had recruited him to get cash and a clean car to get out of town. The caller was to meet Brown that night in East Providence at the Massachusetts state line in the parking lot of a fast-food restaurant.

Law enforcement often gets tips like this that don't pan out, but this sounded promising. We set up surveillance. The team was aware Brown was dangerous, but also coy and surveillance conscious.

At around 8:30 p.m., I sat in a vehicle with Don Kennedy and Dave Dias, both outstanding detectives, backed in at the rear of a large parking lot.

Dave slouched down in the back. We focused on the fast-food joint. I'm far-sighted, and my eyes are attracted to just the slightest of movements. While we were looking across the street, I caught movement to my far left. I noticed there was no wind, yet the branches in the bushes kept moving.

Then, I saw his face peering through the branches.

I told my partners not to turn their heads because he was looking right at us. They got a look at Sgt. Brown as he crawled out of the bushes on his stomach and began a fast, weird-looking crab walk on his hands across the parking lot.

There was one other car in the lot, and he got in it. It turned out to be stolen. Good thing we didn't check it out ahead of time or he would have watched the whole thing.

We radioed the other cars as we were heading out of the parking lot. I said we would cut in front to block his lane of travel; I needed the others to prevent him from backing up. Within twenty seconds, we were out of the parking lot, casually sitting next to Brown in the stolen car at a red light on the state line.

Don, David, and I agreed the other cars would not make it before the light turned green. We had to rush him. The light turned, and on three, we jumped out so fast we caught him by surprise.

I mistakenly ran between the two cars, ending up face to face with him. He looked horrified. I pointed my gun right at his face. It was obvious what would have happened if he accelerated.

Dave took a crouched position while Donald and I pulled Brown from the vehicle. At first, he offered resistance. We fell to the ground, both cutting our heads on the blacktop. As I was subduing him, Donald patted him down for weapons. He kept yelling, "It's over, I'm all done, no weapons. I'm all done."

Brown and I were both bleeding from the awkward takedown, but I still felt I needed to make sure he couldn't move. Within seconds, twenty State Police detectives were at the scene. The takedown was rough, but we were dealing with a guy trained to kill. He'd demonstrated Harry Houdini-like skills in his escape, I would not let that happen again.

We took him to State Police Headquarters, placed him in shackles, and held him in a room under guard. He talked freely about his military life but would not speak about secret missions.

It wasn't our business to ask questions relative to his military service but all other aspects of his life were open season for us.

It was sad to see a guy so dedicated to his country yet so sexually demented he would commit such a despicable crime. Now, he sat in a room in Scituate, RI covered in blood, surrounded by state troopers, with no future but jail. This country owes a debt of gratitude to guys like Sgt. Brown. But on this day, because of those crimes, he was just another felon.

At about 10:30 p.m., the door opened and in walked Attorney General James O'Neill and Colonel Walter Stone. We all jumped to attention and saluted.

As a token of respect, or force of habit, so did Sgt. Brown.

Colonel Stone looked at him, smiled, and said, "Very well gentlemen, job well done." You could tell the old man was proud of his troopers and their trophy. Brown later waived his right to a speedy arraignment and lived at SPHQ for at least a week.

Brown gave a statement admitting to his crimes and was very remorseful. Questions remained. How did he get the restraints off? Was there a car waiting for him? But he was only willing to give himself up.

Should we have expected any more from a member of Delta Force? The military part of his persona masked the criminal element. His assignment as a special forces soldier in Delta Force was in conflict to the crimes he'd committed.

Sergeant Jim Mullen led the follow-up investigation, coordinating with law enforcement agencies throughout the country where Marshall served various assignments.

Once our investigation was over, we released Marshall Brown to military officials. Before leaving the state, he appeared in Providence Superior Court before Judge Vincent A. Ragosta and pleaded no contest to fourteen charges. Nine of those charges were in connection to the rape of two young Rhode Island women.

On those charges, Sgt. Brown received fifty years at the ACI; twenty-five to serve and twenty-five suspended. He also received concurrent time for the escape. Brown's confessions of crimes in other states went to the appropriate authorities, and the military took him into custody.

Cases like this leave criminal investigators with mixed emotions. There were contradictions to the two versions of Marshall Brown. One was a dedicated and highly trained special forces warrior. The other was a predator.

Was he a sexual predator before he became one of our elite commandos, or did the stress burn out his brain? It is a question worth considering. Do we offer enough care to members of the military given the enormous demands we place on them?

Chapter 23 Bobby Walason

The story of Robert "Bobby" Walason's life reads like a troubling fiction.

Tossed out of his house, on Christmas Eve, when he was twelve years old, his exit down the stairs of the three-floor tenement punctuated by his father tossing the Christmas tree right behind him.

He survived in the streets, never returning home

Not that it ever was a home. His alcoholic father beat Bobby and his siblings with furious brutality. His older sister, Patty, also left home at twelve because of the father's abuse. It was not home by any stretch of the imagination.

At sixteen, Bobby found himself the second youngest person sentenced to the adult prison, the ACI. By the time they sent him to jail, he had spent several years in and out of the Rhode Island training school.

He'd escape, be recaptured, only to vanish again; committing housebreaks to survive during his periods on the run.

Eventually, his physical skills—he was powerful and a feared fighter—caught the attention of the wiseguys. Taken under the wing of Nicky Bianco who sent him to work with Bobo Marrapese, it was only a matter of time before he drew more attention from others.

Walason soon found himself in the crosshairs of the State Police Intelligence Unit.

Bobby Walason is unique among the many individuals with whom I came into contact. He eventually became a self-proclaimed honest man, but he was lucky between point A and point B.

Bobby established an extensive resume in the Rhode Island Court system. More interesting was his ability to avoid the ultimate sacrifice of his profession; a lengthy prison sentence or an early grave.

I'm not implying that he made deals to keep himself on the street because that's not the case. I know him, and we had an unconventional relationship. He was always very cordial but would provide no information. He would give a long speech about having more street ethics. More than once, he said he'd rather die than become an informer.

He almost did.

He respected the fact I would never "manufacture" a case against him. He knew I had a job to do, and I wouldn't cut corners just to make a case. Feared on the street, some considered him a threat. In that world, when you're a threat, you face elimination.

One sunny afternoon Bobby was in the Olneyville section of Providence. He and a crew of men working for his moving company were packing some commercial furniture. They parked in a crowded parking lot in front of an old mill. Walason knew he had adversaries out there, so he was always on guard.

While directing the crew, Bobby noticed a young Latino male walking toward him with a purpose. He instinctively knew this was not a cordial visit, then saw a handgun in the guy's right hand. Bobby ran toward Manton Avenue, and the gunman followed, opening fire.

Witnesses reported multiple shots. It was a wild scene in the streets and alleys of Olneyville. Bobby bobbing and weaving, running for his life from a life that had finally caught up to him.

As he ran up a hill leading to safety, one round caught him in the back. He collapsed against a passing car. The woman driving slamming on her brakes at the sight of the bloodied young man staggering in front of her.

Bobby later said he felt disbelief more than anything else. Disbelief it had come to this. Disbelief the life he tried to leave behind wouldn't let him go. Disbelief about dying in the street.

The streets whose rules he refused to obey did not take kindly to being ignored.

The woman screamed as Bobby leaned against the car, frozen in time. The sole assailant walked up behind him, ignoring the horrified woman watching the scene unfold in front of her.

Lowering the gun to Bobby's forehead, he pulled the trigger. Twice. Click, click. Out of bullets, the assailant ran from the scene.

Bobby's brother drove him to the hospital, where he underwent surgery for several hours. I called Providence Police when I heard. Bobby told the Providence detectives he didn't know the young man who shot him, so they assumed it was a hired hit. I provided some other intelligence information, then went to the hospital.

At the hospital, Bobby told me that even if he knew who shot him, he wouldn't say. He made it quite clear he would handle it himself. Bobby spoke of our friendship, an implication I should leave it alone. I made it quite clear that if I could put him in jail for a hundred years, I would.

He just smiled.

As I was leaving, he said, "Brendan."

I turned to look at him. The smile had faded, replaced by a look of determination.

"You know these guys will pay for this, right?"

I just walked away. There was little I could say to change Bobby's mind. Whatever came of this, we would deal with it.

Over the years, we would see each other occasionally. Bobby continued to engage in a "catch me if you can" game. We came close, but his luck held out.

We had a covert camera in a precious metals manufacturing plant in Providence. The CEO of the company was aware, but no one else. The company suspected one employee of taking thousands of dollars in gold bars.

A private detective named Nicky Fernandes brought us in. He'd done a fabulous job putting the case together. They captured the suspect, an executive of the company, secreting gold in a magazine. He would walk across the production floor and directly out the back door.

Company executives are often exempted from following rules. Security Policy and Procedures 101 violated. This executive took advantage of this lapse in security.

On several occasions, surveillance would watch the suspect meet with an unknown male. A handoff would take place, then this unknown subject would drive directly to a location known by us to receive stolen goods, including gold and silver.

The location, Saccoccia Coin, later gained notoriety as the center of one of the most extensive money-laundering operations in the United States.

Stephen Saccoccia and his wife, Donna, would be convicted of laundering millions of dollars for a Columbian drug cartel. Stephen still sits in jail, serving a 640-year sentence. His wife also served time and is now out of prison. But at the time, we knew the location as a place one could sell precious metals with few questions asked. Our investigation was nearing an end.

We felt we had enough probable cause to take down the next meeting. On game day, June 29, 1990, Fernandes notified the State Police surveillance team on standby. We watched the perpetrator meet with the same unknown subject, later identified as Robert "Bobby" Walason.

We needed Bobby to take possession of the stolen property. It appeared to the team he did. We moved in, took down the pair, but the company executive still had the goods in his car. Bobby looked at me and smiled. We charged both with Felony Receiving Stolen Goods and seized money and property from the company executive. The case against the company executive succeeded, the case against Walason did not.

The court granted a motion to dismiss the charges against Bobby for lack of evidence. I tried to make a deal with the company executive to cooperate in the conspiracy case against Walason.

When I approached the man, he said there was no way he could testify against Bobby. I can still remember the guy's words and the look of sheer terror on his face.

"Seriously? Seriously? You think I want to testify against that animal? I'd rather do my time."

Chapter 24 Rudy Earl

According to filings in Federal Court, on the afternoon of October 5, 1977, Raymond Patriarca, Jr., Nicola Leonardo, Antonino "Nino" Cucinotta, Matthew Guglielmetti, Frank "Bobo" Marrapese, William "Blackjack" DelSanto, Pasquale "Patsy" Galea and Rudolph "Rudy Earl" Sciarra, drove from Providence to Boston to receive their buttons from Gennaro Angiulo, the longtime undisputed mob king of the North End and his then-East Boston Capo Joe "J.R." Russo.

The eight men represented a large class of new inductees into the world of the mob and made men. While some might argue Raymond Jr. was a legacy inclusion out of respect for the old man, the others were all long-standing earners and operators within the Patriarca organization.

Despite the doubters, Junior would build his own reputation within the organization.

Some ran bookmaking operations, some were loan sharks, some were good with their hands and guns, some did a little of everything. Each had earned respect to move to the next level. They'd made their "bones," and their status rose.

These guys were the rising stars, beginning their "career" as made men just before Brendan started his career as a Trooper. It wouldn't be long before their paths would cross.

One guy that always stood out as a man's man was Rudolph Sciarra, aka Rudy Earl. Rudy was a loyal soldier to Raymond Patriarca, Sr. An old school enforcer who would do time in solitary confinement or in lockdown rather than cooperate. Raymond loved Rudy. Young, up-and-coming mobsters respected Rudy because he'd paid his dues.

One day around November 1997 an informant told me Rudy took a daily walk in the Memorial Park in Johnston. He said it was incredible because Rudy—the center of so many street wars and suspected of killing several serious guys—walked in the park with no protection.

I asked the source how to approach Rudy under the guise I was a bookie, tied in with someone he might not reach out to. I reassured my source Rudy was one of the few connected guys who hadn't met or seen me.

He told me to be there on Wednesday at 1:00 p.m. When you see Rudy, walk laps near him and call out his name. When he turns, tell him that you're the son of an old friend from Central Falls and your dad was a book. See if he remembers him in his old age.

That Wednesday, when I saw Rudy, I walked up behind him, but not too close to freak him out. I shouted out, "Hey Rudy." He turned and shook my hand. I told him my make-believe story.

"Oh, Central Falls," he said. "We used to call it the city of sin."

Rudy and I walked for miles. He would talk about his old friend Raymond, and he'd even talk about other guys I knew. I would just make up stories as I went along for the walk. He'd tell me the way it used to be. He'd talk about his days in prison and what it was like on the run.

During one walk, I saw his nephew Tony pull up in a beautiful blue Cadillac. I had to veer off because the nephew, an old fighter, knew me from years ago at the gym. Tony was a solid puncher and was looking after uncle Rudy. If he saw me, the game was over.

Rudy did considerable prison time. When he was through doing time, while the other guys were out running around, Rudy was home on North Olney Street in Johnston taking care of his ailing wife, Lucy.

Called “the Captain,” Rudy mentored Rocco Argenti and Eddie Lato, among other wiseguys, in the ways of the mob. He was close to Anthony "The Saint" St. Laurent, Sr. St. Laurent was an earner; Rudy was an enforcer. St. Laurent was generous, and he took care of Rudy.

The intelligence was good, but the approach never worked out. I tried to get Rudy to introduce me to someone else that could lead us to a criminal enterprise. Rudy wasn't interested in bringing in an outsider.

He may have been getting up there in age, but he was still sharp. I may not have persuaded him to introduce me to anyone but talking with him was a master’s class in the mob and added to the base of knowledge we’d build future cases on.

Rudy died on March 14, 2012. They just don't make guys like him anymore.

Chapter 25 Great Cases and Small Disasters

One day in 1989, Brendan received a call from the Detective Commander, Captain Mike Urso, for a special assignment. Mike was a man of few words and got right to the point. He was loyal to Colonel Stone, and whatever the boss wanted, Urso tried his best to deliver.

Urso told Brendan that the Colonel received information regarding a prostitution operation in the city of Warwick operating under the guise of a hairdressing salon and massage parlor. People in high positions in government were frequenting the establishment.

Urso ordered Brendan to investigate the case.

Urso explained that the woman running the business took care of the massages and whatever extra came with it. She went by a nickname, Trixie.

But there was more to the matter than a simple prostitution case. The information indicated the woman had connections to the wiseguys. Perhaps, if the State Police could make a case against her, they might develop a valuable source of information.

My assignment was simple. Infiltrate the back-room operation and get the probable cause for a search warrant to see where, or to whom, any evidence may lead us.

If I'm solicited, or I must ask and she agrees, the case ends there. Urso said the offer was enough. I'm very thankful for that.

Now having received many pieces of information related to vice-type operations, my career experience tells me nothing goes as planned, and the information is usually off a little. Sometimes it's better, and sometimes it's worse. This one really couldn't have gotten any worse from my viewpoint.

Time to put this together. Patience was not a strong suit for Colonel Stone or Captain Urso. They wanted results, and they wanted them yesterday.

I hadn't shaved for a week, wore a blue jeans jacket and pants, a baseball hat on backward, a tape measure on one side of my belt, and an open hammer hanger on the other. A lady who seemed in charge met me at the front door. I introduced myself as Danny. She said she was Trixie.

Okay then, the nickname was right. Maybe this would work out.

It was a narrow building with women sitting on the left and right, those old-style, giant, noisy hairdryers engulfing their heads. More a scene from a science fiction movie than a beauty parlor.

The women were killing time by reading magazines, not paying much interest in me. I could see the only private room was all the way down the back.

I explained I was new to the area, working construction, and had hurt my back. Hoping that a deep tissue massage would help ease the pain. After answering a few questions, she told me it was forty dollars for an hour's massage then gave me an appointment for later in the day because she explained, it was just too busy.

Not a hint of any other services.

With seven women there, and Trixie juggling both operations, I agreed to come back. I took it as a good sign. Maybe she wanted fewer witnesses.

When I returned, I came with outside roving surveillance if something went wrong. We wanted to tape this for evidence, and for my protection, so I wore a wire hidden in my clothes. It would be a juggling act to get it right since I'd be removing most of those.

We tested the wire; it worked well, although I worried the stone foundation of the building might create a problem with the signal. I told the detective with me to lay on the horn a few times if he lost the audio.

I walked in and said hello to my lady friend. Trixie was about twenty years older than me, making this whole scenario even more uncomfortable. She brought me to the backroom, directed me to strip down and to get under the covers. Whichever way I felt comfortable.

I was anything but comfortable at that moment. I opted to keep my underwear on.

I noticed right away that the place wasn't as clean as I'd hoped. I'm a germ freak, and I wanted to get rid of the light blanket. It looked like it hadn't seen the inside of a washing machine in years.

Would it seem weird if I requested new or fresh sheets? Oh boy, I was grossed out already. I didn't want my police career ended by some infectious, incurable disease.

As Murphy's Law would have it, my partner tooted the horn. Great, now I was gonna be inhaling biotoxins, and no one would hear my last moments. Killed in the line of duty getting a massage. Not quite as I imagined it.

Too late to rearrange anything, here came Trixie.

She was very nice, massaging my back while asking questions about the pain. She wanted to know, on a scale of one to ten, how much different pressure hurts me. I could hear the horn occasionally, so I knew the recording wasn't catching this, or, at best, bits and pieces.

And then it was over. Sometimes an hour can seem an eternity.

The possibility of nothing being on tape was disconcerting. I wasn't sure if I should just scratch the plan or not. Maybe it was partially intelligible. As indecision roiled my brain, Trixie told me to dress and pay at the front desk.

She didn't solicit me. Made no happy ending offers. What the heck was going on? So far, the only thing this information had gotten right was her nickname.

I was face down, looking at the plastic exposed from the massage table, and I had to say something because she was about to walk out. Oh boy, this was embarrassing, but I had to say it. My conscience was reminding me of how disrespectful this was if the information was bad. This was crazy...

I just blurted it out using words I never imagined myself ever saying in front of a woman.

She didn't take it well.

Beep, Beep, Beep went the horn.

"What the fuck did you just say? Get your fucking clothes on and get the fuck out of here."

Beep, beep, beep went the horn.

Oops.

"Okay, thank you," I said. "Sorry if I offended you."

Beep, beep, beep.

My thoughts were, holy shit they've got the wrong information. All those years of Catholic education screaming at me in my mind. She could have been someone's mother trying to make a few bucks to raise her family. Something was wrong with this whole thing.

She slammed the door so hard one picture fell off the wall. Mortified doesn't even come close to what I was feeling. I wanted to climb through the back window to escape. Now I was convinced the information is wrong. I dressed quickly and walked out with my money in hand, fifty dollars including a tip which I was thinking wasn't the best idea.

Meanwhile, the horn was blaring outside to remind me of this disaster in progress. Beep, beep, beep.

When I took my first step into the front room, it was like slow motion. Every woman in the place abandoned their magazines and stared me down like a freak or a weirdo. Several women made terrible facial expressions projecting disgust. I wanted to apologize to everyone in there. It was apparent she told them the story.

I put the money on the counter, said I was sorry, and walked out. I wanted to run, but I knew it wouldn't help. The laser stares of the women burned holes in my back.

I walked around the corner, away from the building in case anyone was looking out the window, and my partner picked me up. I felt terrible. Even though I was doing my job, it's against my character to talk like that in front of a woman. To think it might be lousy information made me feel terrible. I learned some of it was on tape, but we would have to enhance the audio if we needed it.

We didn't need it. All set. My memory of the nightmare enhanced it enough for me.

I returned and told the Captain.

His response made me sick to my stomach. He said the boss won't like it because he feels its credible information. With little room for discussion, he said, "Go back in."

"BACK IN?" I was incredulous. "Are you serious? I can't go back in. I don't even think she'd allow me to come back. With all due respect, I'm almost certain it's bad information."

"Do you think you got made? Did she know you were undercover?" Urso probed, not wanting to let it go.

"Who knows? I guess it's possible, but why wouldn't she expose me right there if that was the case? Captain, can we go with a controlled phone call?"

Captain Urso agreed.

I gave it a day and called back. On a taped call, I explained who I was and apologized for my behavior after the massage. I told her the massage helped my condition and got me back to work. I asked if it would be okay to come back.

She said, "As long as you don't pull that stuff again." Which was precisely what I was about to do.

She went through the calendar and picked a date a few days out. I was cringing and wincing because now I was going to pop this question again. Remember, I went to a Catholic high school where they taught me to respect women.

Then, I had a thought. If I didn't use the crude term, it might make it better. I was grasping at straws here but wanted to make the case if the information was right. In closing out the call, I said, "That's fine, but do you think after the massage you'd reconsider and let me know, you know, what a little extra would cost?"

"Don't even bother coming here again, you son of a bitch."

Slam, dial tone, call ended. The recording worked perfectly for this part of this disaster.

"Okay, thank you." Case closed.

Later, when I ran for Congress, I often wondered if some of those women remembered my face and voted against me.

Chapter 26 The Ghost

In the spring of 1994, the State Police Intelligence Unit met with Middletown Police detectives about a local drug dealer. Middletown is a charming New England beach town that abuts Newport. All the charm of a beach community without the summer traffic and fanfare.

The dealer was a guy named Charlie Tuz.

Tuz had a reputation as a connected guy and the guy to see if you needed to resolve disputes. Whatever the illegal activity you wanted to engage in on Aquidneck Island, the body of land Middletown is on, Tuz was the guy.

If he couldn't provide the service, he'd point you in the right direction. Brendan attended the meeting to assess just how current and valid the information was.

The Middletown detectives, accompanied by their Police Chief, Billy Burns, a good cop and previously the Newport Police Detective Commander, attended the meeting. I was with Lt. Jackie Scuncio, an expert in the installation of electronic intercepts, and Detective John Blessing.

The information Middletown had on Tuz impressed me. Information we considered enough probable cause to put a listening device in his house or on his phone, known as a wiretap. Blessing, a young detective, was connecting the dots. I could tell by the way he was processing the information he was thinking of a wiretap.

I knew Charlie Tuz had connections beyond criminal activity on Aquidneck Island. He was an old friend of Charlie Kennedy, Gerard Ouimette, and Anthony Fiore.

Ouimette, as we know, had a reputation that preceded him. Kennedy was a significant mover of drugs and a mystery man. Anthony, or Tony as he's known to his close friends, was an accomplished bank robber. Tony had the backing of Gerard Ouimette to do just about anything he wanted to do. Fiore also had his own connections from New York City to South Boston.

His alliance with Gerard sanctioned Fiore to pull off whatever heist he had in mind. If it wasn't cutting into a protected area. In the early 1980s, I used to see Charlie Tuz hanging out with those guys at Fiore's Gas Station on Branch Avenue in Providence, owned by Tony's father.

I always wondered what Tuz did to get into that crowd. But by the time the information from Middletown PD came up, those guys weren't hanging around Branch Avenue anymore.

OJ Simpson had just been arrested for the murder of his wife Nicole and *The Lion King* just hit the movie theatres. The New York Rangers had just won the NHL Stanley Cup, the Houston Rockets won the NBA Championship, and Evander Holyfield was the World Heavyweight Boxing Champion.

Gerry Ouimette was serving a life sentence in federal prison, and Anthony Fiore began a lengthy sentence in federal prison for his part in the attempted Wells Fargo Armored Car robbery.

Fiore, with three other career criminals, were arrested as they waited in a parking lot a few miles away in Cumberland, Rhode Island. They planned to hit an armored car at the Emerald Square Mall in nearby North Attleboro, Massachusetts.

Rhode Island State Police and the FBI arrested Fiore and his pals as they were passing out an arsenal of guns to the other participants. Tony looked like he was in shock when we moved in on him. It was excellent surveillance work by Lt. Jim Mullen of the RI State Police and his team.

Time moves on, and Charlie Tuz had his own thing going on. John Blessing brought the information about Tuz to Bill Ferland. With his experience running the Organized Crime Unit at the AG's office, he not only understood the who's with who, but he understood what the potential obstacles would be and helped navigate around them.

Charlie Tuz had a small cottage in Middletown within walking distance to Newport's 1st Beach. His house was the target location of the intercept because this was before cellphones became common.

We rented a command post not far from his house. It was a long summer listening to Charlie talk cryptically to his underlings, often until the early morning hours. We had to follow him on his delivery runs. The surreptitious way he would conduct his meetings was comical. We couldn't tell whether he was distracted or if his constant pulling over was part of a counter-surveillance attempt.

In the evenings, when he would be making deliveries at some of Newport's most prominent nightclubs, he would call a cab. He was surveillance conscious and feared a stop by the Middletown or Newport Police.

Tuz didn't know me, so I wore my Newport scene attire and beat him to the locations he mentioned during his early evening calls. But he would only pop into the club, make a quick delivery, and leave. The hand to hand deliveries were tough to catch.

One night, at about midnight, he nearly walked into me on Bannisters Wharf. He was a tough guy to follow on foot because he'd pirouette in mid-step and turn in the opposite direction. We kept people in our command post because he was known to jump back in the cab, take a five-minute ride home, and start power dialing again.

It made for a surveillance nightmare.

He fancied himself a lady's man and had a lot of college-aged women as friends and customers. We interviewed some of those customers after the whole thing was over, and the stories were sickening. Soon, we identified who his supplier was and how he communicated with him.

The supplier was Charlie Kennedy.

Tuz would call him the "Ghost" to others because when he would call him, Kennedy wouldn't talk. If someone picked up the receiver, Kennedy was obviously home. Tuz would then pick up from a prearranged location. Kennedy said nothing incriminating on Tuz's phone.

He wouldn't call from his home phone; Kennedy made him use a payphone. With this new information, our priority changed. The main target became Charlie Kennedy.

Kennedy had an incredible contact list of criminal associates. He could deal with rival factions. He was a close friend of Joe Bevilacqua. Jr., the prominent criminal defense attorney and the son of the former Chief Justice.

While the case was ongoing, we learned through federal and state prosecutors that the Drug Enforcement Administration (DEA) had an investigation going on Kennedy. The obvious inference was since we're all on the same team, we should work it together.

The DEA case agent was a good guy named Russ Holske, but the State Police-DEA relationship was less than amicable. It would be like asking the Red Sox and the Yankees to share the same spring training camp.

Going after major players in Rhode Island offers limited targets of opportunity. One would think this would be a good thing, presenting a prospect for success. Instead, it fragmented what should have been a unified approach.

Each agency had its own reasons for mistrusting others. Some of it valid, some of it based on ancient and clouded history. All of it an impediment to operations. It made for uncomfortable and sporadic cooperation.

There's a lot of competition in law enforcement, especially in a small state. We fish in the same little pool of water for top echelon informants. But we all needed to do the right thing. Setting aside our reservations, we started negotiations between Bill Ferland and AUSA Ken Madden.

Ken was an Assistant United States Attorney, a former prosecutor in the Attorney General's office, and a good guy. He represented DEA's side of where the case should go, and Bill spoke for us.

We knew Bill was pragmatic in splitting a case, and Ken was all about doing the right thing. We had put a lot of work into this and weren't about to just give it away. DEA had also put a lot of work into their side and wasn't about to walk away either.

Agreements were reached and the case progressed.

In December of 1994, after establishing a plethora of evidence on Tuz and his confederates, we took him down. Arrest warrants and search warrants were issued throughout Aquidneck Island.

We also arrested Charlie Kennedy weeks later based on our evidence through this case and follow-up interviews. We removed the veil hiding The Ghost.

During the Tuz takedown, I explained how he might help himself. The danger in offering deals is you must be able to follow through with whatever offer you make. Informants, like tracer rounds, work in both directions.

Someone feigning interest in cooperation could just be fishing for who we were looking into. A detective is only as good as his information. In criminal cases, it too can work in both directions.

Which is exactly happened in this case.

At Newport County Superior Court, during the arraignment for Tuz on numerous counts of Manufacturing and Distributing Controlled Substances, I bumped into his attorney, Joe Bevilacqua, Jr.

He approached me after he had just met with his client in the holding cells. He looked very disturbed and angry.

"Is this the way we're going to play? Is that the deal you're offering?"

It was apparent his client told him his name had come up in our conversation about cooperating. I just smiled and walked away. I was doing my job. Given the circumstances, and based on what I knew at the time, Joe was of legitimate interest to us. He soon would face more pressure coming his way. We took our shot, Tuz chose loyalty over saving his own skin.

Tuz later hired a well-respected attorney named Chris Gontarz. Gontarz was a good guy, but he wasn't allowing his client to talk with me.

Bill Ferland handled all the discussions about any plea negotiation. While the talks went on, the court ordered both Tuz and Kennedy held without bail.

The Ghost finally got out, but DEA swept him up on a Federal Indictment using their information and some of ours. Charles Kennedy went to trial and received a substantial federal sentence for running a major cocaine operation.

Joe Bevilacqua, Jr., during the Buddy Cianci trial, represented a co-defendant. He was disbarred for leaking evidence to TV reporter Jim Taricani. For his refusal to reveal his source, Taricani paid an eighty-five thousand dollar fine and served time in home confinement.

In another case where he served as a defense attorney just before his disbarment, the FBI accused Bevilacqua of fraudulently receiving money from a defendant in exchange for a false promise of getting a reduced sentence. Convicted, Bevilacqua served eighteen months in federal prison.

The twists and turns and interrelationships within Rhode Island are an interesting, yet often troubling, phenomenon.

Chapter 27 Victim or Racketeer?

The inner city didn't have a lock on organized crime activity. The Providence-based mob wasn't averse to traveling. Misquamicut, a beautiful seaside community in the southernmost point of Rhode Island, is a section of the town of Westerly. Like any other New England beachfront resort, it's quiet in the winter and busy in the summer.

The mob saw an opportunity here, as well, alongside the seafood restaurants, bars, and beachgoers.

Jimmy Armenakas stayed busy all year. Some of it legitimate, some of it not so much. Jimmy owned a couple of bars on the beach in the late 1970s, 1980s, and into the 1990s. He built a reputation as a serious drug dealer and a guy who played by his own rules.

He was Westerly's wiseguy.

It's a dangerous reputation to have if you don't have the muscle to fight off the sharks. If a guy is made, then it's a different story. But Mr. Armenakas, who was originally from Connecticut and of Greek descent, didn't have the backing of LCN unless he was paying "rent." If he wasn't paying rent, he was a target of opportunity.

Jimmy Armenakas knew how to make money, and he relished his freelance status. He soon came on the radar of the real wise guys.

Gerard Ouimette knew how to make money from those he controlled and how to take control of those he didn't. Long before his life sentence, Ouimette was busy building his reputation, and his crew, into a force to be reckoned with. Jimmy and his drug business presented an irresistible target.

Gerard contacted Jimmy Armenakas to explain the new rules of their "partnership." A partnership where Jimmy would remain a silent partner if he wanted to keep his business and his pulse.

In April 1978, a source reached out to then Cpl. Mike Urso to tell him that Armenakas was in trouble.

The source information didn't know if Jimmy was being extorted to pay rent or street tax, or if he'd sought Gerard's protection.

Jimmy wouldn't cooperate with State Police inquiries, but Cpl. Urso ran surveillance in the parking lot of one of Armenakas' nightclubs called The Wreck. What the troopers saw proved intriguing.

Three men traveled down from Providence to meet with Jimmy. Cpl. Urso's source said the men threatened Jimmy in a heated discussion. The meeting caused Jimmy to leave town for a while.

The three men who visited Jimmy were Joe Timpani, George Basmajian, and Gerard Ouimette.

This was a trio with a resume for bad things.

A year later, Timpani received a substantial federal prison sentence for guns, loansharking, bookmaking and other racketeer related offenses because of an FBI raid of his home.

Just months after the meeting, State Police found George Basmajian dead in the back seat of a stolen car. Jerry Tillinghast, who was close to Gerard Ouimette, and his brother, Harold Tillinghast, were charged and convicted in his murder. After this surveillance, Gerard just kept being Gerard until his actions earned him a life sentence.

Absent Jimmy wanting to talk about Ouimette, there was nothing the State Police could do. It was business as usual for Jimmy. He was one of those well-schooled criminals who could spot surveillance, suspected the police put undercover officers in his bars, and wouldn't talk in front of anyone out of fear they were cooperating with police.

Every time he saw Detective Ron Gwaltney from Westerly P.D., Jimmy would be on alert. He knew Ronnie suspected what he was all about. Some local folks thought Jimmy was a good guy. A hard-working guy, he'd be the first to buy a beer for someone with any influence, if they'd accept it.

Many did.

Throughout the years the State Police Intelligence Unit took a few runs at Jimmy, all to no avail. Confidential informants, numerous surveillances, and interviews of area drug defendants all fell short.

For a few years, he got out of the trafficking business. But the lure of the money was too powerful.

In 1999, the Intelligence Unit, based on new information, took another look at Jimmy's activities. In April 2000, RI State Police Detective Les Dunbar infiltrated Jimmy's operation in an undercover role. Dunbar looked the part of a beachgoer and spent considerable time in Misquamicut hanging around with Jimmy.

The State Police assigned Les to the FBI as part of a drug task force. The task force included a top-notched agent named Jeff Cady and, as karma would have it, Westerly P.D. Detective Ron Gwaltney.

After months of small talk and small deliveries of cocaine, Jimmy Armenakas became fond of Les, who went by the undercover name, Nicky. Jimmy became so fond of him, he nicknamed him "Nicky Blue Eyes."

Jimmy took Nicky Blue Eyes under his wing. Talked to him about running a scam at the Foxwoods Casino, bookmaking, and moving or distributing illegal football cards. Les, or Nicky Blue Eyes, would spend four to five days a week with Jimmy. Sometimes that would be an all-day event at his beachfront home in Misquamicut.

The surveillance team had their hands full because they had to keep moving. Despite the ease with which TV cop shows portray surveillance operations, they are complicated and manpower intensive. It is challenging to keep an eye on a guy or a nightclub where everyone knows the owner is a target. The combination of paranoia and self-interest in protecting drug connections makes covert infiltration over long periods difficult.

Unfamiliar faces who become familiar without ever doing business are always suspect. They saw undercover cops everywhere, except, due to the excellent work of Nicky Blue Eyes and the task force, standing right next to Jimmy. They would brag about smelling a cop a mile away. This skill apparently didn't work in close quarters.

Most of this activity took place in the summer where bar patrons, parking lot attendants, bartenders, waitstaff all knew Jimmy. They were his willing eyes and ears. But as the case went on, Jimmy became so comfortable with Nicky Blue Eyes he sold him a full kilogram of cocaine for $25,000.

A kilogram back then—cut up (packaged into smaller quantities) and stepped on (adding bulking agents to increase the amount)— could net over $100,000 street value.

The long, arduous investigation resulted in Jimmy's arrest and conviction. Sentenced to five years in federal prison, he died of a heart ailment while serving his sentence.

The intrusion of Gerard Ouimette into the business of drug dealer in Westerly Rhode Island was significant for two reasons.

It showed the reach of the wiseguys on the Hill. They went after revenue streams of easy money wherever they could find them, and it underscored the stubbornly persistent fallacy of the mob not dealing in drugs.

Sometimes cases unfold in a matter of moments. More often, they take weeks or months. Then there are those cases where luck or opportunistic intervention drags them on forever.

In this business, persistence is a virtue. Good cops never give up.

Part III: A Changing of the Guard

Chapter 28 The End of the Stone Age

Colonel Walter Stone served as a Providence Police Officer, Chief of Police, and Superintendent of the Rhode Island State Police in a law enforcement career spanning the era from just before World War II to 1990.

He testified before the United States Congress about New England Organized Crime and led the Rhode Island State Police with an iron fist, building a national reputation as a premier law enforcement agency.

As time and society changed, the organization needed to change. Walter Stone was of a different era of law enforcement, and those days were fading into history.

In due time, the old Colonel began to slip. What was once a man who walked tall in the most difficult of times was now having trouble walking. He was in his 70s, and time was moving quickly.

We had a new Governor who wanted to replace the Colonel. There was a gender equality lawsuit against the State Police and some morale issues among the rank and file, so the Colonel wrapped it up in 1990. This was big news for Rhode Islanders and law enforcement throughout New England.

Walter Stone was like Wyatt Earp, the sheriff in town; he walked tall and carried a big stick.

Those mentioned as his successor were a former Providence Police Major, retired State Police Captain Ed Pare, and retired State Police Lieutenant Vin Vespia, who at the time was Chief of Police in South Kingstown, RI.

The man who made it through was Edmund Culhane, the number two in command of the New York State Police. Word was there were no politics, no personal connections, and the outside candidate was what RISP needed at this time: a non- connected guy to get us through some problematic morale issues.

Ed Culhane was a nice guy, and he had a vision toward the future. I mean when a guy doesn't know how to turn on his own computer, yet has the foresight in 1990 to computerize the entire department and to insist that all learn the skills to create paperless department files, etc. That's innovation.

Shortly after his arrival, I had the luck of solving a homicide and taking down two armed robberies in progress. Timing is everything. It was Col. Culhane that called me to assign me to the banking crisis investigation. It was around this time the focus was shifting from "Public Enemy Number One" being wiseguys to public corruption and computer crimes.

Rhode Island's reputation for criminal activity wasn't exclusively due to the mob. Public corruption was a motivation for many state and local politicians. As the mob aspect began its slow descent out of the forefront of the headlines, corrupt politicians took over first place.

Among the most troubling of these was a charismatic but complicated former prosecutor, popular talk show host, and twice Mayor of Providence, Vincent A. "Buddy" Cianci.

Everybody had a Buddy story. Some were heartwarming, some were shocking, some were criminal.

Public corruption, involving Buddy and other prominent officials, and one of the most devastating fires in American history soon captured the headlines and the attention of the state police.

This became the new focus of law enforcement.

Chapter 29 Wiring the Governor

In the early 1990s, Whitey Bulger was still running the rackets in Boston. Protected, it later turned out, by renegade FBI agents. The New England La Cosa Nostra (LCN) was in a state of flux. The 1989 FBI taping of the NE LCN Induction ceremony in Medford, Massachusetts was a shock to the secrecy of their world and the code of silence known as Omerta. Junior Patriarca presided over the conciliatory meeting to induct new members, but also to appease rival factions in Boston.

The taping of the ceremony did little to enhance his reputation as boss.

Several Rhode Island members were on trial during this period (August 1991) in the Hartford Federal Court, including Nicky Bianco and Matthew Guglielmetti. When Brendan testified, he identified voices from the Medford bug. Philip Leonetti also testified that week. He was the former underboss of the Bruno-Scarfo family in Philadelphia and Atlantic City. Leonetti testified about the day-to-day activity of a Mafia family.

A lot happened. Rhode Island had a new Governor named Bruce Sundlun. He was a no-nonsense guy with a command presence; a hold-over from his days as a command pilot flying a B-17 Flying Fortress named Damned Yankee on bombing missions over Germany during the war.

On his 13th mission, the plane suffered massive damage from anti-aircraft fire, losing one engine. Struggling to get the crippled plane and his crew back to England, Sundlun was forced to fly slower than usual.

Several German fighters attacked the slow-moving aircraft and shot it down. Sundlun crash-landed the plane, steering it away from a nearby French town. Four members of the crew died, and the Germans captured five.

Sundlun manage to escape back to England with the aid of the French Underground.

He was a handsome, powerful man. Brendan came to know him better after Sundlun left office. He had an honest reputation and did not tolerate corruption. He gave the State Police the tools to do its job effectively.

One day toward the end of his tenure as governor (1991–1995), I received a call to go to Sundlun's house as soon as possible. The governor wanted us to cover a meeting where he believed someone would attempt to bribe him. I sent a message to the Superintendent that the Governor would have to let us record the meeting to memorialize the conversation.

The Superintendent agreed.

I arrived with my partner, Det. John LaCross. The Governor's assistant told us we needed to wait for the Governor, still tied up at the State House. It was around 5:00 p.m. and the meeting was to take place at 5:30. With the time getting tight, we asked where the Governor would typically hold meetings at his residence. The assistant led us to the street-level office at the South Main Street side of the home. John wired the office with a recording device. We tested it, and it was perfect. Hiding the wire in a book on the table, you could hear a pin drop.

Shortly after setting up the wire, the Governor arrived. He explained that the guy told him they should meet in private. The guy said it was in the Governor's best interest to meet and keep it quiet. He had a bad feeling about the meeting but agreed to meet the guy.

We stood there while the Governor unbuttoned and removed his shirt. I told him that the room was all set. He asked, "What do you mean all set?" I told him the place was bugged/wired and ready to go. He looked at me, eye-to-eye, and said, "No, I think it would be better if I wear the wire."

I tried to tell him it wasn't necessary, but he had that authoritative look and voice. He insisted that he wear the wire. I wasn't going to argue with him. But that wasn't the type of intercept device we brought with us. We'd have to improvise.

John went out to his car and brought in the white athletic tape he had bought for his hockey game that night. After showing the Governor how we would use the tape to secure the wire to his chest, he decided that wearing the wire the way he imagined it wasn't critical. The thought of us yanking the tape off after the meeting was enough to change his mind. He decided we would tape it to the outside of his t-shirt. We weren't concerned about the guy trying to pat down the Governor looking for a wire, but you never know.

The guy arrived and broke down, crying about his financial troubles. He begged the Governor for a job. There was no bribe or tacit implication. No one could ever bribe Bruce Sundlun.

Years later, he would joke with me about it. I never knew why it was so important to wear the wire. Perhaps he'd watched too many cop movies. But he was wise enough to know it wasn't worth having John LaCross and I yank that tape off his skin just so he could have the full undercover cop experience.

Apparently flying through enemy anti-aircraft fire, getting shot down, or having German patrols hunting and trying to kill him didn't scare him. Two troopers yanking athletic tape off his skin terrified him.

Chapter 30 Whitey Bulger and Southie

The entire sad saga of James "Whitey" Bulger is now well known. But before the revelations of some FBI agents working toward a cross purpose, Whitey was in the crosshairs of several agencies. Cooperation, stilted and inconsistent, was rare but nonetheless official policy.

Interagency rivalries are a pox on law enforcement. The bigger the target, the more jealousy interfered with a willingness to share.

A case with more than one agency involved often dragged on because of this internecine bickering. Yet things were changing. Cooperation slowly improved between local, state, and federal agencies. The old ways fell to the realities of a more technologically connected world.

Where once identifying an individual whose criminal record came from California took days, now took seconds. Where investigators had to climb telephone poles to install wiretaps, now a few keystrokes on a computer connected a criminal target's cellphone to law enforcement monitoring equipment.

Cooperation, once considered outside of normal operating parameters, became more commonplace.

But it took time and effort to build such interagency relationships, and the Bulger case did little to help the progress.

There is no need to revisit the unholy alliance between James "Whitey" Bulger and the FBI. That is a story for a whole other book. Brendan and his troopers continued down a path of cooperation as much as humanly possible. It wasn't always perfect, but it was getting better.

In Rhode Island, we worked closely with the FBI and Massachusetts State Police (MSP). Both had talented investigators. I was close with Tom Foley, who later became Superintendent of the Mass State Police. He was the epitome of sound ethics, and he had a PhD. in the streets. Foley was a little close-mouthed when we would talk about the Bulger crew because he knew we worked closely with the Bureau. If he shared intelligence information with me and asked me not to share with any other agencies, I honored his request.

Unfortunately, there were even personality conflicts with the Providence FBI office. I felt like I was in a horse race and caught in the middle. I knew them all and got along with them well. Just another senseless obstacle to overcome.

I was in Los Angeles at an Organized Crime conference at the outset of the Massachusetts State Police investigation of Whitey Bulger. I met John Gamel, the head of the Boston office of the FBI. John was a perfect gentleman. I'm sure he didn't know how severe the Bulger damage was because he wasn't there during that period. But he was trying to figure it out.

He knew I had a close relationship with the Massachusetts State Police, most notably Tom Foley. John wanted to see me. I met with him for a drink, and he told me about the lack of camaraderie with the MSP troopers. It was about the unhealthy discourse and tacitly implied wrongdoing and innuendo. It didn't make too much sense because who would compromise themselves for a mobster?

John asked me to just talk to Foley to see if I could be a conduit to repair their relationship. I agreed. I thought, and still believe, he was just trying to create harmony and rebuild what was torn down rather than stop what was to come.

It's one of those moments where I realized that I'm really sticking my nose in an area where it doesn't belong. I didn't have all the facts. I had no idea where the MSP case would lead, or who might be involved.

On the plane ride home, I decided not to be the intermediary. I never heard from John Gammel again. I never told my friend, Tom Foley, the FBI asked me to help create kumbaya between their agencies. The rest is history.

Several years later, on July 27, 2014, Ambassador Ray Flynn invited my brother Chris and me to his 75th birthday celebration at the St. Augustine Chapel in Southie and then over to a local pub to an Irish party. Like any other neighborhood loyalist, you take the good with the bad. Ray was a revered neighborhood guy. He was also in constant conflict with the Bulger political machine and the Bulger criminal enterprise.

Raymond didn't back down, but those who know him know the spiritual side of him trumps all feelings.

Senate President William Bulger wasn't too complimentary of the Ambassador in his book *"While the Music Lasts."*[5] When leaders and combatants get older, they try to mend fences.

---

[5] Houghton Mifflin ISBN 978-0395720417 by William M. Bulger

At the Flynn reception, I sat right next to Billy Bulger and his lovely wife. I was surprised, but my brother told me they'd buried the hatchet. When introduced to Billy, I told him I was retired. I wasn't going to ask him about his murderous brother, no matter how much I would have liked that conversation, but we did talk politics and the Irish culture.

Just before the meal, we joined in with Billy as he prayed.

A week later in *The Boston Globe*, an article appeared about the movie *Black Mass*. The movie was based on the relationship between Whitey Bulger and FBI Agent John Connolly, reopening the wound done to law enforcement in Boston.

Knowing Ray the way I do, I'm sure he and Billy have put their political rivalries aside for the good of their soul, their families, and their community.

Old feuds sometimes find their way to resolution or forgiveness. That's a hard sell to the Irish. The saying goes that Irish Alzheimer's is forgetting everything but a grudge. I know some Irish guys who hate another guy but don't remember why. They just remember they hated the guy for something. The reason doesn't matter.

That's not to say Ray would be visiting Whitey any time soon. Back in the day as they say, Whitey threatened Ray, both overtly and tacitly. Ray prefers not to talk about ancient history.

Irish Alzheimer's reminds me of several years ago during the "troubles" in Ireland. I was driving through Belfast with my brothers, on Falls Road to be precise, looking for the murals of political prisoners.

Bobby Sands, Kiernan Doherty, and Paul Hill were big names. I then took a random turn and drove through Belfast neighborhoods. At one point we drove by a bus stop. There were eight or nine kids, ranging from about seven to ten years old, waiting for a bus.

Now, remember the political and socio-economic environment was challenging for kids growing up in that city. Armored vehicles traveled the streets, and heavily armed British soldiers walked the sidewalks. It was more occupied territory than a neighborhood.

To those kids, we were either tourists or people on the enemy side of their parents' conversations.

We slowed down to get a good look. We wondered what challenges these poor Irish kids endured, living in Ulster County under British rule. Many lived in abject poverty. Coupled with cultural and religious differences cutting so deep in their surroundings. They suffered under conditions hard to understand by those not living in their environment. It made for a hard existence.

As we looked at their faces, sad yet angry eyes stared back. We felt terrible for them. They responded to our interest the only way they knew; shouting obscenities and giving us the middle finger. The older ones yelled, "Fuck you, Yanks."

It was shocking. These kids didn't know why they were supposed to hate us, they just knew they were.

These animosities sometimes carried over to those who emigrated to the US. But time has faded the differences.

The old Italian and Irish neighborhoods are few in our days. Southie has become a yuppie, gentrified, and diverse enclave attracting a younger crowd of Bostonians buying real estate like it's going out of style.

The Federal Hill section of Providence has changed drastically as it relates to demographics and the make-up of the side streets. It's much like Hartford, CT or Arthur Avenue in the Bronx.

The Italian heritage is alive and well, but the neighborhoods are not all Italian anymore. Yet, in Providence, Atwells Avenue on Federal Hill is still the place to go. It's like Hanover Street in the North End of Boston.

Change is good, or at least inevitable, but we love our culture and need to respect and hold on to it if we can. Once it's gone, it's gone forever.

One guy who I had the opportunity to spend a day with, and who loved his Italian heritage, was Governor Mario Cuomo.

It was 1990, and he arrived at TF Green Airport early in the morning. When I picked him up, he was with a squared away member of the New York State Police. I took him to Cookson America and Brown University. I pointed out Federal Hill from our car.

He talked about family and how to stay close to your children and gave me advice as to how to best present yourself. Dress for success. Read as often as you can. Never pass on an opportunity to learn. We were in the car for a while, so I soaked up the opportunity.

It was like being in an accelerated course on how to reach your potential. I spent the entire day with him, but I wished it was a week. At the time, many considered him a potential Presidential contender. He had not announced whether he'd be running yet, so there was a lot of media.

At one point I had pulled up to the sidewalk in front of Cookson America in Kennedy Plaza where then-Mayor Joe Paolino presented the Governor with the "Key to the City" and a gift basket from Federal Hill.

Other people brought baskets, as well, and I filled my trunk with them. One basket was the size of a shopping carriage. I mean, really? What is the poor guy supposed to do with all this fruit, cheese, and meats? Every city he visits must give him the same thing. The large basket was full of prosciutto, pepperoni, salami, soppressata, provolone, parmigiana. You name it, we had it in the trunk.

It was getting late in the afternoon, and we had to get back to TF Green Airport. As Governor Cuomo was getting in the front seat and the NY Trooper in the back, Providence Journal Reporter M. Charles "Charlie" Bakst jumped in on the passenger's side rear seat.

The New York trooper glared at Charlie; Charlie smiled and held up his press pass. The trooper wasn't impressed. He looked at me as to ask if I'd invited Charlie, making eye contact in my rearview mirror. I shook my head, no.

Charlie said, "I'll just take the ride to the airport and back."

The trooper said, "No, get out." Just his tone should have been enough, but Charlie was not easily intimidated.

Charlie looked at me and asked why he couldn't accompany us to the airport. I wanted to say, "Really, Charlie? Do you really want me to get into policies, procedures, security protocol, and the fact that other reporters are standing on the sidewalk thinking they should have jumped in too?"

It was an awkward moment because Charlie was one of the lead political writers in New England and, although politicians loathed the sight of him, I liked him.

As I explained to Charlie why this would not happen, Governor Cuomo got out of the passenger's side, stood on the sidewalk, and granted Charlie a one on one interview with other reporters getting a piece of the responses. Most questions centered on if he'd run for President of the United States.

They spent around five minutes asking the Governor questions. He thanked them, then jumped back in the car. That shortened our window of time to get back to TF Green Airport. He had a private jet, but they needed to stick to their schedule.

Rhode Island trooper Ed Stapans led the way in a uniform car which helped us make better time. Then Governor Cuomo asked if I was hungry? I remember thinking, *Oh, my God, if he wants to stop, I'll never get him to the plane on time.*

I told him I was hungry, but it was not a good idea to stop because of his tight schedule. He agreed and told me there were enough calories and cholesterol in the trunk for a hundred people. He said he'd take a couple back to New York, but he wanted me to take the rest.

Dropping them off at the private hanger, I had enough Italian meats and cheeses for the rest of the year. Cuomo was quite a guy.

Chapter 31 The Station Nightclub Fire

On February 21, 2003, one of the deadliest fires in the history of the United States occurred at a nightclub in the town of West Warwick, Rhode Island.

When the Station Nightclub incident was over, one hundred people were dead, and two hundred and thirty people injured. First responders faced a horrific scene with bodies wedged tightly together in the panic to escape the fast-moving flames. From the early reports of a fire to the area-wide request to surrounding fire departments across Rhode Island and Massachusetts to "send everybody," the nightmare would haunt those at the scene for a long time.

For the families of those lost, life would never be the same.

Not much can derail the State Police from a focus on the mob, this was one of those cases where the State Police used every resource in helping the victims and seeking justice.

Brendan was a Major and acting Executive Officer. Colonel Steve Pare, then the Superintendent, and Major Jack Leyden, the number one and two men in the department command structure, were out of town. In their absence, Brendan was in command of the State Police and the senior State Police officer at the scene.

It was about 1:00 a.m. that I received a call at home about a bad fire in a night club in West Warwick, Rhode Island. Our department was assisting West Warwick Fire, Rescue, and Police at the scene.

Troopers on the scene reported that the situation was so bad it required mutual aid from other cities and towns. Several people were dead and unknown numbers transported to local hospitals with varying degrees of injury.

As the acting Executive Officer, I offered whatever resources we had available. I asked for another update when we had a clearer picture of fatalities and if they needed any other resources. I never imagined while I was waiting for more numbers and the exact magnitude of this tragic event that it would become the deadliest tragedy in the state's history.

A few hours later, I received another call that the death toll reached several dozen, and the number of injured overwhelmed the local hospital emergency rooms.

I made my required phone calls to Colonel Steven Pare and Command Staff members and then headed to the ad hoc Incident Command Center (ICS), a side room at the Cowesett Inn. The Cowesett Inn is a popular West Warwick restaurant located across the street from the site of the deadly fire.

Many of the injured, suffering severe burns, ran from the building to the Cowesett Inn looking for shelter and aid while the inferno of the Station Nightclub raged behind them. The blaze, sparked by an unwise pyrotechnic display inside the club, burned out of control.

People were dead or dying, and the blaze still burned.

Great White, the band playing that fateful night, set off pyrotechnics which ignited flammable sound insulation foam in the ceilings and walls.

The use of pyrotechnics and the insulation later became significant factors in the criminal investigation and prosecution. Early on, I met with State Police personnel, West Warwick Police Chief Peter Brousseau, and other first responders to determine what we needed to do.

Where do you start?

We were assessing what we needed to do and to prioritize the tasks. Priority one, making sure there were no more injured people still alive in the rubble. We had to deal with the dead bodies already retrieved from the burned-out building while fire personnel, State Police Criminal Identification Unit members, State Fire Marshal's Office located more bodies.

Areas the victims thought would be safe havens turned out to be death traps.

The numbers of fatalities were staggering. As the scene went from a medical rescue focus to a recovery and identification action, the possibility of a criminal investigation required specific protocols to preserve evidence.

We didn't have immediate confirmation as to what sparked the fire. The chaos of the scene, coupled with the magnitude of the loss of life, made it impossible to be certain. But survivors intimated a troubling possibility. Some reported exit doors blocked, limiting avenues of escape. Some mentioned fireworks. Determining the cause would come later.

Around 8:00 a.m., the death toll was somewhere near fifty and rising. That number eventually hit one hundred. The scene was chaotic and the challenges almost insurmountable in the early stages.

But words cannot describe what the first responders saw that night. That goes for the good Samaritans too. People saw things that would haunt them forever.

The owner of the Cowesett Inn, Jimmie Paolucci, left his business open all night to accommodate those who survived and made it over for shelter. He left it open all week for police and fire officials to take breaks and as a meeting place for other necessary personnel. It was the venue for our first organized meeting to take care of and address the needs of family members, recovery efforts, and the need for a criminal investigation.

People from the Red Cross, Critical Incident Response Team, clergy, police, fire, rescue, Governor Don Carcieri, Attorney General Patrick Lynch, Senator Jack Reed, and Adjutant General Reggie Centracchio all attended a 10:00 a.m. meeting in the restaurant. Governor Carcieri took a quick leadership role in assisting families, and Senator Reed spoke of utilizing federal resources as needed.

As more information came in, Attorney General Pat Lynch and I recognized the need to conduct a criminal investigation. Lynch assigned Assistant Attorneys General Bill Ferland and Michael Stone to the case. Having two career prosecutors assigned full time to an incident in its initial stages is somewhat unusual, but this was anything but a usual situation.

Father Anthony Marciano became more than a priest. He was an ad hoc social worker, psychologist, and a friend. Later, a third seasoned prosecutor, Randy White, joined in. I assigned Detective Sgt. Brian Casilli, along with several other State Police detectives. West Warwick Police dedicated numerous members, including Detective Ronald Coutu. The State Fire Marshall, Jesse Owens, and his deputy, Mike DiMascollo, joined the investigative team.

Early on, we separated the criminal case from all the other responsibilities. I had conflicting duties, overseeing the criminal investigation, and working with other agencies in identifying bodies. And equally important, I had to spearhead efforts with West Warwick Police Chief Peter Brousseau, The Red Cross, The National Guard, and others in guiding, assisting, and comforting the family members of those identified and those not yet recovered but likely deceased.

Members of every media outlet imaginable assembled in front of the building. Knowing what lay in store for the foreseeable future was mindboggling. It left me in a confused state for a few minutes. It underscored the uncertain nature of my business. One moment I was sleeping at home, the next I was thrust into the midst of a mind-numbing story of immense tragedy with international interest.

I realized the magnitude of interest when I saw media outlets from Europe parked alongside our local media. It was surreal. A word sometimes used too loosely but fitting here.

The recovery of bodies continued, hour upon hour. We found many in an area where I couldn't help but struggle with the thoughts of the panicked victims desperately seeking a safe- haven. Trying to escape the fire and smoke but ending up in their tomb.

A picture of horror and sadness still haunts that memory.

Removing the rubble and collapsed building exposed the horrific scene. Members of the recovery team of troopers, local police and fire, ATF, State Fire Marshals, and others recovered bodies. Others focused on locating and identifying items of evidentiary value. They did their best to show respect and preserve the dignity of the recovered bodies, one at a time. Stopping to remove their hats, bow their heads, and offer a quick moment of silence.

It was their way of saying—*even though we're exhausted, covered in ash, soot, and water, we will stop to pay our respects to you, my friend. We honor you now and will never stop until we learn the truth about what happened here.*

Words cannot describe the level of sadness and downright sorrow. Amid such horror, humans are capable of great things. Although these young men and women were beyond saving, we could still preserve their humanity.

It was the most fitting offer of respect we could bring to bear. Mothers, fathers, sons, daughters, and friends were showing up at the scene with photos. They would ask anyone who looked like they were in a role of authority if they have seen them. It was crushing because we had only a look of sorrow to offer.

How can you tell a mother of a missing son or daughter you wouldn't be able to use the photo because many victims are unrecognizable? In most cases, dental records or corroborating factors such as scars, marks, or tattoos helped identify the deceased. The sheer volume of bodies taxed the resources of the state medical examiner's office.

The Chief Medical Examiner, Dr. Elizabeth Laposata, was exhausted and not adequately staffed to face such a crisis. This was an unimaginable loss of life. When was the last time we had a mass casualty in Rhode Island? The death toll and number of injured such as we faced happens in war zones, not in a small town in Rhode Island.

This was uncharted territory for all involved.

We were all working from early morning to late evening in whatever capacity we served, and the Medical Examiner was no exception. The quicker we transported bodies to the ME's Office, the more backup it created. Learning as we went along, we tried to control the flow as best we could.

The Red Cross—with helpful volunteers, comfort dogs, and other resources—set up at the Inn at the Crossings in Warwick, Rhode Island. They focused on comforting family and friends of those as yet unrecovered but believed to be deceased. We took over a large ballroom with a stage on the south side of the building for updates and announcements.

First responders would come in and out, greeted by anxious relatives of someone not yet accounted for. Exhausted and mentally wounded, they were forced into playing a supportive role for the desperate family members. We tasked some to assist with identification or to run down leads with State Police and West Warwick PD.

Ferland, Stone, White, Casilli, Coutu, and the rest of the investigative team stayed away from the area. They were on a different mission, and it was important not to compromise the criminal aspect.

But I was responsible for both areas of interest. I'd check in with detectives and prosecutors but wouldn't even let anyone in the recovery and identification area know what was going on with that part of the case. Cross interest was no good for the ultimate goals. And those goals were different.

The staging area for the families of victims was off limits to reporters and posted clearly on the doors. However, it was difficult to control because we didn't want family and friends to go through a check-in desk or badging system. They were dealing with the worst moments of their lives and had been through enough. It was on the honor system; we relied on human understanding and compassion.

But not everyone follows the honor system, right? About the third night in we were getting information from family members that journalists from out of state were sneaking notes to family members asking for discrete interviews.

It's a complicated issue to resolve. The media was doing its job. We wanted to give the families of the victims or missing room to think. Some wanted to talk to the press, others wanted no part of it. The reporters were trying to get the scoop and beat other stations.

Our local reporters were at a disadvantage because we knew them. The out of state reporters could just blend in with families. At any one time, there may have been over a hundred people in the ballroom milling about. Everyone waiting for us to announce the recovery of more bodies, or the names of newly identified victims.

Emotions ran high, tension in the air palpable.

At one point a woman in her mid-50's approached me, tugged on the sleeve of my State Police search jacket, and put a photo in front of my face of a young girl about twenty-five years old. The woman, with tears in her eyes, asked in a hauntingly sad and broken voice if I'd seen her daughter.

I don't know what came over me, but I was tired. The emotions just kept coming at you and, most of the time, you'd deal with it. But this time...this time I felt like a rock hit me on the side of my face. My face got numb, and I didn't know what that meant.

There was devastating news coming to everyone I looked at. I met the woman's eyes, and I couldn't stem the emotions flooding my mind. I couldn't talk. My eyes welled up, and all I could do was look at her.

The emotions overwhelmed me. We were supposed to stay strong, immune to the trauma. Tears? Troopers don't shed tears. My pride was too strong to accept that. The crushing responsibilities of my job collided with my humanity. It did for all of us in positions of responsibility in those moments. I faced a woman living a nightmare; a situation no one should have to endure.

At one point, Trooper David Tikoian of the governor's security detail, contacted me to tell me there was an unhealthy tension in the air and that the families were getting restless.

This presented a challenge for Gov. Carcieri and me. There was no standard time for people to be identified via autopsy. Sometimes they had to wait an unbearable amount of time. The medical examiners needed to do their due diligence, but families were anxiously waiting.

Many of the police, fire, and support personnel there had children of their own. They were fathers and mothers, grandparents, aunts, and uncles. Digging through the ashes of a nightmare too devastating to contemplate, each faced the inevitable voices in their heads.

What if this were my child?

As these things unfolded early that first morning, Chief Brosseau looked at me and said, "I think I am going to stop home for a moment."

At first, I was taken aback a bit, then I realized he'd been here all night. Still, there was much to be done.

"We have some things to take care of, Chief." I said, "Lots of agencies need to be coordinated here."

Chief Brosseau looked at me with a profound sadness, reflecting what we all were feeling.

"I know," he nodded. "I'll be right back. I want to go hug my kids."

And I couldn't say as I blamed him for needing that momentary escape from all the horror before us. It was important to remember the living even in the midst of death.

Those waiting for news, turned to us to make things right. To bring them good news amidst their worst fears.

Good news that would never come.

I knew, instinctively if not for certain, at some point I would have to tell this woman her daughter was dead. There can be no worse moment as a police officer than being the bearer of such news. But standing before her, looking into the abyss of sadness in her eyes, I was utterly incapable of controlling my emotions.

I couldn't talk, and I just shook my head "no." I felt like I'd done something wrong, so I tried to speak again. But I couldn't. In my mind, I'd let her down.

What a weird response. People expected more of me. I knew I had to maintain the face of strength, but I failed for a second. I failed that mother, and I felt terrible. I looked in her eyes, shook my head, and softly said no.

She let go of me, walked away, and plunged back into the solitary loneliness of hopeful uncertainty.

Shortly after that, Governor Carcieri and I, along with Adjutant General Centracchio, took to the podium again to announce more names from the Medical Examiner of those positively identified as deceased.

When we would do this, there came the inevitable gasp from those whose last vestige of hope we had destroyed. Muffled crying followed as families gathered around each other to attend to one another's grief.

I witnessed the incredible power of the human spirit for compassion.

As families received the information, no matter how devastating it was, they muffled their grief out of consideration for those still clinging to hope. They knew for most of the other families still waiting that their time was coming soon.

I saw what amounted to acts of courage from ordinary people during that horror. People facing the loss of a child, the worst moment of their lives—the worse moment of anyone's life—still able to show consideration for others. If there could be anything good to come from such tragedy it lies in such acts of kindness and compassion.

It seemed comforting in a way for those hundreds still waiting.

On or about the fourth day, I was walking through the main ballroom area. A gentleman walked up to me, introduced himself as the father of someone still not among those recovered, and handed me the card of a member of the Boston media.

The card contained the writer's name, cell phone number, and a location in the parking lot for an interview if he was receptive. We had told the media not to come in that area reserved for family members.

This reporter violated our trust, approaching the family member in the sterile area who wished to be left alone. The man told me the Boston media guy was standing in the bar area of the hotel waiting for a call. At that, I removed my State Police emblazoned jacket, I was just in slacks with a shirt and tie.

I walked over and introduced myself, showing him my State Police identification.

"Did you know the Hope Valley Barracks isn't far from here? It's a couple of exits up from the Connecticut line."

"Why would I need to know that?" he asked.

"Because," I explained, "that is where you'll be locked up if you return back inside the ballroom."

He gave me a quizzical look and left. I never saw him again.

The media per se was not the problem. I understood and respected their job. It was their indifference to the families of the victims in pursuit of that job I found troubling.

If the family members wanted to talk to the media, they could do so. I felt an obligation to let that decision come from them, not because of pressure from some overly ambitious reporter trying to scoop all the other equally enthusiastic reporters.

Few incidents will redirect the full attention of the Rhode Island State Police from other responsibilities. As crucial as investigating organized crime is, it pales in the face of incidents like the Station Nightclub Fire.

For the other public safety personnel at the scene, the nightmare faded with time. For those who heard names announced over those terrible days, the nightmare never ended.

Chapter 32 Flipping a Wiseguy to Get a Judge

One of the most challenging and troubling aspects of investigating organized crime is the necessity of using informants or, to use the more politically correct term so as not to offend their pride and sensibilities, cooperating individuals.

Recruiting and using such individuals is the definition of a deal with the devil. Those arrested because of this cooperation despise them., calling them rats. That is an injustice to rats. Yet as disgusting as many cops find dealing with them to be, they are a necessary evil.

In the history of organized crime cases, not one nun ever made a case against the mob. To catch bad guys, you need bad guys to do it.

Yet, there was always the danger of the ends justifying the means. When the FBI made La Cosa Nostra their focus, it drove agents to extremes to make cases and build careers. Such efforts went off the rails with Whitey Bulger, but it was not the only example.

In 1968, a jury convicted four men, Henry Tameleo, Peter Limone, Louis Greco, and Joseph Salvati, of murdering a small-time hood named Teddy Deegan. Their convictions were mainly based on the testimony of a cooperating individual.

Tameleo, Limone, and Greco received the death penalty; Salvati faced life in prison. The US Supreme court later ruled the death penalty unconstitutional, and the three had their sentences commuted to life in prison.

The men were imprisoned from 1968 until 2001 when evidence came to light that the informant who'd testified at trial, Joe "The Animal" Barbosa, and another, more recently identified informant, Stephen Flemmi—coincidently a member of Whitey Bulger's crew—lied about the details with the knowledge of FBI agents.

The FBI had also failed to disclose it had intercepted telephone conversations involving Barbosa and Flemmi seeking the okay to kill Deegan and still let the murder occur. The FBI knew the four men convicted had not been involved yet allowed the trial to go forward based on perjured testimony.

The men were exonerated and released, except for Tameleo, who died in prison in 1985.

Barbosa, who was one of the first men to enter the Federal Witness Protection Program, resumed his life of crime. In 1976, another mob enforcer recognized Barbosa and shot him to death.

Informants are a dangerous but necessary tool in the law enforcement arsenal. But they are like junkyard dogs; off the chain they can be deadly.

I guess I'm a product of the environment I grew up in. My dad was all about ethics while my mom believed in "an eye for an eye." My maternal grandfather, Jack Flynn, was a tough street cop who told me crime stories fascinating to a young boy and my paternal grandfather Tom Doherty ran rackets in the same town.

I mean that can be a little confusing, I liked to be on the side of the good guys. But Grandpa Doherty was a good guy too.

I guess it's the psychology of the cops and robbers that makes them self-reflect. I self-reflect often. I would question myself as to why I targeted someone when there are hundreds of criminals out there. Because that's where my information brought me.

Like when a reporter asked Willie Sutton, notorious bank robber, why he robbed banks. "Because," Sutton said, "that's where the money is." I followed the information to where I would find the bad guys.

But I always made sure that my information gleaned through an informant wasn't one bad guy pointing us in another direction. We were there to arrest bad guys, not eliminate the competition for our informants.

Wiseguys question themselves. Some of those guys wished they took a different path in life, but when you can get elevated on the streets, it's a badge of honor. You don't even have to have earned a button. Just being a close associate, no matter how low in the organization, gives you bragging rights on the streets. You can walk with a little bit of a swagger. But it comes back to haunt them all eventually.

Richard "Moon" D'Orio is a good example. Moon was a big guy. He was in Frank "Bobo" Marrapese's crew but didn't have a button. He got jammed up on a serious charge out of Massachusetts where he served some substantial time.

Members of the Rhode Island State Police, including then Sergeant Mike Urso and Major Pete Benjamin, made him an offer he couldn't refuse. It must have taken some ingenuity to commute sentences and transfer time from Massachusetts to Rhode Island, but however it happened, Moon was with us. He flipped, and others followed.

We indicted numerous high-ranking members, including Bobo. It was a vast mob take-down, and Colonel Stone was proud. Tony Pesare, who later became Chief of Police in Middletown, Rhode Island became case agent. Debriefing and guarding the people cooperating with the investigation became a daily event.

I was one of the junior guys, so they assigned me to Moon more often than I wanted. However, Moon was a great cook. While awaiting trial, I always enjoyed our time together in the safe house when he was making sweet Italian sausage and peppers or *pasta fagioli*.

Moon would tell me one story after another. You had to know the players, or the stories wouldn't make sense. I liked the lesser known stories he'd tell about his former colleagues. Stories that would almost humanize these otherwise animals.

He'd tell stories about how a guy cried at his mother's funeral. A guy you'd never expect to cry for anyone. He had stories about Bobo.

Bobo was in the Intake Center of the ACI awaiting trial. He was a big man in the prison and enjoyed privileges not exercised by other inmates. He was sitting at a round table chewing on an unlit cigar while playing cards with a few select inmates. Suddenly, The Reverend Wade Demers, self-proclaimed pastor of Christ's Church in Action approached Mr. Marrapese.

He said something to the effect of, "If I had fifteen minutes with you, Mr. Marrapese, I'd have you preaching the good Lord's word."

To which Marrapese responded, "Reverend if I had fifteen minutes with you, I'd have you stealing fuckin' cars in Olneyville."

Bobo was just a natural comedian, but if someone mouthed off to him, he'd smash them in the face with whatever he could get his hands on. Moon and I would talk all day about crimes he committed and different wiseguys that he liked or didn't like.

Moon would get agitated and nervous the day before a trial or court appearance. I was with him the day before we brought him in as a witness to testify before the Committee to Impeach Chief Justice Bevilacqua. You could understand his frustration because he grew up in Providence, and his family was well respected in the Italo-American community. Yet he agreed to testify against fellow mobsters.

Now he's in another league. To some, he's finally doing the right thing after years of criminal activity. To others, his former partners in crime, he's a rat. In their world, there is no lower form of life on this planet.

The night we brought him to the hearing was one for the ages. They held the hearing in the basement of the Rhode Island State House. We sent a decoy car to the front door where media and spectators were waiting, and we pulled Moon to the side of the building.

We were all set to go in when he shouted that he needed a disguise. What disguise? We never considered a disguise. Why bother?

He knew as soon as he walked in the door, he'd be front and center looking directly at the Chief Justice, his son Joe, attorney Richard Egbert who represented Bevilacqua, and the mobsters and wannabes who made it in before the room reached capacity.

A disguise wasn't going to hide anything.

The tension in our car was almost visible. Moon wanted a disguise, and we knew it was a waste of time. But he was adamant.

One detective, Lou Reali, who was a Miami Dolphins fan, pulled a Dolphins hat out of the trunk and Moon was happy with it. Go figure. We shuffled Moon in through the bowels of the State House, cleverly disguised, and the show began.

He offered testimony consistent with the prevailing theme that the Chief Justice had ties to the Patriarca Organized Crime Family. His testimony caused a lot of speculation. Mobsters were fooled by the sophisticated disguise. Some thought we were hiding Moon in the Miami area. Political figures worried we might use him again in public corruption cases.

It was a challenging venue for Moon because of the one degree of separation that is Rhode Island.

Moon's brother, Ron, Chief of Staff for Governor Ed DiPrete, had an office upstairs. Disguise or not, everyone knew Moon had crossed the line to the other side.

But one day it ended for Moon. The trials were over, and so was Moon's sentence. He went off to the Witness Protection Program, never to be seen again.

...well, almost.

A couple of years later, Moon showed up, unannounced, at State Police Headquarters. His vehicle—registered with an out-of-state tag and parked in front of the building—was something we wouldn't want anyone to see.

We needed to get him to a secure place. Then-Captain Mike Urso called me to meet him at Headquarters right away. Moon's older sister was coming in to talk to him. It was a very uncomfortable meeting. She was not happy with him and the way he'd embarrassed his family. She lambasted him, and he sat in a chair and took it.

It was really something to see. A mobster scolded by his older sister. No come back. No argument. Sat there and took it. He was ashamed. Before she left, she ordered him to stand up and gave him a hug. She said something in Italian, and he acknowledged with a nod.

She then turned toward Captain Urso and me and stared. I looked away because I thought she'd yell at me. Instead, in an authoritative voice, she told us that the meeting was over and to take care of her brother.

Hours later, at the request of Captain Urso, I stayed at a secure location with Moon for the night.

It was an isolated location, and a second detective was supposed to meet with me, but that never happened. I was okay with it because no one knew where we were except Captain Urso.

Moon couldn't make a call. Who could he call?

I was unconcerned, even though I was technically violating some department policy. But Moon was not an inmate, either. He could go, but I had to stay with him for safety reasons until daylight.

There we were. Moon was trying to sleep, I had to stay alert. Moon's bed was about ten feet away, and I could hear mumbling. He was upset. The room was very dark, and the moonlight was brilliant outside but offered little light in the place.

I knew this would be a long night because Moon kept talking about all the damage he'd caused and that he never wanted to be a mobster. He'd embarrassed his family. He'd been a good student but liked the notoriety of being a wiseguy. I was a captive audience to the incessant whining of someone who'd never considered the consequences of his actions.

Bobo convinced him to do bad things yet treated him poorly. It seemed as if he saw his life from a different perspective. The once bright prospect of being part of Bobo's crew was now a dark, sinister chapter in his life.

He talked of the time he complained to Bobo about needing a new car. A car with a sunroof is what he needed, he told Bobo. He kept complaining. Wouldn't let it go.

In his mind, he saw the lack of a sunroof in his car as a reflection of his low-level status. He deserved a sunroof as if that would mark him with respect.

This was a grown man, involved in dangerous criminal activity, a feared member of a violent and volatile crew run by the notorious Bobo Marrapese, and in his mind, the benchmark for his success, or failure, was a lack of a sunroof.

You can never make this stuff up.

Moon said Bobo became irate, went out to Moon's car with a saw, and cut a hole in the car's roof.

"Now you have a fuckin' sunroof," Bobo told him.

These stories continued for several hours. Each more nonsensical than the others. Then came a troubling change.

"That's it, I'm going to kill myself," Moon said, a culmination of the long recitation of his failure to succeed as a wiseguy.

Still lying in the pitch darkness, I asked, "How are you gonna do that, Moon?"

"With your gun," he said. "When you fall asleep, I'm going to get your gun and shoot myself."

I thought to myself, *this is great.* I had a snub-nose.357 Magnum on my side. Alone with a suicidal ex-mobster suffering from a guilty conscience. Regretting not staying loyal to his criminal pals yet hating them for mistreating him. I was exhausted, and this guy was going to wait for me to doze off to solve his problems.

This was not one of my favorite moments.

I thought for a second, then said, "Moon, if you even try to grab my gun, I will beat the living shit out of you. So, go to sleep."

Eventually, I heard him breathing heavily, snoring, but I quietly emptied my gun just the same. I put the bullets in my pocket and the gun halfway into my pants leg. There was no way he'd get to it. Not without paying the price.

A short time later, some uniform troopers sent by Captain Urso stopped by to check on me. It broke up the time.

It was a weird night, but that's the life I chose. Little did I know becoming a trooper might involve listening to the suicidal rantings of a former wiseguy suffering from an inferiority complex over a sunroof.

We sent Moon on his way the next day, and this time he stayed gone. He never did try for the gun. I guess my therapeutic recommendation against such action worked.

Chapter 33 A Whole New World

"For the times they are a-changin'"
Bob Dylan "The Times They Are A'changin'"

Brendan's career spanned a significant transition period in both law enforcement and crime. While women made inroads into the once male-dominated profession, the mob clung to its male exclusivity.

Police departments hired better educated, more well-rounded candidates with less emphasis on physicality or political connections, and more focus on skills, both technical and intellectual.

The job was still physically demanding, but the days of backroom interrogations or street justice were fading. The nature of crime changed with computer crimes, sophisticated scams, a more mobile society, and police departments needed to adapt.

The law regarding search and seizure, interrogations, and electronic surveillance grew more and more complex. Technology advanced, and police departments struggled to keep up. Public scrutiny of police actions—once almost off limits to the media and rarely subjected to official review—became more intense and immediate.

The explosion of cell phones and surveillance cameras shed light on the once dark alleys and isolated street encounters.

The responsibility of policing in a multi-cultural world changed the job. Where once white males dominated police work, now new names and faces joined the ranks. The expanding inclusiveness of the job was for the better. That some sought the job not as a calling but as just another job because of the improving benefits was not.

In the world of "La Cosa Nostra," the direct ties to Italy faded. Some clung to the past, others saw the change for what it was and adapted. The once reliable supply of young Italian men looking to join a crew by earning it dried up.

Reality shattered the myth of Organized Crime's prohibition on drug distribution. Too much money and too many ways to make it made it impossible to ignore.

The new breed of those rising in the ranks of organized crime differed significantly from the old-school Mafioso. Men who grew up in an Italian influenced society, but one based in a multi-cultural environment of the United States, differed from those raised in Sicily or Palermo. The once inviolable rule of "making your bones" on the street gave way to nepotism, impatient greed, and intrigue.

America's impatient fast food drive-up window entitled attitude changed the mob as no law enforcement agency ever had.

All these factors brought change to organized crime, the focus of the State Police Intelligence Unit, and the nature of crime and law enforcement in America.

Time moves on, cultures change, techniques improve, characters remain, and so it goes.

I remember an attorney who hung around the halls of the courthouse trying to drum up business and undercut other attorneys. This guy couldn't get you out of jail if your time expired, but he'd play the halls looking for desperate defendants without the funds for a good lawyer.

His was a slick sales pitch convincing defendants or relatives of defendants he was the guy. A fast retainer paid, a couple of brief client meetings, and almost every one of them pled to what the attorney said was a great deal.

One only he could deliver.

Then there are the small-time hoods and hustlers that infest every major city. The guy who wants to buy influence, so he becomes a groupie with local politicians and cops. Cops on the job but who don't work the job. They work the angles. CINC, Cops in Name Only. You know the type, there for a paycheck, loaded with detail pay and perks, but little interested in catching bad guys.

Some cops, when it comes to the street, can hear the grass grow. Some, a small minority, yet every department has them, are chiselers. They get out of the academy with a badge, a gun, and little drive to make a difference. Chiseling their way through their career.

They live by a simple philosophy.

Big cases, big problems. Little cases, little problems. No cases, no problems.

I'm not saying they're corrupt, but they know where the good deals are. They gravitate to the influence guys, hang out in the popular bars and hot restaurants, and weasel their way into promotions or cushy jobs.

Jobs that get them off the street.

They grease people, do favors, and ingratiate themselves. It becomes a symbiotic relationship. Cops, conmen, hustlers, politicians, and wannabes engaged in a game of what's-in-it-for-me.

They "have a guy." They all have a guy. A guy for anything you can think of. If you need a city or town license or permit, he's got the guy. If your nephew needs bail, he's got the bail bondsman in his contacts. Need a suit? He's got the best guy for that. How about tickets to a show or a concert, even the Red Sox versus Yankees? He can get them and, if he's good, it's at cost or on the arm.

If it's for you, it should be at cost, but for someone else, he may say he's got to get his piece. If you need a high-end car, I mean really high-end BMW or Mercedes, don't just go to anyone because his guy gets 'em at cost.

It's just human nature. Trying to survive and prosper in a dog-eat-dog world. But when police officers engage in the practice, it demeans the badge, the profession, and the course of justice.

One day, I walked in my barbershop. I saw fellas sitting around, chatting about the track and the casino. Typical barbershop talk in the city. They were all hang-around, kick-around guys from Smith Hill, the old Irish section of Providence.

I didn't grow up there but knew a lot of them from my days at the Civic Center. In the middle of these guys was a cop I knew. A tough kid, but I heard he was still hanging with neighborhood guys. Guys who only rode in the back seat of police cars.

Some guys were harmless, but they were still loan sharks and hustlers. Some were informants one day, wearing a white hat, then they'd hustle some poor bastard the next day.

But the cop I knew seemed savvier than that. I thought he was smart enough not to hang with these guys. The cop was a good guy, but I'd heard he wasn't too excited about getting bad guys. He went through the motions. Answer calls but don't look too hard beyond the minimum.

The officer recognized me. He stood up and saluted me; I returned the salute and said hello to the fellas. The para-military protocol display derailed the conversation. Seeing him in a compromising situation, I pulled him aside and told him he should never let someone put him in that position. It's an honor to wear the department uniform and not one to take lightly.

I told him he needed to be more selective about who he hung around with. He gave me the neighborhood line about not turning his back on his old friends.

Later, I talked to my friend, a ranking officer on the same department, and told him the story. He told me to forget about it. I wasn't the first one to try and straighten him out. The cop was too far gone. Shortly after that, the department terminated the officer for his ties to a neighborhood criminal.

The hustle and glitter of the street jam up a fair share of people. The fast-track lure of deals and money, without having to work hard for it, is a promise more gorgeous than its realization. Some get out and turn their lives around, but it's rare. I've seen a lot of kids with talent and potential eaten up by it.

It reminds me of a young man I was trying to help in the city, a young boxer with a lot of promise. My son, Matt, fought with him. They were stablemates for the Golden Gloves competition in Lowell, MA. They respected one another but came from very different backgrounds.

I wanted this young guy to go on to college. He enrolled at CCRI, but life dealt him a few bad cards. I wish I had known he was struggling. He died young. His family and friends didn't have an answer. The city, the night, the darkness and unknown ate him up. We loved him, but there was nothing left but prayers. It reminds me of Bruce Springsteen's Jungle Land lyrics.

> *"Outside the street's on fire in a real death waltz between flesh and what's fantasy and the poets down here don't write nothing at all, they just stand back and let it all be..."*[6]

We all want to do well, and we all want to make our families proud. We chase the American dream and try to leave this world in better condition than we found it. But our legacy is our family and friends. Aesop, a Greek writer and philosopher, said, “A man is known by the company he keeps.” I believe that is true.

I try to practice civility and respect for all people, but if a guy is a bully or mistreats others, especially women, I don't have time for him. I always joked with my wife about my gravestone. I want it inscribed with these simple words.

"He always did the right thing.”

Some might ask what that means because the "right thing" is so subjective. True, but if you are trying to do the right thing and you have only good intentions, you'll usually do what's right.

---

6 Songwriters: Bruce Springsteen
Jungleland lyrics © Downtown Music Publishing

When I was a kid, a neighborhood bully called my friend "fat boy" within earshot of my mother. My friend was heavy, and he was accustomed to the name-calling because kids are brutal. But when my mother heard it, she asked me what I would do.

"Are you going to let him call your friend *fat boy*?"

I knew I had to do the right thing. I took care of it, right in front of my mother. No kidding. Right in front of the school, I gave that kid the beating of his life because he picked on my pal. The irony of this is my pal was one of the toughest kids in the neighborhood. He could have done it himself. But my mother told me I should straighten it out, so I did.

He never called my friend fat again.

My friend and I went our own way at sixteen, he later went to federal prison. I don't know if beating his tormentor was the right thing to do, but it's the way it was.

I'm talking about ethics and civility when I talk about doing the right thing and finding your true north. We're constantly challenged with twisted values. I know nasty guys, and I know how they think. I used to try to out-think them and to understand their rationalization. Why does a criminal do the things he does?

When we look at crime and punishment, we must examine the risk versus reward. What's the penalty? Why do you want to risk your freedom for this life of crime? Is it a learned behavior? Chasing career criminals for long periods hardens you; it creates a certain cynicism. Yet, when you've done it long enough, it becomes an art that has no equal.

If you work at it, strive to become good at what you do, there is no better career choice.

When you are in the middle of the game, you test yourself repeatedly because it is not an exact science. My grandfather went to prison for violating the Volstead Act. Family rumors tell me he controlled alcohol, gambling, and perhaps had a loan shark operation.

He was one of the nicest men I've ever met.

Now I'm targeting bookies, loan sharks, boosters, and people that some in society view as perpetrators of victimless crime. Who was I to focus on these guys just because they took a little action? Just because they fell under the umbrella of the "Patriarca Organized Crime family?" These Goodfellas of the neighborhood.

Sometimes these crimes lead to other crimes. Usury or loansharking is a byproduct of squaring away gambling debt. A beating may follow, but most of society doesn't see that. When I was chasing these guys, they operated in well-defined territories and boundaries. Borders as dangerous and as well guarded as post World War II Europe.

When things go wrong, it can be a brutal, even fatal mistake.

Times, as they are wont to do, changed. While we were attacking illegal gambling operations —not the mom-and-pop, nickel-and-dime type store — with an organized hierarchical structure, states got into the action.

It seemed almost as if states adopted a more practical approach to gambling. Perhaps they realized gambling became part of society shortly after the invention of the wheel. My cart is faster than your cart.

If you can't beat 'em, replace 'em.

They built the first casino in New England just forty minutes from Providence. Why bother Mafioso running a high-stakes card or crap game when a corporate giant is raking it in down the street?

The casino does the same thing, legally, with the blessing of the state.

Then, a second casino pops up, and before you know it, we've got two of the largest casinos in the world competing against what?

The last legacy Mafioso, a boss with interest in racing cars and property development more than extortion and bookmaking, inherits a La Cosa Nostra family from his father. He is not without skills or propensity to using violence, but times have changed. Like inheriting a company that makes rotary dial phones, once in every house in America, in the age of cell phones. What the hell did he inherit?

The mob faced competition; it could not threaten or whack the government; the state co-opted the mob. Street bookies, once in almost every bar and barbershop in the city, went the way of big-box stores in the face of Amazon online ordering. They were still around, but they were on life support as a career choice.

Law enforcement needed to change. Every time we would conduct a wiretap, round up a bunch of bookies, we'd get pushback from the community and prosecutors.

"Why are these guys chasing geriatric wise guys?"

The way I saw it, after listening to the transcripts of the induction ceremony and looking at the real property of some of New England's biggest racketeers, they still need attention. Guys were getting murdered. People paid for protection. Gambling debts, collected under duress, got paid one way or the other.

Why should we turn a blind eye? Casinos offered legal avenues for gambling. They did not legalize gambling at large. The risk, threat, and cost to society from illegal operations still existed. In our minds, nothing had changed.

Bookmaking, loansharking, threats, and intimidation still permeated the streets of Rhode Island, and until directed otherwise by those in charge, we continued our investigative efforts.

I took an oath, and I accepted an assignment with my guys to decimate organized crime. Did I have to put myself in check sometimes? Of course, but I was fair and honest. If we could build a legitimate case against you, as far as we were concerned, it's "game on." If I can get you, and get you clean, you're going to jail. We enforce the law; we do not make the policies.

We also saw signs of change. With legal gambling in Rhode Island, the focus of law enforcement had to change. The mob no longer had a lock on gambling, but it still had considerable interest. It could infiltrate and corrupt the political process, worm their way into a piece of the pie, and this would become our new focus.

Chapter 34 Family Ties

There is a public perception about unwritten rules and certain activities within organized crime. One of them prohibits targeting cops and their families. Mostly, particularly with the old-school wiseguys, this is true. At least with those who've earned a button or worked their way into positions of power.

But much of the rank and file are bone-breaking trigger men not on staff because of their intellectual prowess. More robot than human. Expected to follow orders without question.

They either don't or can't consider the consequences. The risk of one going rogue in some misguided attempt to protect his boss or improve his own standing within the crew by targeting cops is real, yet unlikely.

There is a more significant risk from those in the "disorganized" crime world.

Unaffiliated freelancers, gang members, or next generation wiseguys, lacking the dedication to tradition, sometimes operate without rules. The nature of a police officer's job is to interrupt a criminal's activity. Some accept this as a cost of doing business, others do not. And the bigger the case, the higher the stakes.

In 1988, the Rhode Island State Police Intelligence Unit received a Christmas card sent from the ACI (Adult Correctional Institution) and dated Christmas day. The note made little sense, gibberish and nonsensical ranting, yet mentioned how I would soon meet my demise.

It mentioned 'jake-brake' which a friend told me was a trucking term. The insinuation being some large vehicle would turn me into a hood ornament or road pizza. Not rising to any real level of concern, the incident faded from memory.

A few years went by, and I heard no more. Then, in May 1992, complaints came into State Police Headquarters from tow truck companies. The tow operators complained I treated them rudely and swore at them when having a car towed.

One woman called in to talk to me about showing up at her house late at night to yell at her about her driving habits. She said she refused to let me in because I was so angry, yelling through the door. She said the way I knocked and rang the doorbell frightened her. She thought it would be better if we talked on the phone or I talked to her attorney.

Now, remember I was in the detective unit and didn't deal with motor vehicle offenders. Even if I did, we wouldn't visit someone late at night unless it was serious. I explained to her that someone was using my name and a couple of detectives, who will clearly identify themselves, would meet with her for more information.

Meanwhile, we were running down leads on the tow company issue. Someone was towing legitimate vehicles from streets in the city of Providence. The State Police were dealing with the repercussions from the vehicle owners and tow companies.

In most occupations, people use a style of talk or nomenclature. Whoever was impersonating me talked that talk. After three or four days of this insanity, a more ominous call came in from a woman saying someone approached late at night in a parking lot identifying himself as Trooper Brendan Doherty. The fake trooper said he was investigating a DUI case. We decided to step up the pace of our real investigation.

The woman broke down on the phone while speaking to a detective and said she would call back. We never discovered what happened in the parking lot because she didn't call back. But her description of the man who claimed to be Brendan Doherty, six foot four, two hundred forty pounds, matched my description. The detectives knew it wasn't me, but I'm not sure the woman believed it. The situation became more serious, and more complaints came in.

An attorney called me and told me how disappointed he was that I would mistreat his staff at the office. He knew me from representing various defendants I arrested. Both he and his clients were very familiar with me.

When I explained the situation, he agreed that the story from his staff seemed out of character for me or anyone in law enforcement.

I went to his office to speak with the staff. Their description of the guy was consistent with those from the other incidents. They told me that while in the office, he showed a photo of me from a newspaper story several years prior.

In 1987 a national committee selected Rhode Island troopers as the best-dressed police officers in the country. David Letterman invited us on his show. The Providence Journal published an image from that appearance. I wore the traditional leather coat with boots and breeches. This guy was showing the photo as a sort of proof of who he was. He also held a police-type radio. I wondered how far this would go. Up to now, it amounted to little more than a nuisance.

Then, it escalated to a more personal level.

My family got a few hang-up calls. My number didn't appear published under my name, but this guy may have been able to access a personal file or even pulled my rubbish—who knows?

The State Police arranged for a security detail at my house, and the Cumberland Police did house checks. Four or five days into this nightmare, a woman called to report that the fake Detective Doherty called her. The phony detective had her registration data and demanded to meet her.

She told him she worked downtown and could meet him at her car after work at 5:00 p.m. He knew her vehicle and where she parked. What the hell did he have planned?

Detectives set up surveillance on a parking garage on Westminster Street in the city of Providence. Det. Lt. Jack Scuncio spotted someone my size waiting in the garage near a car later identified as belonging to the woman who'd called us.

She walked out of the door of her office building and headed for the garage. The suspect watched her. Scuncio didn't want him to hide or spot the surveillance team, so he pretended to be walking to a nearby car then planted the guy against a car.

Scuncio asked him his name.

"Brendan," he said.

Wrong answer, right guy.

Scuncio placed him under arrest and returned to State Police Headquarters while other detectives reassured the young lady, visibly shaken by the experience.

We identified the suspect as Albert Labonte of Providence. Recently out of jail, with an extensive criminal record, Labonte was an enigma. He wasn't very forthcoming about why he'd done this. We applied for a search warrant for his apartment.

Bizarre doesn't even come close to describing the scene there.

We found another photo of me on the wall. Nearby, next to his telephone, were notes with practice lines for contacting the Registry of Motor Vehicles.

"Hello, this is Detective Brendan Doherty of the State Police, and I'd like data on Rhode Island registration…the code word is 'beach'…"

Every month the registry provided a code to the police to secure telephone inquiries on registration or license data. How did he get the private phone numbers and the codes? Well, for a little while, he was Brendan Doherty, and I guess he was just good with his social networking.

I paid Albert a visit and spent a little time with him in his cell. I explained, in clear and unambiguous terms, why it would be unwise to ever use my name again. He got the message.

In court, we arraigned him on a variety of charges including felony impersonating a police officer. We never learned the full extent of his activities, but his note pad contained a lot of registration data and personal information on people. With his rap sheet consisting of larceny, B&Es, forgery, stolen motor vehicles, and other serious felonies, the State Police conducted follow-up investigations, but the investigation brought no additional charges.

Dealing with people of diminished capacity or asocial behavior always has risks. This case was an example of an extreme, but the outcome turned out for the best. Yet, in the back of every police officer's mind, we wonder if the last person or the next person we arrest will cross the line into violence against our families or us. The job offers those who accept the position an opportunity to accomplish good in the world, yet the risks are real and a fact of life.

This wouldn't be the only time my family got dragged into things.

Chapter 35 Unholy Focus

The second time I was concerned for the safety of my family came from a case we put together against self-proclaimed Mafioso, John Feole.

John was born in Italy and moved to Providence based on the recommendation of people from his hometown. He settled in Glocester, Rhode Island, a small town known more for school cancelations during snowstorms then mob-connected wiseguys.

Johnnie Feole was an unknown to the Intelligence Unit until a call came in about the extortion of a Johnston construction worker. The guy borrowed somewhere around four to seven thousand dollars from Feole. As with most loan sharks, the "vig," or interest, was exorbitant. Feole claimed, after about four months, the victim now owed seventy-seven thousand dollars and threatened him.

Clearly violating the state usury statute.

We met with our victim. He came from a large Italian family in Rhode Island, who were all hard workers and good people. The man was understandably nervous and fearful. But we couldn't just take his word on what had transpired.

We needed to hear the threat for ourselves.

After wiring our guy up, we had him make a controlled telephone call. Feole discussed the loan and made implicit threats with both his words and tone. Our victim was a mess.

Feole gave him a certain amount of time to pay. Our victim said he would call back, that he needed time to find the money. Knowing Feole would not be very patient, we arranged another call.

For the second recorded call, we told the victim to low ball Feole with an offer of a three-thousand-dollar payment. Feole would not react kindly.

Feole knew the victim's family and that they could quickly come up with more than seventy thousand dollars to take the pressure off their brother. During the call, our guy offered three thousand dollars. Feole told him to take the money and "buy a casket." He told him ways the victim could get the money and there better be "no funny business."

Our interpretation of "funny business" was talking to law enforcement.

After discussion with our prosecutors Gerry Coyne and Bill Ferland, we arrested Feole on February 15, 1995. He showed great disdain for the case agent, me.

Several months later, we took the case to trial in Rhode Island Superior Court. Feole was as angry and threatening with his eyes as he was with his voice in the recorded calls.

The jury convicted him on all counts. The victim's family attended the verdict. Feole was pissed. Judge Domenic Cresto allowed him to remain on bail until sentencing. His rage roiled and surged as he awaited sentencing. Not satisfied with the normal appeal process, Feole took things into a dangerous direction.

Approximately one month later, Det. Elwood Johnson and Chief Jamie Hainsworth of Glocester PD called me. They told me they had a source hired to ring the doorbell of one of the family members and shoot whoever answered the door.

The hired hitman turned out to be a cooperator for Chief Hainsworth (who later became U.S. Federal Marshall). The investigation resulted in more taped conversations between Feole and the cooperating witness. Feole provided a list of addresses and a gun to the informant.

We arrested Feole on August 1, 1997, for criminal solicitation for murder. He was still out on bail from the usury case. We located him standing in front of his lawyer's office.

He smiled and yelled my name as I approached.

"Brendan, I have been with my lawyer for hours."

He thought he had an alibi. We placed him under arrest, put him in the back of an unmarked police car, and sped off to State Police Headquarters.

Johnny had nothing to say on the way back other than his insane rant of having nothing to do with anything that might have happened today. He was giddy with certainty he'd outfoxed us. Repeating my name, exaggerating the pronunciation, obvious disdain in every sentence. Confidant being at his lawyer's office for several hours would win his release.

“Brendahnnn, Brendahnnn I have been here minding my own business.” Followed by a crazed smile.

Operating under the delusion he was in the clear for the “murder” he believed he'd cleverly arranged, we let him savor his moment of ignorant bliss.

We didn't tell him the truth until later; his hitman buddy was a cooperating witness. It was something he'd get in the discovery process, anyway.

Back to Superior Court went John Feole to once again face Judge Dominick Cresto. Judges don't like it when they allow you to make bail, especially after a conviction.

Bail conditions require you to keep the peace and be of good behavior, not go out and hire a hitman to kill a family member of your victim.

There were children in those homes, and the cooperating hitman had asked the question.

"What if a kid answers?"

"Anyone who answers the door," Feole told him, all on the tape.

The judge heard the recordings and reacted. He sentenced Feole to fifteen years. He served about eight years.

While he was away, a correctional officer contacted me. He thought it necessary to tell me about Feole's attitude and interests while incarcerated.

One might think he'd be a model prisoner since he was 65-years old now. Perhaps it would be reasonable to expect him to be somewhat remorseful or possibly engaged in some rehabilitative program. Or, at least, mastering crossword puzzles.

That's not the message I received from the officer. It was the contrary. I learned that Johnny talked about me with anger and hatred on a daily basis. I learned that any time my name was in print, Johnny would clip it out and tape it on his wall. He particularly liked photos of me from local newspapers. The officer warned me, "You have a problem with this guy when he gets out."

John Feole was released and went to a half-way house in Central Falls, Rhode Island. Shortly after his release, I had his activity monitored, but there was no apparent attempt to even any scores. I kept it in the back of my mind; he was not a fan of mine.

There were a couple of unique events, though. These stories come from the "you can't make this stuff up category," Rhode Island style.

A good family friend of mine, Scott Partington, who happens to be an attorney, was driving through Glocester, Rhode Island. He spotted a guy with long white hair walking in the road in the pouring rain in a secluded area during daylight hours. My friend Scott decided to pick the guy up as he looked in distress.

You guessed it. John Feole was the road-walker. Scott is the son of the legendary lawman, John Partington. Scott grew up in the house I purchased from his father, John.

I told you this is a Rhode Island exclusive story.

Scott had no idea who Feole was but quickly learned that he didn't like Brendan Doherty. An accomplished attorney, Scott didn't want to get involved in the unsolicited dialogue about me but, he later told me, what he learned from the brief encounter was troubling.

Feole hated me.

As soon as Scott told him he was an attorney, bells went off.

Feole asked, "Do you know Brendahnnn"? He pulled out affidavits from the case. Scott just wanted to get the guy to a safe area and get him the hell out of the car. Eventually, Scott pulled over and asked Feole to get out.

Scott obviously didn't want to get involved but thought he had to let me know. I knew there would be an inevitable encounter with Johnny Feole.

We stepped up our intelligence on Johnny.

I had to do something I never wanted to do; show my family a photo of someone who might be a threat to both warn them and inform them. Feole's combed-back white hair and angry scowl was not a pleasant sight. Now to have to face the fact this guy held a grudge, especially considering what he had tried to do in the past, was not a comforting thought.

I'd never had to do that before. We always kept the job away from the family. I never wanted to involve them in the crazy world I lived in. I tried as best as I could to leave the job at work. I never wanted my children affected by the life I chose.

I told them to call me immediately if they ever saw someone near the house or looking at them in a crowd or making them in any way uncomfortable.

I'm a law-abiding person. I wanted to enforce the law while standing up to the worst of society. I also wanted to always play by the rules. I was never afraid of anyone. I showed respect for the bad guys but would show no sign of fear.

Now I found myself in some weird game. If I was single and lived alone, I may have been more amenable to the gamesmanship, but I had a college-age daughter home on summer break.

If someone showed up at my house to hurt my family, they'd never make it off the street alive.

I didn't think Mr. Feole was capable, at least physically capable, of showing up at my house. But I had first-hand experience with his propensity toward soliciting violence. He had a history of trying to arrange a murder.

While this was playing out, a friend named Jeff Angus, who my daughter Shelby didn't know, arranged to meet me at my house. We were working together on a charitable event.

Jeff pulled up to my house early. I was about twenty minutes away. Jeff waited in the driveway, sitting in his pickup truck, wearing dark sunglasses, and sporting his combed-back white hair.

Coincidence will get you every time.

Shelby looked out the window, looked at the photo I'd given her, and dove to the floor. She grabbed her cell phone and rolled under the bed.

Shelby called her mother to tell her the bad guy that wanted to get her was in the driveway. He looked mean and had the signature combed-back white hair.

It was him.

Michele called me right away to tell me that the bad guy I was looking for was in our driveway. Shelby was trembling under the bed. Another call from Shelby interrupted our conversation. She said the bad guy was now knocking on the door.

You can imagine what's going through my mind, especially since I forgot Jeff was meeting me. Traveling at a high rate of speed, trying to get there as fast as I could, I called the Cumberland Police and State Police to send cruisers.

Another call interrupted me. Jeff called to let me know he was waiting for me in the driveway.

Poor Shelby was shaking for another hour. I can only imagine the experience my friend Jeff would have had if the troopers and the cops got there before he called me.

Mr. Feole did not try to contact me, nor did I make any attempts to contact him…directly. He did get a message, and we never spoke again.

Chapter 36 Small Town Corruption

Rhode Island's reputation for mob-influenced or plain old greed-driven political corruption was well known throughout the country.

A short recitation of facts would lend credence to this contention. Aside from Buddy, we have had several judges, a couple of mayors and Speakers of the House, a governor, plus a plethora of local officials, move from political office to a prison cell.

The mob might have the lock on organized crime, but they did not have a lock on greed and lust for power. Organized crime had a competitor. Perhaps, one might argue, a more sinister one, operating under the guise of legitimacy in government.

If one had to say something good about the mob, it would be that they knew they were the bad guys and would accept such a title. Crooked politicians were a virus on society, ingratiating themselves with smiles and handshakes and then altering the DNA of government for their own enrichment.

The mob was what it was. If ever there was an example of the devil you know, this was it.

While the Feds went for the big, newsworthy cases—they could afford to be choosey—it left the majority of cases to the State Police and local agencies to investigate. The State and Local police held their own investigating and prosecuting significant cases, even without the resources of the Justice Department.

During the Cianci matter, the FBI relied heavily on investigators from the State Police to build the case.

Often, it would seem, the Feds focused more resources on one case than any state or local agencies combined ever could. To the exclusion of other matters. Leaving State and Local police stretched to the breaking point with the demands for investigations, but still sought after for their expertise and contacts in local matters.

Some took place in Providence, Woonsocket, or Pawtucket. Well known cities in the state. Others happened in less familiar, sleepy villages not known for public corruption. But nowhere is immune from greed and lust for power.

Considering Rhode Island is the smallest state in the nation, the number of villages is impressive. There are over one hundred named villages, most of which are unknown even to those who live in them. Names such as Usquepaug, Canonchet, and Quonochontaug reflect the influence of the Native American tribes who once dominated the land.

Quonochontaug had such a unique and intriguing name, it became the hometown of the mother of David Duchovny's character on the TV series, X-Files.

The name alone spooky enough for the X-Files conspiracy theory concept.

And like the mysteries on the show, the truth about a few of these villages was out there.

Lime Rock, a part of Lincoln, Rhode Island, is one of these villages. It's known for the few remaining, but once numerous, horse farms connected to the former Lincoln Racetrack, and residential developments with large stately homes.

It has its share of oversized and upscale houses, many occupied by corporate executives, attorneys, and doctors. There are a few organized crime figures who, trying to appear legitimate, settled in this section of town. The migration to suburbia even includes the mob.

Today the area is known for Twin Rivers, the massive casino in Lincoln, and the beautiful sprawling Lincoln Woods State Park around the corner.

In early 2001, information percolated regarding Lincoln Planning Board member Robert Picerno. At the front and center of these rumors were his political machinations and his alleged connections to organized crime.

Picerno had the look, charm, and demeanor of a character from central casting in the hit HBO show, *The Sopranos*. But members of the State Police Intelligence Unit had never heard of him. If he was a mobster or connected to them, he was a new name. Picerno was an unknown commodity in a relatively insular world.

Picerno sat as a member of the Lincoln Planning Board and as such maintained authority over builders and developers looking to build in this upscale section of town. A middle-aged man with wavy gray hair and a charismatic personality, Picerno used his name and his Italian heritage to convince many of his connection to the wise guys.

Mob connections in Rhode Island often had benefits; it opened doors and discouraged opposition. Robert Picerno was one never to miss an opportunity. He could benefit off this patina of mob affiliation that many people seemed to revel in, or fear.

Adding to the Picerno mystery, we noticed an unusual situation. Lincoln Town Councilman Dean Lees, a political contrarian, often butted heads with other members of the town council. He questioned things Picerno may have a hand in. Picerno despised Lees.

Two men assaulted Lees as he left a store in Providence. The assailants added a message to the mayhem. If Lees continued his ways in Lincoln politics, there would be more.

And it would be worse.

Councilman Lees refused to let the incident quell his participation at council meetings. The State Police solved the Lees beating in short order, arresting two men. Both men had long arrest records. They were convicted of several charges related to the assault and intimidation of a public official.

Neither man would talk about who sent them after Lees, choosing jail time instead. A beating, some threats, and refusing to cooperate, all straight out of the operating manual of the mob.

With little more to go on, the case faded. But our interest in Picerno continued.

In the summer of 2001, Picerno started visiting construction job sites, soliciting payments to ensure a smooth transition through the planning approval process in town. He also sold tickets for a fundraiser for the Lincoln Town Manager. One contractor acquiesced to the pressure and purchased five thousand dollars' worth of fundraising tickets, well above the allowed one-thousand-dollar maximum political contribution.

Picerno was a master of subtlety and inference. He intimated connections with personnel in Lincoln town hall, including the Town Administrator. Picerno had his eyes set on a building along George Washington Highway, the town's central business thoroughfare.

The former H&H Screw Company, a large commercial building, sat on a sizable parcel of land with frontage on George Washington Highway, was the focus of Picerno's plan. The town-owned the property because of unpaid back taxes and wanted to sell it. Picerno positioned himself, covertly, in the middle of the sale efforts.

The information about this potential irregularity found its way to the Rhode Island State Police Financial Crimes Unit. The financial crimes unit had its origins a decade earlier on the heels of the Rhode Island Credit Union Crisis. Its primary mission was to investigate large complex white-collar crime cases and public corruption matters at both the municipal and state level.

The unit had its share of successes, and many local police departments would refer matters to them regularly.

They operated on the adage, "follow the money."

Information regarding Picerno made its way to honest people in town and eventually to a well-respected member of the Lincoln Police Department. The Lincoln police officer, Al Martel, understood the ramifications of the accusations and took a bold step. He referred it directly to the State Police financial crimes unit. Avoiding the internecine complications of local politics set the case on the right path.

The critical issue for the investigation, designated Operation Lime Rock, was whether those approached for payments would cooperate. Typically, many refused. Here, contractors and others agreed to cooperate, and a full-scale investigation of Picerno's activities and shakedowns began.

Because of the confidential nature of a public corruption case, particularly in a small town like Lincoln, discretion and information security was critical. Two people can keep a secret if one is dead.

Detectives would have to limit the list of need to know participants and remind those involved to keep quiet. Det. Sgt. Brian Casilli, the lead investigator, needed to decide whether the investigation would continue covertly or whether we pursued it overtly by interviewing witnesses immediately.

I met with Casilli, along with his partner Sgt. John Lemont, in my then capacity of Detective Commander. Casilli had a reputation as bright and thorough. Lemont, an attorney, was a no-nonsense guy and thrived on taking down corrupt public officials.

We met with prosecutors Peter Neronha, Steven Dambruch to discuss the most practical approach and the benefit or risk of pursuing the case long term.

Peter Neronha later became the U.S. Attorney for the District of Rhode Island and then successfully ran for Attorney General winning eighty percent of the vote. Steven Dambruch later became the acting U.S. Attorney and is one of the most effective prosecutors I've ever met.

During our meeting, we felt confident the people assisting or cooperating, from the Lincoln police detective and his Chief to the contractors, had been faithful to their word and not talking. We knew the Police Chief, William "Bill" Strain, a highly respected Chief and former Rhode Island State Police Lieutenant, was all in and trustworthy.

At that point, we decided on an innovative move. To uncover the full breadth of Picerno 's schemes, the State Police would need to intercept his phone calls. This would be the first-ever court-authorized wiretap into public corruption in Rhode Island.

After months of investigation, including surveillance, monitoring of incriminating calls, and the controlled delivery of bribes, we arrested Picerno and his associates.

The operation was a seventy-two-hour rolling takedown.

The first associate taken into custody was a local businessman involved in one specific instance of bribery and conspiracy.

We arrested the businessman after a pretextual traffic stop on the side of Route 195. After providing a full confession and agreement to cooperate, the local businessman delivered a twenty-five-thousand-dollar bribe to Picerno, while under close surveillance. The State Police let Picerno walk out the door with the cash in hand to continue the investigation.

The next day, a home builder cooperating with the State Police delivered an additional bribe to Picerno while a surveillance team monitored the contractor's office. We arrested Picerno as he left the office.

Later that Friday evening and into Saturday morning, we explained the options available to Picerno. He agreed to cooperate, implicating the Town Manager in a bribery conspiracy scheme to purchase a large commercial property from the town by tax sale.

The deal was a one-hundred-five-thousand-dollar check to the town of Lincoln and cash "on the side."

Picerno agreed to deliver a bank check and ten thousand dollars in cash to the Town Manager, Jonathan F. Oster, on a Saturday morning at Oster's private law office on Old Louisquisset Pike in Lincoln.

Besides being the town manager, Oster was also a long-time practicing attorney. A surveillance team, set up in a parking lot at the former Lincoln Greyhound Park, tested the recording device and a transmitter. All were in perfect working order.

The racetrack sat across the street from Oster's law office. The surveillance team kept a close watch on Picerno as he walked in the rear entrance.

One member of the surveillance team sat in a car "broken down" along the side of Rt-146 S/B. A perfect spot for video and audio surveillance monitoring. The breakdown lane is just forty yards from the rear door of Oster's office. With the then new technology, it was like being in the room with them.

The audio and video recording were pivotal.

The audio captured Picerno and Oster discussing the possibility the law office was "bugged." They debated if there was probable cause or reasonable suspicion for the bugging to occur. Picerno and Oster left the building because of these concerns. In most cases like these, the electronics fail, something blocks the camera view, or other unforeseen circumstances interfere with the evidence gathering.

Not this time.

In an ironic twist, Oster's paranoia sent him right into the sightline of a video camera. The two men now chatted in full view of the camera and on high-quality audio. The video captured the moment the hand to hand exchange of money took place. I can't overstate how critical those items of evidentiary value were to the case. This video recording would prove priceless in securing the arrest and indictments of two public officials in the town of Lincoln and one prominent business owner.

Once the meeting ended, the State Police put the law office on lockdown and obtained a search warrant for the premises. The search team recovered the cash in Oster's law office.

After three long days, the operational phase of Operation Lime Rock ended, and so did the long-time political career of Jonathan Oster.

The trial attorneys assigned to prosecute the Picerno and Oster cases were two of the best. Bill Ferland, who've I've mentioned before and Bethany Macktaz, then a rising star in the AG's office.

Macktaz, a tenacious and highly regarded prosecutor, worked for more than fifteen years in the Attorney General's office, ultimately heading the Organized Crime and Narcotics Unit.

With the assignment of these two prosecutors we knew the cases were in good hands

Every time I saw Mr. Oster at State Police Headquarters, or later in court hearings, he would tell us he wouldn't serve one day in jail. Despite the thousands of dollars in bribes given under the video and audio monitoring of the State Police surveillance team, he felt comfortable in saying that.

Picerno's influence and standing in the town disintegrated. While the operational phase ended in early 2002, the legal wrangling would drag on for six more years. Expectedly, Picerno and Oster assembled one of the most exceptional legal teams Rhode Island has seen. The high-powered defense filed seemingly endless motions, some of which succeeded in limiting evidence, while others failed.

Robert Picerno pled guilty in 2004, and the court sentenced him to the Adult Correctional Institute for eight years, three to serve five suspended.

The trial for Jonathan Oster would begin in early 2008 and last for several weeks. Ultimately, the jury returned a guilty verdict for Oster for bribery and extortion.

Tragically, within twenty-four hours of the verdict, on a Saturday morning, Oster returned to his law office, placed a handgun to the side of his head, and took his life. The suicide had a powerful impact on all those involved, including the jurors. The loss was most tragic for his family.

Oster's statements he would never spend a day in jail became a self-fulfilling prophecy. In a final twist to Operation Lime Rock, the court vacated the verdict in the Jonathan Oster case. The law allows for a convicted person who dies before sentencing to have the decision set aside.

Under our judicial system, Oster is an innocent man.

Operation Lime Rock shows how a man, with no genuine ties to organized crime, could use the aura of the mob to influence people's decision making. Many people believed Picerno had mob connections.

The pervasiveness of the mob's influence in Rhode Island made it a real possibility. This perception was enough for credible people to make rash decisions handing over thousands of dollars needlessly to a man out for nothing other than self-enrichment.

It was the ultimate scam. Just the specter of Organized Crime was enough to make rational people do irrational things out of fear.

Chapter 37 The Art of the Deal, or No Deal

Every state has its icons, and Rhode Island is no exception. Despite what many may see as the negative connotation of this, one of the best known in Little Rhody is the late, great, study in contrasts, Vincent A. "Buddy" Cianci.

Buddy's life reads like an improbable fiction. Doctor's son, Army officer, lawyer, Special Assistant Attorney General, Mayor of Providence, featured speaker at the Republican National Convention, potential Vice-presidential running mate with Gerald Ford.

Resigned in disgrace Mayor of Providence, talk show host, again Mayor of Providence, recurring guest on the Don Imus show (who called him the thug mayor, but Buddy held his own with the sharp-witted Imus.)

Named in Federal Indictment, tried and convicted in Federal Court on one count of RICO violations, resigned Mayor of Providence II, federal prisoner (or, as Buddy put it, guest in a federally funded gated community,) returned talk show host, failed candidate for Mayor III.

Everybody in Rhode Island has a Buddy story. He is one of the most well-known Rhode Islanders, for both good and bad reasons. Never was there such a charismatic Jekyll-and-Hyde person to come from the littlest state in the Union. There was only one Buddy and, love him or hate him, almost everybody knew him.

In 2000, while Buddy Cianci was wielding power in his second round as mayor, I was the Detective Commander of the State Police. It is a position of power and responsibility. You need to stay on top of all significant cases under investigation and have a working knowledge of those cases. Some may even extend beyond State Police cases to local or federal agencies seeking assistance on other matters.

The detective commander often facilitates state and federal strategy meetings on matters of mutual interest. I held myself and my detectives to a high ethical standard. If the people of the state can't count on us to do the right thing, who can they count on?

One day I came home from work, and my wife Michele told me it was time for a career change. She saw a job posting at a small suburban high school for a business teachers' position. Michele thought she had the requisite experience. She was the office manager and business editor for a medical publications company, been in business for several years, was a graduate from Bentley College and held a teaching certificate.

She applied for the open position and wanted the chips to fall where they may. She was clear about not wanting anyone making calls and no letters of recommendation.

I was to do nothing.

Michele didn't like that manner of doing business even though people in the corporate world do it every day. I was excited for her, but I got the message.

"Stay out of it."

And I always do what Michele tells me to do.

A few weeks went by, and I had forgotten about her applying for the job. I had heard nothing from her about it, and if there were something I needed to know, she'd tell me.

I was walking into the Providence Superior Court and said hello to an attorney I knew to be a political operative. He said, cryptically, that he realized how fierce the competition for a teaching vacancy could be. If I needed any help, I should let him know. I didn't know what the hell that even meant other than it must have gotten around that my wife applied for that teacher's job. I thanked the guy, told him I was all set, and moved on.

The next day I got a call from the Speaker of the House, John Harwood. John and I knew each other well as we had mutual friends. He was once a hell of an athlete and loved to talk about sports when I'd see him.

But not on this call.

He was very matter of fact. He told me that he knew my wife had applied for a job at a local high school and, although it was none of his business, wanted me to know if I needed any help, he'd be there for me. John explained he also wanted me to know my wife would face resistance. He told me he knew how I felt about political cronyism but wanted me to know he had gotten calls from some serious players about the position.

He told me he backed off when he heard my wife was in the process and, if I preferred, would just step back altogether and not help either side. I asked who was on the other side. He couldn't say, but he was undoubtedly closer to me.

I asked that we just let the chips fall as they may.

When I hung up, I remember thinking, *"Why can't my wife just apply for a damn job just like anyone else? Why do people have to get involved?"*

I understood Harwood's point. Somebody asked him to get me to back off. Instead, he took a pass and, without divulging those involved in the other conversation, let me know I'd be in a fight if I wanted Michele to get the job. But a fight with whom? Over an entry-level high school business teaching job?

It was absurd.

Another day went by and I got a call from a friend in the know about the situation. My first thought was to shut him down, tell him thanks but no thanks. I didn't want to talk about it. He explained a war had broken out over this. The guys on the other side were angry because nobody was willing to have me ask my wife to withdraw from the job process.

My first response was to do just that. Ask Michele to withdraw because of all the political involvement in the hiring process. The guy said not to do that. The people in on the selection process were getting pressure from all sides.

Some wanted them to make the political decision and go with the mayor's choice. Others wanted it based on Michele's qualifications for the job. The selection process came down to Michele and another lady. Michele was likely to get the job.

I told him I didn't want my wife to know any of this nonsense was going on. I knew her, and she'd withdraw because of the unprofessional nature of the politics. We would not be beholden to anyone.

I asked why the other candidate would want this job so badly.

"She doesn't," he said, "Buddy Cianci and Frank Corrente want her out of City Hall."

And there it was, another chapter in the Bad Buddy story.

The guy explained the woman worked at City Hall in Providence and they wanted her out. She was friends with someone, and Buddy was afraid the media would find out. They thought they could land her this job and move her out that way. The school department was resisting the pressure, and it looks like the more qualified candidate would get the job.

Evidently the media had already been poking around and her friendships or relationships. It would not bode well for Buddy. He was irate with his Chief of Staff.

I asked my friend to stay out of it and let the chips fall where they may.

A few days later, I got a call from a Providence Police Detective close to Providence Police Chief Barney Prignano. I also knew of his close relationship with Buddy and Frank. He was a good street cop, but with his friendships and method of operating controversy swirled around him.

The detective said he was calling to smooth over the friction between Frank Corrente and me. I said I didn't know there was any friction between Frank and me, especially since I had never even met the man.

He said, “Come on, Brendan. It's about the teacher's job. He is irate, and Buddy is pissed off at him. They need that girl out of there, and your wife is the only thing stopping that.”

Then he said, “It'll work out fine because your wife will get a better paying job at City Hall.”

Now, as I was listening to him, I'm was thinking, *"You've got to be kidding me. I'm supposed to have my wife back off, let their friend get the teaching job, and then Michele gets a job at City Hall. Oh, and by the way, I'm part of this shady, backroom deal while I'm the State Police Detective Commander. And it's assumed I'd be comfortable with this."*

I would rather ask Michele to drop from the process than compromise my ethics, and I knew she'd feel the same way. I'm not going to be beholden to Buddy or Frank or anybody, period.

No thanks. No deal.

He conveyed an invitation from Frank to come over to Frank's office the following day to work this out.

"Frank wants to see you," he said.

I was angry, incensed by the callous nature of these political hacks who considered this normal and acceptable.

"Tell Frank to go fuck himself."

Perhaps not the most delicate approach, but it suited the character of some of those involved in this backroom deal-making nonsense. Corrente, Cianci's Chief of Staff, would later serve federal prison time in the same case as Cianci. It would not come as a shock.

The process continued, and they offered Michele the job. She accepted, and I heard no more about it. Buddy later told me he respected the way I handled that. If you stood up to him, and he didn't have the ability to cut your throat, he thought of it as gamesmanship.

Another Buddy story in the growing chapters of Buddy's colorful life.

And it was far from the final chapter.

Chapter 38 Rising to Superintendent

From the moment Brendan entered the hell that is the Rhode Island State Police Recruit training school, through all the time working the road as a uniform trooper and all the cases he handled as a detective, his rise through the ranks came as little surprise to those who knew him.

It was almost predestination he would one day wear Trooper #1 and the full-bird Colonel insignia as the Superintendent of the Rhode Island State Police. He fulfilled the motto on the patch worn proudly on the State Police uniform, "In the Service of the State."

On April 27, 2007, Governor Donald Carcieri swore me in as the 11th Superintendent of the Rhode Island State Police, holding the rank of Colonel.

Later, I would also serve as the Public Safety Commissioner for the State of Rhode Island overseeing other law enforcement components; The State Fire Marshal's Office, Capitol Police, Justice Grants Administration, E911, and anything else the Governor deemed necessary.

Wearing several hats and juggling the responsibilities required more time and work. But this was the job I'd aspired to and I accepted the burden willingly.

The Governor's office asked what I thought would be fair as additional compensation. I passed. We were heading right into the recession, and I didn't think it appropriate to seek more money when many in the state were in difficult times. The Governor needed me to take these on, so I adjusted.

Throughout my tenure as Superintendent, I was spared any controversies, major internal issues, bias complaints, or complicated legislative challenges that accompany many police administrator's jobs.

We continued to build on a cooperative effort with local and federal agencies, recruit a broad spectrum of new troopers to the ranks, and modernized the operation in the ever-changing world of law enforcement.

It may not have always been smooth—there were disagreements both public and private over policy decisions and other issues—but in retrospect there is little I would change.

Having risen to the highest rank in the department, one considers the next step. Where do I go from here? In the four years I would serve as the Superintendent I had one overarching goal: to leave the department in better condition than when I assumed command. I, aided by the incredible dedication and commitment of the women and men who served with me on the State Police, believed I'd accomplished that goal. I felt the time was right for a change. As much as I loved the job, loved that each day differed from any before it, and loved being a trooper, the time had come for me to seek a different course in life.

This decision led me down unexpected paths, a road less taken, but I embraced it with the same commitment to doing my best, to always being squared away as I'd learned as a young recruit and faced the new challenges.

But before any of that happened, I faced several new challenges in the changing world of organized crime and law enforcement.

Chapter 39 Buddy Déjà Vu

The early 1990s was an exciting time in New England for the Rhode Island State Police, the changing nature of crime, and politicians. Governor Ed DiPrete hired Colonel Edmund Culhane to replace the legendary Walter Stone, who retired after decades in Law Enforcement, marking the end of the Stone Age.

DiPrete himself would end up in prison because of a State Police investigation of bribes. After DiPrete's conviction, the then Governor's office received a phone call from Who's Who in America. They wanted to confirm that DiPrete, once the Mayor and a lifelong resident of Cranston, Rhode Island, still lived there. The Governor confirmed that DiPrete did still live in Cranston as the address of the prison, where DiPrete was serving his term, was also in the city.

John Rowland was on his way to become Governor of Connecticut, and he, too, later went to federal prison for conspiracy to commit honest service fraud, mail fraud, and tax fraud.

In 1991, Buddy Cianci became Mayor of Providence for the second time. In 2002, a federal grand jury convicted him under the RICO (Racketeer Influenced and Corrupt Organizations) Act. The judge sentenced him to federal prison for five years. Or, as Buddy described it, an all-inclusive vacation in a federally funded gated community.

Buddy got out of prison in April 2007, the same month Governor Carcieri swore me in as the 11th Superintendent of the Rhode Island State Police.

Buddy and I shared the top of the fold in the Providence Journal on April 27, 2007, for my return to the State Police and his return to society as a free man. It underscored what many people in Rhode Island would find equally impressive, a new Superintendent of the State Police and a recently paroled felon. I'm not sure what drew more attention, but I suspect it was not me.

In May, Buddy started back on his popular radio show on WPRO broadcast throughout Rhode Island and parts of Massachusetts and Connecticut.

Much has been said and written about the charismatic Mayor of Providence, good and bad. He was funny, tiresome, and would appear at the opening of an envelope. Even if asked not to. He was charming and loved his city, but there was another side of him that most people never saw.

He could be vindictive to the point of being dangerous. Most politicians practice a little retaliatory payback, but Buddy brought it to another level. While some considered payback toward their political opposition an option, Buddy considered it an obligation

He resigned the office of mayor for the first time in the early 80s after a highly publicized assault of a Rhode Island contractor. He returned to office again in 1991 and was forced to leave in 2002 because of his federal indictment.

I didn't testify in the trial, but I did produce a valuable witness who assisted the prosecutor, Assistant United States Attorney (AUSA) Richard Rose with necessary background information. Because I didn't testify, Buddy may never have known that I provided the witness or information. I always wondered about that because he always spoke well of me on his radio show, which was incongruent with his retaliatory mindset.

One day I agreed to an interview on Buddy's show about criticism leveled at the State Police over a sensitive issue. I felt the need to appear in the media to defend the department.

While I was on hold, listening to the commercial talking about me as the next guest, my private line rang. I noticed the number to be a back-room number of WPRO because I've called it before. I knew I had at least one minute before the show returned from station break, so I answered.

An unmistakable voice came on the other line.

"Colonel, it's Buddy, what do you want me to ask you?"

After giving him a couple of softballs for my interview, he said, "Okay, but be direct and say it with conviction."

You can't make this stuff up.

Buddy served twenty-one years in office, albeit not consecutively, making him the longest serving "big city" mayor in U.S. history. After seven years as a popular radio host, Buddy ran again for mayor.

In 2014, he announced his candidacy for Mayor of Providence. He had many supporters but his old nemesis, *The Providence Journal*, whacked away at him daily. Also, a group of neighborhood leaders from Providence's affluent east side mounted a significant campaign against him.

In August of that year, I got a cold call from him. He told me he was up in the polls and could win the election, but the media kept attacking him on his past indiscretions. They harped on the fact this would just be another corrupt political administration. He tried to convince me his past "shenanigans" were just that, in the past. He wanted me to know that. There was slight desperation to his tone.

By this point, I had retired from the State Police and run unsuccessfully for U.S. Congress. But I think, when all was said and done, my reputation remained intact. I fared well in a poll for governor, which I did not pursue. I had political options but pursued other interests.

First, Buddy told me how well he was doing. Then he said his advisory committee believed the campaign needed a game-changer. They agreed one guy fit the bill. I asked why he was explaining this to me, searching for a way out of the inevitable. I tried to beat him to the punch. I wished him well but said I couldn't get involved in his campaign.

I was trying to deflect, pivot, and maneuver my way out of what I knew was coming next, but Buddy would not be derailed.

“You're the game-changer,” he said. “You're the guy people trust. They know you wouldn't allow any wheeling and dealing.”

I'll never forget that call, because it was sad.

“Colonel,” he continued, “I need to be able to report that you will be the Director of Administration.”

Frankly, I would have loved to run the city, but I'm not naive. I know what would happen if I agreed. The first time I told him I would handle all finances in the city, contracts, or other matters involving money, I'd force him to fire me.

I'll admit, I gave it some thought. I knew I could run the city ethically, but I also knew from my familiarity with Buddy's history that when there were contracts to award, he'd try to interfere.

Even if it were legitimate, the appearance of impropriety would be too disturbing for me. The optics of working for Buddy would disappoint many people. I needed to maintain my reputation for the troopers who used to work for me, the organization, and the people throughout the state who believed in me. I knew I could have helped him, and probably kept him straight, but it was a matter of appearances.

Perception is reality.

I politely told him no, but he wouldn't accept it. No is not a word Buddy understood when it applied to something he wanted.

He had friends call me. He even got to my brother Chris. Chris knew Buddy through their mutual friendship with former Boston Mayor Raymond Flynn. Ray was the former Ambassador to the Vatican and a family friend. Buddy put Joe Paolino on the mission. Joe was the former Mayor of Providence and another pal of Ray Flynn's. Joe was also the Ambassador to Malta and a successful businessman in Providence.

Buddy was relentless.

I was on vacation on Cape Cod, and Ambassador Paolino kept calling and texting. He invited me to a Red Sox game, to a Billy Joel concert, and out on a yacht in Newport to discuss the opportunity.

All to no avail.

I agreed to meet them for lunch but told Joe I would be accepting no position. I was a former Colonel of the State Police, and Buddy was an ex-con. It just wouldn't do.

I appreciated their confidence in me, but I would not change my mind. I wasn't afraid of dealing with Buddy, I could stand up to the best of them, but my reputation and the reputation of the organization I once led were paramount.

I hated to look Buddy in the face and tell him this stuff. But I had no choice. Buddy was a shadow of his former self. The dichotomy of the two versions of Buddy, the good and the bad, the public and the private, engendered sympathy. I believed he was sick. This was his last hurrah. Buddy, Joe Paolino, and I met at Joe Marzilli's Old Canteen Restaurant on Federal Hill. I told them not to "waste any more time on me."

"I'm out," I said.

Buddy was undeterred, reiterating everything he had told me. I stuck to my guns, “I'm out.”

After I left, Joe continued to have more people contact me trying to change my mind. In our last text, I wrote, “It's more complicated than I can explain.” He said something to the effect of, “That's what makes us the men that we are.”

I never spoke with Buddy again. He was angry I wouldn't support him; he wouldn't look at me at public events. I think he needed my support as a validation in the eyes of others. I believe he saw my support as a form of redemption. A *mea culpa* for all his past sins. His legitimate friends respected me, and I think that would have helped cleanse him. I just couldn't damage my own reputation for his legacy.

Buddy went on the lose the election. Even if Brendan had agreed to join his campaign, most believe it wouldn't have been enough. Buddy had his second chance, and the voters were not convinced a third term offered anything different than the first two.

Time for the city to move on.

Despite everything he'd been through, Buddy maintained a razor-sharp sense of humor. A short time before he passed away, he appeared at the unveiling of his official, if controversial, Mayoral portrait.

Never one to shy away from the limelight, as they unveiled the portrait, Buddy said, "You know, it's not the first time I've been framed."

Buddy died January 28, 2016, at age 74. May he rest in peace.

Part IV: A New Path: Career Decisions

Chapter 40 Higher Aspirations

"I shall be telling this with a sigh

Somewhere ages and ages hence:

Two roads diverged in a wood, and I—

I took the one less traveled by,

And that has made all the difference."

"The Road Less Traveled" by Robert Frost

In April 2011, Brendan resigned as Superintendent of the State Police and Commissioner of Public Safety. He'd spent twenty-eight years in law enforcement, much of that time investigating organized crime.

A world of opportunity lay outside the confines of the Rhode Island State Police. The politics and nature of the job were continually changing as was organized crime.

It was time for Brendan to explore the possibilities.

It was time for a change.

What do you do now after leaving such a challenging and demanding job? This was more than a career; it was a calling. It became part of my life and personality. Moving on would not be easy; like losing an intrinsic element of my being.

But it was time for a road less traveled.

My wife was more than supportive during all those years. The crazy hours working drug, organized crime, and political corruption cases. The late-night phone calls. The disrupted family plans. I thought it time to slow down. Whether I could do so was the question. There were options. The local media had me doing well in polling for a Senate or Congressional bid.

I had research to do. Michele gave me the impression this was not what she had in mind for my career change. However, she is a sport. If I wanted to consider it, she'd go along. I put a focus group together to decide whether I'd run as a Republican or Democrat.

I'd been a Democrat most of my life. JFK's picture had a prominent place in my parents' home. They loved their Democratic politics. My uncle Jack worked for Hubert Humphrey in Washington, and we had constant political talk around the house. A big fan of Democratic Governor J. Joseph Garrahy, as was the rest of Rhode Island, my appointment to the State Police came under his administration. But I saw my political views changing.

As Superintendent of the State Police, I remained unaffiliated. I needed to maintain an impartial role. The President's numbers were low. The incumbent representative had low approval numbers because of budget issues in his previous job as mayor of the City of Providence. So, I considered a run for US Congress as a Republican against Congressman David Cicilline.

David and I go way back. He was a criminal defense attorney representing many organized crime figures and high-profile criminals. He was without question one of the best criminal defense attorneys in New England. But like many in that profession, there's burnout. He wanted to move on from representing the same mobsters and high-profile criminals that his dad handled. His father had a name as a hard-nosed win at all cost defense attorney whose reputation spread far beyond Rhode Island.

There was once a conversation, recorded on an FBI wiretap, between John Gotti and his attorney, Bruce Cutler, discussing business in New England. Gotti advised Cutler to check with Jack Cicilline on a matter. That was the wide extent of his reach.

Jack's philanthropy to some causes resulted in rumors of a large accounts receivable file. He would represent the right person, regardless of their ability to pay. And then some people, like a battered woman from Glocester charged with murdering her husband, he represented for free.

Jack was a tough guy, a tenacious lawyer, but he had a big heart.

David always appeared to be more concerned about civil liberties issues and constitutional issues than the wiseguy world. We had a few battles during his days of walking the halls of State and Federal Court. The Coppola forfeiture hearing became contentious, and one of his clients sued me. It led to some tense moments.

Early in his career, when I would pass him in the hallways, I might get an acknowledgment or a subtle nod, but he was never overjoyed to see me. David ran for state representative and lost but ran again and won. He spent several years in the Rhode Island House of Representatives.

In 2002 he ran for Mayor of Providence after Buddy Cianci went to jail. Running on a reform platform, he won. In 2010 he ran for US Congress in the 1st District after Congressman Patrick Kennedy's decision not to run.

While political office never was an aspiration, I am a big fan of seizing an opportunity. I felt I could benefit the people of Rhode Island, and the moment was before me.

I announced my candidacy as a Republican for 1st District seat in May 2011.

Early on we were up in polls by fifteen points, but astute advisers told me the gap would close-up in the last two weeks of the race. The media enjoyed the battle between a career law enforcement guy and a career defense attorney.

People also tried to get me to buy into other differences. I preferred to focus on the issues and avoided mudslinging politics. I hired a campaign manager named Ian Prior. A brilliant guy who was a quick study, identifying my strengths and weaknesses. He kept me on message and away from the quicksand pitfalls of my political inexperience.

Going into 2012, with the election about six months away, we were still up by fifteen points. A change in the national picture had an effect here. President Obama's approval numbers were rising. He was a rock star in Rhode Island. One thing I learned from the race was that a Presidential year matters.

David understood it.

As the election neared, David wrapped Governor Romney around my neck. Perception is the reality, right? Romney, the Republican Presidential candidate, was not popular in New England. He was a likable guy, but he wasn't faring well in the polls.

David and his campaign cast me as friends with Romney and Paul Ryan. I had met Mitt Romney once for two minutes and didn't know him well, but I knew Paul Ryan. Congressman Ryan ran a fundraiser for me in Washington and offered his help.

The political rhetoric at the time had Romney and Ryan wanting to change Social Security and Medicare. Topics of great concern to Rhode Island voters. It implied, as a candidate who was friends with them, I would want the same. No matter how hard I tried to correct this misinformation, it became a reality to some seniors.

While I knew Romney and Ryan's policies were not so simple, Ian Prior wanted me to maintain a distance. He refused to let me put photos with Romney, Ryan, or Eric Cantor on the website. I thought, in my political naivete, showing a connection to national figures was helpful.

Prior disagreed. "Not here, not in New England, not this time," he would say.

I learned the hard way he was right.

The national race became corrosive and divisive. On the advice of a Washington consultant, so did ours. The sad reality of political campaigns in the United States is negativity works. Like people drawn to look at a car accident, people pay attention to candidates slamming each other. It drowns out the issues and inhibits rational discussions.

The theory is when someone's number improves, you "tear their numbers down." We did, and his numbers came down, but negativity, like tracer bullets, works in both directions. My numbers declined toward the end.

President Obama, along with Speaker Pelosi, Congressman Kennedy, and former President Bill Clinton all came out to Rhode Island to stump against me. Hard to compete with such high-powered name recognition.

I had no one toward the end except a great group of loyal supporters.

Not because I was a Republican, and not because they thought I had some magical recipe, but because they believed in me. For that, I am forever grateful.

In the last few weeks, David stayed on message. He tied me to the Republican machine and political donors I didn't even know. I don't blame him; we were trying to do the same. But it cut both ways.

Hello, why are we doing this? I wanted to talk about the issues facing the country and the state, yet the political strategists knew it was a waste of time. Attack, demonize, and target the opponent. Go after their weaknesses. That's how one wins an election.

It's a numbers game, and Rhode Island is a Democratic state. I knew that, but I thought I could flip Independents or the unaffiliated. It would be a painful lesson. It became a graduate course in politics. Sincerity, integrity, and commitment to doing the right thing is useless fluff in a campaign.

In politics, winning isn't everything; it is the only thing. If you can't win, you can't make a difference.

I learned that the lion's share of Independents in Rhode Island lean Democratic. It meant their mothers and fathers were Democrats and, while they may not be willing to be a registered Democrat, they lean toward those principles on election day.

I learned no matter how much you help the kids in the inner-city, no matter how much you advocated in your prior career for seniors and senior's safety, traveling senior center to senior center with identity theft tips or other messages relevant to their well-being, it gets drowned out in the other messaging.

There were Republican candidates nationwide making outrageous comments, and the media would call us asking for a response. No matter what we said, the mere fact that the comments came from a Republican reflected on our campaign.

House Majority Leader Eric Cantor pulled me aside in Washington.

"I'd like to help you," he said. "You're welcome to call me for messaging advice or anything else we can do, but you don't want me in Rhode Island. Your base might like it, but most of the state won't."

Politics is a treacherous arena.

I felt like a guy alone on an island. The insider Republican neophytes only supported me because I raised enough money to scare everyone else out of the race. By the time we had to ask for the endorsement, I didn't want it.

Another guy wanted to run, and he showed up to tell me. He was about thirty years old and had just moved to Rhode Island. He came over to me, shook my hand, and let me know that he was considering running, but he wouldn't say for a day or two.

I said, "Well, sounds like something you need to give a lot of thought to. I wish you luck."

Then, I had one of our campaign advisers follow him out to tell him one thing he might want to consider is my campaign had over two million dollars, and we'll use every dime in the primary against you.

He dropped out the next day. I may not have liked the rules of the game, but I was learning.

There were a lot of distractions, and the stigma of the national Republican candidates was the gift that keeps giving for the other side. One guy I could embrace was my old friend, Senator Scott Brown. At the time he represented Massachusetts in the Senate and now serves as the Ambassador to New Zealand and Samoa.

Scott and I played basketball together as kids. We were in a basketball camp together at thirteen years old, and both made it to the finals of the one-on-one tournament. We faced off against each other. He won, but I always tell people he fouled me so often the referees should have disqualified him.

One night, at an event at the Metacomet Country Club, Scott told the story a different way, laughing through his version. He said it was me committing the fouls, he won fair and square, and it's a shame because "Brendan's still crying about the game some forty years later."

Scott was a good sport to come by because he was in his war against Elizabeth Warren. The race continued into November 2012 as one to watch by Politico. Brown lost the close election.

Many aspects of campaigning left a bad taste in my mouth.

I did not approve some commercials produced for the campaign. One was an ad for television depicting David's brother, John Cicilline, also a lawyer, walking through a smoke-filled room with a background mob music. The inference being the brother and the mob held influence over David. I knew that wasn't true and didn't want the ad linked with my campaign.

One guy asked why?

“Because David's mother is alive and well,” I told him, “and I don't want her to have to watch that.”

John Cicilline served federal prison time after a conviction involving drug clients. I didn’t want to cause the mother any more heartache.

Other distractions and nonsense were going on toward the end. We had a campaign worker who appeared to take a Cicilline campaign sign. But he took one of ours as well for a political project he planned on his return to college. He wanted the signs for props.

The poor guy ended up in the news with a valuable lesson on attack politics.

I also had campaign workers I fired for acting in inappropriate ways. That didn't make to the news, but if it had, it would have been headline news for nonsense.

We also discovered that we had an inside guy feeding the other side. A double agent. Much like an informant ratting to the other side. I didn't want to believe it. I floated a false story to him, and the media called me to respond to the rumor.

Part of the story was correct, but only the guy leaking information knew the fabricated piece. I denied the aspect we'd invented, but it verified the identity of the double agent. We shut him down, and he quit after that. It's too bad to have something like that happen.

I remained kind to his son, but the internal spy was a coward.

The show goes on, and you do the best you can. I recall people telling me I should be careful. Politics is a tough game. What a joke. Politics isn't a tough game. I was in a tough game. Cops are in a tough game. Politics is a confusing and sometimes disingenuous game, but it's an injustice to call double agents and people who exhibit no moral compass tough guys.

I'm not saying this describes all political figures, perhaps just the segment people would consider difficult to deal with. A lot of the actions one would describe as tough are moves out of fear. Some of these people could not survive in any other forum, so they become political sycophants.

They are part of a parasitic relationship. They remind me of a barnacle, hanging on and living off the boat until it's all rotted and decayed, or until someone scrapes them off.

Others are genuine and worthy of respect. They believe in public service yet become engulfed in the noise of negativity.

I lost the election 53% to 40.8% with 6.1% going to an independent candidate. Despite the loss, I felt comfortable. I maintained my integrity and commitment to the high road throughout the campaign. I accepted the voice of the voters and moved on.

Chapter 41 Marvin Barnes and Street Politics

Among the other characters coming from Rhode Island was an immensely talented, if often troubled, basketball player from South Providence named Marvin Barnes.

Marvin's skills brought him to the heights of college and professional sports. His demons took him to Hell.

But this being Rhode Island, he also believed he could help Brendan win an election.

And so it goes.

Many funny stories took place during my run for Congress. One of those happened at the wake for legendary basketball coach Dave Gavitt. Dave was a Hall of Fame coach for the Providence College Friars for many years, the first-ever Commissioner of the Big East and coached the 1992 US Olympic "Dream Team" with a short management stint with the Boston Celtics.

He was beloved by all walks of life. Dave died in September 2011, and the wake was on Providence's east side. I had been friendly with Dave through Jim Skeffington, a prominent Providence-based attorney. We attended many Red Sox and Patriots games together with Dave Gavitt and others.

At the wake, as is the custom, everyone was somber and whispering while waiting in the line which snaked around the building inside and outside. Sports luminaries from around the country were there to pay respect. I could overhear a few guys in front of me who were from New York and in front was Jim Calhoun, the legendary University of Connecticut coach.

Then I saw him. Coming through a corridor where people maintained the long line was Marvin Barnes.

Marvin, known by his friends as "Bad News" or just "News" was an All-American basketball player for Providence College and 1st round draft pick in the ABA—American Basketball Association.

Barnes later played in the NBA after the two leagues merged.

Marvin was a significant part of Dave's success and vice versa. Marvin loved Dave and Dave loved Marvin and tried to keep him out of trouble. Having helped Marvin out with his Rebound Foundation, I knew he would spot me. Marvin would have something comical to say because he was just full of charisma. He was preoccupied, talking with someone I couldn't see behind the wall. Marvin looked up, saw me, and yelled, "Chief, Chief."

I was just hoping he'd quiet down, but he didn't care. He enjoyed the commotion. I wanted to crawl under the rug.

Wearing a smile from ear to ear, he said, in his less than subtle voice, "Hey, Chief, I heard you're running for Governor."

My title was never Chief, and I was not running for Governor, but I just waived and said, "Hello, Marvin."

The whole room turned to look at me. A spectacle is not something I wanted to be known for at Dave's wake, but now I'm in it, and I know it will not get better soon.

Marvin is pumped and on a roll.

I loved the guy, but I was embarrassed under the circumstances. But no one silences Marvin.

"Chief, I'm going to get you the black vote," Marvin said.

"Thank you, Marvin."

What else could I say?

Everyone in the room was snickering now, and he pulled the guy he'd been talking to from around the wall. Ernie DiGregorio, one of the most exceptional passers ever in basketball and Marvin's former teammate, smiled back at me.

In the same breath, Marvin said, “Ernie will get you the Italian vote.”

I just wanted to disappear. I waved hello to Ernie. Then Marvin reached back further into the hallway and pulled Kevin Stacom forward. Another of the great Friars, Stacom spent six years playing with the Championship Boston Celtics.

Marvin, realizing Kevin was Irish, said, “Oh I forget about that, you already have his people.”

This was like a standup comic act at a wake. People in the line laughed. It was a *Saturday Night Live* skit. The best part was anyone who knew Dave knew he'd find humor in it too.

Marvin was a character. One night he called me and asked me to meet him at the Providence Oyster Bar on Federal Hill. He had a special guest in town. I told him I was with Attorney General Patrick Lynch. Marvin asked me to bring him along. On the way, the Speaker of the House called and asked what we were all going to. Marvin had contacted the speaker.

Only in Rhode Island could a guy like Marvin, who we all admired but understood he had a propensity to get himself in trouble, call the Colonel of the State Police, the Attorney General, and the Speaker of the House and assemble us at the last minute. We showed up. A few others were waiting, including Senator Steven Alves who could start an argument in an empty room.

Shortly after that Marvin arrived looking fresh, top hat and all. His guest was none other than Bob Costas who started his career in St, Louis where Marvin was a rookie with the Spirits of St. Louis in the ABA. Costas credits Marvin for helping him at the start of his career. Salutations aside, an argument ensued within minutes between Costas and Steve Alves. A bizarre disagreement about the pronunciation of names at the past Olympics. Who does that?

And so it goes.

Marvin had his demons. He knew a lot of wiseguys. He ended up in a little trouble, spending time inside a state-funded gated community. When Marvin was in high school, rumor has it, he allegedly attempted to rob a bus driver in the downtown section of the city. The story has him wearing a basketball letter coat with the name Marvin prominently displayed on the front. Now based on those rumored facts and the stature of the culprit being six-foot-eight or nine, the Providence Police had some leads to work with.

Who knows if it's true? History, as the saying goes, is only a bunch of lies agreed upon.

Before his time in jail, Marvin became friendly with some of the old neighborhood racketeers. One friend was Dougie Gomes who ran the south side of Providence in the '80s. He and his brother, Dennis "Cadillac" Gomes, were feared on the street. Dougie was the arch rival of Gerard Ouimette.

One of the cases used against Ouimette to convict him under the "three strikes you're out" life without parole statute was an assault of Dougie Gomes. In 1982 at Sullivan's Café, Providence Police walked in and saw Ouimette drop a handgun, later found to have an obliterated serial number.

Around the same time, I was on surveillance on the south side late at night and spotted Dougie Gomes in a car with several career criminals. The surveillance targeted Gomes for potential weapons possession and his propensity for crimes of violence.

My partner and I stopped the car and, low and behold, in the back seat sat none other than Marvin Barnes. We asked everyone to step out and patted them down for guns, there were none. I was disappointed that Marvin would hang with this crew. At the time, Marvin was on one of his many sabbaticals from the NBA. He was suspended or on waivers, a common theme during his playing days, and the better part of his career was over.

Marvin didn't know me back then, but I figured I'd just give him a little friendly advice. I pulled him aside away from the others. I had to be cautious in talking to him. I wouldn't want his guys to think he was cooperating or in their world, snitching or ratting. When he took a couple steps toward me, Dougie yelled, "You got nothing to say to him, News."

I told Marvin I watched Dr. J the night before and how he was lighting up the court. Then, in a lower voice, said, "Why are you hanging with these guys, Marvin? You've got more going for you than this. Shouldn't you be working hard to get back in the NBA?"

Marvin, always a consummate gentleman with law enforcement, acknowledged what I said, said nothing in return, and headed back over with his pals.

Years later, I helped Marvin with his Rebound Foundation. There were no more second, third, or fourth chances. The music stopped playing, and the paychecks stopped coming.

Marvin's career and his lifestyle as a professional athlete were over. He opened a charitable foundation to help at-risk kids in the inner city. I helped him land a few speaking gigs, and I contributed to the cause.

Marvin was a talented athlete and had a heart of gold. But the lure of the old neighborhood, despite the heights he'd reached in his college and professional career, was something he could not escape. Where once the world admired him, now just the street thugs were his only fans. To them he was "News," to the rest of the world he was another sad footnote.

A talented but flawed individual misled by the lure of inner-city streets. How many Marvin Barnes' never had the chance to leave the dark side of every American city? That such a talented, personable, and charming man fell victim to an environment he had a chance to escape is a sad testament.

Chapter 42 Twilight Days of Organized Crime

The mob is dead, long live the mob.

This twist on a king's passing and the continuity of the monarchy also rings true for organized crime. And like most monarchies, the mob evolved from a level of absolute power to one of reduced, yet still significant, influence. The mob exists in a different form in a very different world.

Some people miss the days of Mafia royalty, others never noticed the absence.

Long gone are the days of wiseguys shaking down legitimate businesses. Long gone are the days of loan sharks standing on the street corners waiting for their customers to show up to pay the juice; a never-ending cycle of paying a bill you can never pay off.

Long gone are the mom and pop stores, on street corners all over New England, taking bets on a numbers game or horses at Narragansett or Lincoln Downs. Or the stores in Maverick Square East Boston, taking bets on Wonderland, Raynham, or Taunton racetracks. Replaced by Daily Numbers, Mega-millions, and Powerball. The "Office" has a new name, *The Rhode Island Lottery* run by a very different "Commission."

If ya' can't beat 'em, replace 'em.

Today's bookies are more discrete, offering the same credit betting on sportsbooks outside state supervision. Sanctioning by the wiseguys is passé. Yet long ago in a place just around the corner in Rhode Island, the bookmaker was an earner for the mob and held an essential status in the community.

Everyone knew it was wrong. Everyone knew where the uncollected debt would end up and who would come to collect, but there was something cool about the bookie.

At least in the eyes of those who didn't have their legs broken or businesses taken from them.

The cool, well-dressed bookie on the corner, a large roll of bills in his pocket, hanging around on Mondays for square up time, is an anachronism. Obsolete in our web-connected, instant message, tweeting, online American culture.

Long gone are the days when you'd drive by Coin-o-Matic on Atwells Ave— otherwise known as 'The Office"— and see Raymond L. S. Patriarca, Sr., the Old Man, the Don, the *Capo di Tutti Capi* (Boss of Bosses) holding court.

The same thing goes for the North End of Boston. People have forgotten the power of 98 Prince Street back then. Run by the three Angiulo brothers, Donato, Francesco, and Gennaro.

Gennaro "Gerry" Angiulo, the Underboss to Raymond Sr., ran the show with the able help of his brothers. They operated the same way, the same style. Old school Mafioso.

When Gennaro was on trial, he'd come into court singing, "I'm just a racketeer that's everything you hear..." to the tune of *"Just a Gigolo."* The swagger, the demeanor, the caustic refusal to operate under the law masked by a warped sense of humor.

They don't make'em like that anymore.

New centers of power opened. Not only in Providence but in other cities. Raymond died. Gennaro went to prison because of an FBI bug in his office. New bosses, bred in a different, more privileged world, assumed command, but their lack of experience—having made their "bones" under less challenging circumstances—brought chaos rather than continuity.

The changing world brought its own stresses. Technology created virtual offices, popping up with different initiatives and different values. No longer did one have to venture out to a bar or store to place a bet. The cautious glances over one's shoulder, looking for cops, replaced by discrete concealment of a smartphone screen.

In Boston, Providence, Hartford, Springfield, or New Haven, the issues once important on Prince Street or The Hill may have no significance today. In Connecticut, the rules are different. When Raymond was alive, his gravitas could control various factional problems. But Connecticut has several families now, including the remnants of the New England mob.

I'm not saying it's over, but it's shattered.

This 'Thing of Ours" is now the domain of aging mobsters fifty years too late or wannabes emulating television shows and old movies. It is a shadow of its former self. For a variety of reasons, including federal and state prosecutions aided by the RICO statute, the once structured, rigid, and organized hierarchy of the mob is no more.

Like the lines from the Jimmy Buffett song, "A Pirate Looks at Forty."

"Yes I am a pirate, born two hundred years
too late...
This occupational hazard being my
occupation just not around"[7]

The heyday of the mob is behind them. They are a dysfunctional family if ever there was one.

[7] Songwriters: Jimmy Buffett
A Pirate Looks at Forty lyrics © Universal Music Publishing Group

Long gone are the days of hearing about Frankie "Cadillac" Salemme, Vinny "The Animal" Ferrara, and Bobby Carrozza in Boston or stories about Louie Failla or William "Wild Guy" Grasso in Hartford. Even the legendary Gaetano Milano, the once ambitious Patriarca soldier from Springfield convicted of the Grasso murder, renounced his involvement in the Mafia at sentencing.

The Grasso murder in Connecticut was a big deal. Today many of the new up-and-coming mobsters wouldn't even know him or his confederates. Representing the Providence mob at that funeral were Anthony "The Saint" St. Laurent, Matthew "Matty" Guglielmetti, and Pasquale Galea. I could see the fear on faces on the Connecticut mobsters.

They didn't know who would get it next.

But the Providence guys kind of walked in with a little swagger.

Long gone from the Hartford area are the stories about Grasso and his friends John Castagna, Frankie and Louie Pugliano, or Frank Colantoni. Failla was a defendant in the Hartford Trial along with Milano and several others. The same trial also convicted Nicky Bianco.

Nicky, as we know, was a close associate of many New York factions and close loyalist to Raymond, Sr. Convicted in Hartford of his managerial role in running the criminal enterprise, he was the last of the guys with the gravitas and background to run the organization. The trial and conviction derailed the process but didn't end it. Amyotrophic lateral sclerosis, Lou Gehrig's disease, did.

Bianco died in federal prison in 1994.

Sometimes, even among the most hard-core wiseguys, a long-suppressed conscience can rise to the surface. Many of the old-time wiseguys express remorse for their misdeeds. Some, like Milano, renounce their involvement with the mob. Others, like Nicky Pari, gave law enforcement information from their death bed. Not as an informant but to come clean, incriminating just himself.

Nicky Pari was a tough guy. A jury convicted Pari and his partner, Andy Merola, of murder in the 1978 disappearance of Joseph "Joe Onions" Scanlon, despite the lack of a body. After their conviction, they remained close in prison.

The leading theory had "Joe Onions" body disposed of in Narraganset Bay. After many years in prison, they paroled both Merola and Pari.

Andy Merola opened a restaurant on Federal Hill called Andino's. Located across from the "Office" and next door to the old Vincent's Restaurant, where someone shot and killed Raymond "Slick" Vecchio. While Andy was busy running Andino's in the legitimate world his pal Nicky Pari was dabbling in stolen goods and other crimes.

For many years Nicky operated out of flea markets and by reputation alone he could get his part of the take.

In 2007, Andy passed on from a bout with cancer. His mobster friends would remember his addictive laugh and eternal smile. He always appeared to be positive and upbeat. That's kind of rare in a business where you never know when it's your time. But he also knew his lifelong pal, Nicky Pari, always had his back.

In November 2008, State Police arrested Nicky on charges related to running a crime ring at a local flea market. Now seventy-one-years old, the once debonair and flamboyant mobster faced going back to jail as a violator of the terms of parole. And, a more dire situation, one even the most hardened mobster in the world couldn't challenge, confronted Nicky.

Nicky Pari was ill with throat cancer. The prognosis was grim.

The detectives handling the case confirmed Nicky had but weeks, perhaps days, left. He had a gauze wrapped around his neck and appeared very weak while sitting and awaiting his court appearance in the cell block. The detective who made the case showed him compassion.

His past was his past, but when a man is sitting on a metal bench in a dank cellblock telling you he'll be dead soon, it calls for empathy and kindness. The detectives did what they had to, but despite it all this was a human about to leave this mortal coil.

Detectives interviewed Nicky. He offered to tell us where they'd buried "Joe Onions" body, but nothing else. He wanted the family of Onions to have a decent burial.

I was the Superintendent and didn't often come down to the cellblock to greet an old adversary, but this was a unique circumstance. I went to see him alone.

When I walked in the cellblock, he looked up and smiled. I smiled back.

"Hi, Nick."

"How are you, Doherty?"

We traded small talk. I touched on the Onions situation. Holding his throat, in obvious discomfort, he was clear it was as far as he would go. The location of the body and nothing more.

I told him I understood. In his world, although ready to meet his maker, he would never give up anyone still living. Never break the code. He would offer himself and Andy Merola and nothing else.

Merola was dead, and Pari would soon join him. Like visiting someone in the hospital, knowing they weren't leaving there alive, you don't want to upset them too much. However, we had to get as much as we could, and this was something worthwhile.

I thanked him for showing that respect for the Scanlon family and wished him well. He smiled, and I walked away. I looked back, and Nicky fixed on me with a saddened face. I gave him a thumbs up. He couldn't undo the past, but it showed he still had some trace of human empathy.

Out of curiosity, I went to the scene of the dig. Nicky hit it right on the money; accurate all those many years later. I watched the backhoe sifting, swinging back and forth, scraping away the dirt inch by inch from what we believed to be Joseph "Joe Onions" Scanlon's grave.

It was a slow, methodical process.

For over an hour, the backhoe continued, getting deeper and deeper until one of Mr. Scanlon's boots appeared. The backhoe withdrew, and we switched to shoveling by hand. They uncovered remnants of his shirt and jeans along with bones. All of which we later identified as belonging Joseph Scanlon.

A crowd gathered. Without knowing who or what we were digging for, rumors rumbled through the onlookers. Guesses ranged from missing persons to missing mobsters. When we were through, there was one less missing person in Rhode Island. Joe "Onions" Scanlon was no longer unaccounted for.

There were no additional charges. The two people involved in the murder were dead or dying. Nicky wasn't offering any other information about why they killed Scanlon or who ordered the hit.

Those secrets he would take to his grave.

Yet the unearthing of "Joe Onions" helped close out another chapter of New England wiseguy lore. The story appeared in papers from *The Boston Globe* to *The New York Times.*

The whole world loves a mob whodunit.

Nicky Pari died three weeks after we dug up "Joe Onions." The three actors of a tragedy had played their parts, the lights went out, and the drama faded into history. Like Shakespeare said,

"The evil that men do lives after them; the good is oft interred with their bones."

Long gone are the days when someone could drive up to the hill and see where they gunned down Jackie "Mad Dog" Nazarian or point out where the biggest crap games took place.

Long gone are the days when one might see where Alfred "Chippy" Scivola conducting his business or where Felix "LaLa" DiBenedetto offered the latest line on a game or George "The Kook" Najarian peddled knockoffs before they were in vogue.

Long gone are the days when people tried to guess where Bobo hid the stolen La-Z-Boy chairs.

You haven't heard about the La-Z-Boy chair hijacking?

Fuggetaboutit[8]—It's all over.

[8] Fuggetaboutit: Rhode Island-speak for forget about it.

Chapter 43 Thoughts on the Mob Mystique

There is an inexplicable fascination for many with the Mob, La Cosa Nostra, the Mafia, or whatever they know as organized crime. From its Sicilian roots, brought to the shores of America with waves of immigrants, to its rise to power during Prohibition, there has always been grudging admiration for those who lived the lifestyle.

In Rhode Island, disabusing people of the myth of organized crime would be like disproving their memories of the good old days. You might be right, but you would not be popular with those from whom you've stolen their fantasy.

And it is a fantasy.

The mob, like any other business, is market driven. Gambling succeeded liquor as the lifeblood of Organized Crime, followed by drugs. Although the official line of the mob was they didn't deal drugs, the fact is the mob would sell cancer if they could profit from it.

Each activity punctuated with bullet-ridden bodies or the grotesque faces of garroted mob associates found in shallow graves. Some they never found. Men who'd outlived their usefulness, stepped on the wrong toes, or fell victim to pure greed.

The bodies belonged to bad guys. No one paid attention to the deceased except their families, and the cops tasked with tracking down the killers. In their world, it was a Herculean task.

Mob funerals, if there was something to bury, were a form of a retirement party. Except, instead of giving you a gold watch, they took it back. And those in attendance, eyes scanning the crowd, looked for signs of who might be next. Fond memories of the deceased were their last consideration. Not ending up like them was their first.

Is Vito the Ax staring at me? Who are those two mugs over there? Why are they watching me? How come Johnny Cornflakes didn't shake my hand?

Paranoia is a job perk for those who join this profession.

Such activities did not happen in a vacuum. While the mob provided the service, ordinary Americans plopped their money down to chase the gambling dream. If they followed the rules—collect their winnings or pay for their losses—they stayed safe and unharmed.

Although safe was a relative state in the status quo.

One might consider anyone who places a bet with a bookie, no matter how small an amount, part of organized crime. And like the changing demands of post-Prohibition society, across the country, people can now walk into a casino, buy lottery tickets at gas stations and Mom & Pop variety stores, or install an app on their phone and gamble away.

One need only look at the scene across from the Lincoln State Police Barracks to see how things have changed. Where once troopers and detectives noted known bookies coming or going from the racetrack, now a specialized unit works within the casino targeting fraud, card counters, and others trying to game the system.

Some troopers and police officers spent their entire careers chasing bookies who engaged in activities we now deem legal under state supervision. The bookies are now tax-paying employees of a licensed gambling entity.

Yet the myth and the nostalgia for the heyday of the mob persists.

Some truth lies in the legend of safer streets in areas controlled by the mob. Raymond L.S. Patriarca, Sr. practiced a form of community policing. He lived in the neighborhood, listened to people's problems, and offered solutions.

He made them go away.

How they went away was of little concern to the day-to-day life on Federal Hill. The lack of problems was all that mattered.

There was little of the random violence plaguing cities today. In a perverse way, targeted killings of guys who'd fallen out of step with the dictates of the mob boss are arguably better than drive-by shootings by roving gangs of immoral thugs injuring innocent people more often than the intended target.

Given a choice, many would return to the amoral world of mob control on the hill than the immoral randomness of violence today.

Patriarca had an unwritten—but enforced—rule about cops. Cops he could not corrupt should never be disrespected or targeted. It may not have been altruistic—it was more smart business policy—but it made dealings between cops and mob guys less fraught with uncertainty.

As to those he may have corrupted, they crossed the line. It was their choice.

It is difficult to put into words the attitude of many toward the mob. While it is clear the net negative effect of society eluded many because it was difficult to see, it doesn't alter the fact the mob preyed on society while using a well-orchestrated, if self-serving, publicity campaign of keeping streets safe.

Think of it this way. If one were to look at the bravery and dedication to duty of many of the soldiers during wartime, setting aside for the moment the cause or side for which they fought, one would be in awe of the actions of many of these men on both sides.

It is the same with the Mafia. They made the streets safe for those who had no cause to fear them. They demanded a code of conduct which did not bring unwanted attention to the family business. They operated within a framework of keeping their business successful and not bleeding the community dry.

But like young soldiers sent off under the false umbrella of fighting in a just and noble cause, it is the motivation by those in command that determines the righteousness of their actions.

On every side of a conflict, if one looks past the cause of the struggle, there are heroic acts and self-sacrifice. Sometimes otherwise good men take a wrong path.

Righteousness was not a concern here within organized crime; self-preservation and greed were.

While Raymond Patriarca would never tolerate drive-by shootings or random violence by those who operated under his umbrella, one must also acknowledge, were he alive today, he would more likely have redirected the randomness and casual disregard for innocent people. One might say he did, directing the violence into a more profitable, and less random, operation.

Keeping those who would operate outside the law under his control and to his profit.

It would be a mistake to underestimate the influence of the Patriarca organization. At the height of his rule, Patriarca held sway over all New England and much of the country. Many considered him a wise man among wise guys and deserving of great respect.

His iron-fisted control over his organization was mythological even among those involved in the mob.

There's a story of a conversation between Gerard Ouimette, Jerry Tillinghast, John Gotti, and some members of Gotti's crew in New York. Gotti introduced Gerard and Jerry to some guys.

One of Gotti's guys said, "So, where you guys from?"

"Providence," Jerry answered.

"Providence?" came the reply. "You guys are fuckin' nuts. You kill everybody."

Providence may be a small city, in the smallest state in the United States, yet once, the influence of Federal Hill reached far and wide. For a time, this was a center of the Organized Crime universe.

Those days are over.

A closer look at a rose reveals the sharp thorns concealed beneath. Understanding the reality of the mob unmasks the false perception of wiseguys deserving admiration.

It's just the way it was...

About the Authors

Brendan Doherty

Brendan Doherty provided over 28 years of public sector leadership. He was formerly the Superintendent of the Rhode Island State Police and the first Commissioner of Public Safety for the State of Rhode Island. During his tenure in the State Police, he worked his way through the ranks in the Detective Bureau spending most of his career investigating Organized Crime and Public Corruption. He was involved in the prosecution of some of the state's highest-profile cases. Brendan retired in 2011 holding the rank of Colonel. At the time of his retirement, through his leadership, the state-of-the-art Public Safety Headquarters was built on time and under budget.

While Superintendent of the State Police, he began a Community Outreach Program and fostered a close police-community relationship that encompassed programs such as *Kids, Cops and Christmas, Kids, Cops and Classrooms,* volunteer basketballs leagues and youth mentoring programs.

After retiring from the State Police, Brendan was a candidate for U.S. Congress in 2012. He has lectured at numerous colleges and universities on topics such as 4th Amendment issues, Identity Theft and Ethics. In 2013 he began working as Director of Special Investigations at Blue Cross Blue Shield R.I. focusing on healthcare fraud.

Brendan has been a member of numerous boards throughout New England, including R.I. Special Olympics, Crossroads R.I., Cumberland Lincoln Boys and Girls Club, N.E. Heart Association, The National Healthcare Anti-Fraud Association Training Committee, Chairman of N.E. State Police Intelligence Network, Chairman of Wyatt Correctional Facility, The Beacon Mutual Insurance Company Governance Committee, and Phoenix House of New England. He is a member of the Bishop Feehan High School Athletic Hall of Fame and R.I. Criminal Justice Hall of Fame. He is also a member of R.I. Police Chiefs Association.

Brendan is a graduate of Roger Williams University with a B.S. in Administration of Justice and holds a master's degree in Criminal Justice from Anna Maria College.

Brendan and his wife Michele reside in South Kingstown, R.I. They have a daughter who lives in the Providence area with her husband and a son who lives with his wife and family in the Boston area.

Joe Broadmeadow

Joe Broadmeadow retired with the rank of Captain from the East Providence, Rhode Island Police Department after twenty years. He served in the various divisions within the department, including Commander of Investigative Services. He also worked in the Organized Crime Drug Enforcement Task Force (OCDETF) and on special assignment to the FBI Drug Task Force.

It's Just the Way It Was: Inside the War on the New England Mob and other stories is the third non-fiction book by Joe Broadmeadow

UnMade: Honor Loyalty Redemption (written with Bobby Walason) and ***Choices: You Make 'em You Own 'em,*** *(The Jerry Tillinghast Story),* Joe's first two non-fiction works, were both Number 1 New Releases on Amazon.

Joe is the author of three works of fiction. ***Silenced Justice*** and ***Collision Course,*** featuring East Providence Police Detective Lieutenant Josh Williams, and ***A Change of Hate***, a spin-off of the Josh Williams series, featuring Defense Attorney Harrison 'Hawk' Bennett.

The books continue to garner rave reviews and are available on Amazon, Barnes & Noble, and bookstores everywhere.

When Joe is not writing, he is hiking or fishing (and thinking about writing). Joe completed a 2,185-mile thru-hike of the Appalachian Trail in September 2014. After completing the trail, Joe published a short story, ***Spirit of the Trail***, available on Amazon.

He lives in Rhode Island with his wife, Susan, just a short distance from his daughter, Kelsey, and her husband, Chuck. Strategically close by to respond immediately to care for their dogs, Ralph and Seamus, who do not realize they are dogs.

Thanks for reading! Please take a moment to review the book, it is most appreciated.
http://www.amazon.com/Joe-Broadmeadow/e/B00OWPE9GU
Contact the author: jebwizardpublishing@gmail.com
Website: www.authorjoebroadmeadow.com
Twitter: @JBroadmeadow
Author Blog: www.joebroadmeadowblog.wordpress.com

CPSIA information can be obtained
at www.ICGtesting.com
Printed in the USA
LVHW051247031119
636167LV00015B/59

9 781733 526401